OF JUDGEMENT AND OF MERCY

ROY ROBERTS

 SPIRIT MEDIA

SPIRIT MEDIA INC

Published in the United States of America by

Spirit Media Inc

https://spiritmedia.us

Spirit Media and our logos are trademarks of Spirit Media Inc

8045 Arco Corporate Drive STE 130

Raleigh, NC 27617

1 (888) 800-3744

Religion & Spirituality | Christian Books & Bibles | Inspirational

Paperback ISBN: 979-8-89307-187-0

eBook ISBN: 979-8-89307-188-7

PDF ISBN: 979-8-89307-189-4

Library of Congress Control Number: 2025916862

To DeeDee, Anna, Steve, and Janet—your faith and encouragement helped bring this story to life. May God bless you all.

CHAPTER 1

THE TICKET AND THE TRAP

Phil Gunn lived in a small trailer park right next to the river, where he could fish or swim at his leisure.

The alarm clock rang, and with one eye open, Phil rolled over sleepily to shut it off.

Phil was long and lanky, standing about six foot two and weighing around two hundred ten pounds. He was strong as a bull, though not quite as big. He didn't mind working the afternoon shift because when he got up at six-thirty in the morning, he still had all day ahead of him before he had to go to work at four in the afternoon. By the time he showered and shaved, he was ready for breakfast. It would be warm enough to walk the two miles to Kamish Café, which was on the other end of town. They had the best breakfast around.

He turned on his favorite radio station—the only Christian station he liked—and Rev. Jenkins was giving a sermon on prayer and fasting. This was a subject Phil always liked to hear about. Pastor Stan Keily had touched on it often. Phil, being a born-again Christian, knew this was a strong part of any Christian walk. He liked the worship music but couldn't carry a tune too well, so the only place he sang was in the shower, where he couldn't be heard.

He grabbed a towel and headed for the shower. He had barely stepped out when the phone rang.

"Hello? Oh, hi, Mom... No, you didn't wake me. I just got out of the shower... Oh, you did? How is Jeannie? Well, when you call her back, tell her I'll try to get her some money, okay? Have you had breakfast yet? You haven't? You want to meet me at Kamish Café about 9:30? Fine. See you then. Bye."

As he hung up the phone, he thought to himself that he would help his family where he could, as they were most important to him. Phil knew his mother had probably already eaten, but she would come if for no other reason than just to visit. She lived behind Kamish Café in the Burbank Homes, so she didn't have far to go. He was about the only one who came to visit her, as she didn't get out much anymore. He didn't see her as often as he'd like, so it was good that she would join him this morning.

He was just finishing getting dressed when the phone rang again.

"Hello. Hey, George! How ya doing? How's the new job? Oh yeah? I'll bet driving the Hyster is a lot more fun than the trim saw! Yeah, I wouldn't mind driving it myself—maybe next year. No, I can't meet you right now. I'm meeting my mom at Kamish Café. Sure, you and Marge can come, about 9:30. If you get there before us, pick us a good table, okay? Bye."

Phil said out loud to himself, "I hope I can finish getting dressed before the phone rings anymore."

He went out the front and locked his door. He took a deep breath. "Boy, that smells good," he said out loud. He breathed in the mix of fir trees, freshly mowed grass, and the faint, cool scent of the river. "What a day."

As he walked along, he contemplated how hot it might be at work that night because he was already feeling it. On his way to town, he went back to thinking about his mom. She was a small woman, and with her age, he worried about her health. Getting her to go see a doctor for a checkup was worse than pulling chickens' teeth, since she always claimed to be all right whether she was or not. On the other hand, she fretted about Jeannie being away at medical school and constantly worried about her daughter. Why, he didn't know. Hopefully she would get to do her internship closer to home, and thank the Lord she was almost finished with school.

He had a savings account, but it never seemed to grow. By the time he paid his tithes and offerings and helped family members and others with their needs, there wasn't much left to save. He didn't really care, as helping his family was most important to him.

Then there was Jonathon. The last he heard, his brother was somewhere on the streets of Oakland. Ever since Jonathon came back from the Vietnam War, he had turned to the call of the world—drugs, alcohol, and street life. If you could call it living, because he was a real mess and always down on his luck. Not that he ever asked for help, but love stretches many miles. If it wasn't for a Christian police officer Phil knew in Oakland, he would have no way of sending Jonathon any money.

When he could, he would send it to the officer, who would track Jonathon down and give it to him. Phil wished Jonathon would have listened when he tried to tell him about God, but his brother always changed the subject.

Dear Lord, Phil prayed, *please somehow, someway, bring him to repentance—that he too will be a child of yours.*

Phil often told himself that he would upgrade his trailer to a new double-wide as soon as the small trailer he now lived in was showing its age and wear. For now, he would just have to keep doing repairs and patches. He didn't have much hope of upgrading anytime soon.

Phil looked at his watch. "Better hurry," he mumbled. "I'm going to be late."

By the time he reached Kamish Café, it was 9:30. His mother had already found a table, and George and Marge were just pulling in. George was driving his midnight-blue Dodge 4x4 pickup. It was only a year old, but it still wasn't what George was looking for. He never seemed satisfied with things in life. Nothing could fill the void he had, although he kept trying.

Phil joked, "See ya finally made it."

"Yeah, you probably just got here yourself. In fact, your mom was probably the first one here, wasn't she?" George responded with a smile.

"Okay, okay, I concede. I'm guilty as charged," replied Phil.

All three laughed and walked into the café, where Phil's mother was seated, waiting for them. You could tell by Mrs. Gunn's face and hands that she had worked hard in her younger days, as they were calloused and scarred. She also battled other issues she'd rather not talk about. But now, after all these years, she was just a lonely old woman who loved her family. She smiled at Phil and the others.

"We got company?" she asked.

Phil nodded.

"Good, good—the more the merrier, I always say." She was beaming now. "I'm just going to have some coffee and toast," said Phil's mom.

Phil surmised that his mom had already eaten, and now he knew for sure.

"I'll have my usual. You two need a menu?" asked Phil.

"No," said George. "Just call the waitress. We already know what we want, too."

Phil's mom lifted her hand and motioned to the waitress. "Rosalyn, we're ready to order."

Rosalyn came over. "Alrighty then. Where do we start?"

"Well," Mrs. Gunn said, "I'm just having toast and coffee."

"And you?" she looked at Phil.

As Phil went to give his order, Rosalyn said it right along with him, because she knew it by heart. After all, she had been serving him since he was about twelve years old.

"Bacon and eggs over easy, toast, hash browns, coffee, large milk, large orange juice, and extra bacon," they chimed together.

"Need I say more?" snickered Rosalyn.

Phil laughed. "Well, Dad always told me, if you find a good thing, stick with it."

They all laughed.

Then Rosalyn asked, "And you?" looking at George and Marge.

George stated that he would be having the special—ham and bacon omelet, hash browns, and coffee. Marge decided she wanted poached eggs with bacon, extra crispy, and lightly toasted sourdough. "And oh, make sure the whites are fully cooked too!"

For the next hour they ate, laughed, and made small talk—though most of it was Phil's mom reminiscing about things Phil used to do.

"Boy, I'll tell you what," she said. "You never wanted to leave Phil alone with a screwdriver when he was younger. You'd come back, and he'd have the whole house torn apart."

"No wonder the foreman won't give you a tool belt," spouted George. "He's heard about you."

Phil was laughing so hard now his eyes were tearing up. "Yeah, he must have my number all right."

Marge made a few comments, but they were more derogatory than funny. "You must have been a pain in the butt," she said, half sarcastically.

"No," interrupted Phil's mom, "he was just curious. He just wanted to see what made things tick. He was very smart. In fact, he was the first of my whole family—his father's too—to graduate from high school. If it wasn't for his encouragement and his financial help, I'd hate to see where Jeannie would be today."

"Well, what do you know? I think we've got us a real hero in our midst," mocked Marge.

Phil knew Marge didn't like him, but he could never figure out why.

Marge knew why, though. Many years ago, she had a big brother too—only he was mean and hateful and did things to her that a sibling should never do. He didn't protect her from anything. He didn't care about anyone or anything except himself. It was her brother who got his hands on the inheritance money from their grandparents and squandered it on a business that went belly-up. That was what killed their dad—he couldn't believe a son would do such a thing. Their mother died shortly thereafter of loneliness. Then her brother left her with an old aunt and uncle who raised her so far in the backcountry that it was completely out of step with the times. Because of this, she was constantly humiliated and teased throughout her growing-up years. When her brother died in a car wreck—so drunk he couldn't see—she just laughed. Yes, she hated Phil because he represented everything she could never have. *Never.*

Phil bent over and kissed his mother on the forehead. "Momma, I'll try extra hard to get over to see you sometime this week, okay?"

"Okay, Phillip. Remember too, that Mr. Winters said I could come up and see the house again! You remember him, don't you?"

"Sure do. He's the one I did a little electrical work for a few years ago."

"Yes sir-ee. I fell in love with that old house the first time I saw it, and he told me he'd sell it to me one day. He said I could come see it anytime I wanted to," said Phil's mom.

"Sure, Momma. I'll do what I can to get you over there soon. I think he's a bit sweet on you," teased Phil.

"Oh, phooey." She blushed slightly.

"Well, if I'm going to get anything done today, I guess I'd better get going," said Phil as he grabbed the ticket and started for the register.

"Yeah, we'd better get going too," said George. "Marge and I have some shopping to do before I head off to work."

"That's right," said Marge, "or else there will be no lunch for you."

"Hold up there, Phil. Let me pay our share," said George.

"Naw, it's on me," said Phil as he paid for the entire breakfast.

"Can we drop you someplace, Phil?" asked George.

"Yeah, as a matter of fact, you can. I've got to pick up a few things myself, so I'll tag along. Then, if you don't mind, drop me off at my place?"

After being dropped off at home and putting his groceries away, he decided to hold off on the few things he needed to do around the house and jumped into his 1972 Ford wagon. He drove up to the Stop and Go in Kamish to top off his fuel so he wouldn't have to think about it later in the week. Besides, he really enjoyed visiting with the owners.

He pumped his fuel, then proceeded to go inside. As he entered, Bonnie shouted, "Hi, Phil!" She was a mite older than he was and always had a smile on her face and something nice to say.

"Bonnie, let me tell you something. There are three things I'd really miss if I ever left this town: my momma, breakfast at Kamish Café, and coming here to see your smiling face. What a thrill," Phil said.

"Hey, Buck-o, that's my wife you're talking to," teased Mac, Bonnie's husband, who had come in from the back room. "You keep talking like that and I might be in big trouble. She'll get rid of me and take after you. Fact is, I don't know who'd be worse off—me or you."

All three burst out laughing. They had known each other for many years. Phil thought Mac was very wise and respected him. When Phil needed advice on important matters, he always went to Mac.

"You don't need to worry about that," Phil joked. "She wouldn't want a young pup like me."

"No, but I do have a younger sister, ya know," teased Bonnie.

"I think I'm in trouble now," said Phil. "I'd better pay for my gas and get while I'm still ahead—and single."

"Have a good day," said Bonnie with a smirk.

"You folks too," returned Phil.

For some reason, Phil had a yearning deep inside to buy a lottery ticket. *But that would be wrong,* he thought. Pastor Keily preaches against gambling. *Oh, but what if I won!* It was a huge amount—either sixty-eight million in cash or one hundred seventy-nine million over the next twenty years. *Wow. Wouldn't that be wild?*

As he was leaving the Stop and Go, he felt the pull to go to Klonger's Grocery again. He walked through the door and made up his mind for sure that he'd get a ticket. He picked up a few snacks for work so he wouldn't look so conspicuous buying just a lottery ticket. All the time, he felt guilty but overrode it with *what if?* Besides, what could one ticket hurt? Who would know anyway?

If he didn't win, it wouldn't matter. If he did, everyone would think it was a good idea. He had told himself that if he won, he would share the wealth. So the thought became a plan, and the plan became reality.

On his way home, he went to the post office to get his mail. There was a letter from his sister Jeannie reminding him of the money he said he'd send. So he went ahead and bought a money order and sent it to her, that way he wouldn't forget.

After he got home, he spent the rest of the day feeling dread—but of what, he wasn't quite sure. He decided then and there that he would never buy another ticket again. He then remembered that he hadn't read his *Daily Bread* or his Bible passage, or even prayed today. So he took time to read and pray.

He always read three passages, asking God to show him where to read.

Today, the first passage was in *Numbers* chapter 22. It told of Balaam, a magician, and King Balak, who hired him to curse Israel. King Balak sent for Balaam the first time, but the Angel of the Lord bid him not to go. The second time the king sent for him, he went, and the Angel of the Lord met him on the way to smite him. It was the donkey on which he rode—speaking in the voice of a man—that saved his life.

The second passage was in *II Chronicles* chapter 35. It told how Josiah, one of Judah's good kings, kept the Passover for the first time in many years. It also described his death, how he meddled in something he shouldn't have—a battle ordered by God in which Josiah was not to take part. He was killed in that battle.

The third passage was in *Judges* chapter 16. It told how Samson compromised his walk with God for a Philistine woman named Delilah, who broke him down to learn the secret of his strength and led to his death.

Phil could usually tell right away how to apply what he read to his daily life, but today's passages puzzled him. He didn't realize that by buying the lottery ticket he had compromised what he believed—that he'd opened the door for Satan to take charge. Afterthought set in, and he prayed for guidance and understanding. He still felt puzzled, unable to find meaning in the passages as he always had before. So he turned his mind toward getting ready for work.

As the night went on, his mind kept wandering back to the lottery ticket. *What if I win? What will I do with all that money? The right thing would be to pay tithes and offerings first, of course. But what next? I suppose I could buy Mom that house she loves so much, and then...*

"Hey, Phil, are you working tonight or just daydreaming?" chuckled the foreman.

"Oh, hi, I didn't see you come up. Guess I was a little way away, huh?" replied Phil.

"Well, you can't do much right now anyway. The head rig is down. It's going to be a couple of hours before they get it fixed. Maybe you could do a bit of cleanup and then take your break—even though you seem to have just had one," remarked the foreman with a snicker.

"Right," said Phil. *The only thing that would make it better is if I got off early,* he thought.

Phil was getting a little anxious. The fever of the lottery had taken a firm hold. Under the circumstances, he didn't see any chance of getting off early. Soon the foreman announced that they'd be doing cleanup for the rest of the shift since repairs were taking longer than expected. Phil didn't like cleanup work because the time dragged by, but he figured it all paid the same.

After the shift was over, everyone clocked out and went their own way.

Phil went straight to the Stop and Go. He hurried inside with a piece of paper and a pen. "Do you have the numbers for tonight's lottery draw?" he called as he crossed the floor.

"Yes," said the girl behind the counter, startled by his shout. She pointed. "They're posted on the board over there."

Phil quickly scribbled the numbers and said, "Thank you."

He rushed out the door, the only thing on his mind was getting home to check his ticket. He pulled into his parking space next to the trailer, barely braking, shoved the car into park, and swung open the door. Forgetting his lunch box, he slammed the door and half ran up the steps to his porch. He fumbled with the keys, finally got the door open, and flicked on the lights. His cat, Sparky, wove between his legs; he jumped a little, then regained his composure.

He grabbed the ticket off the counter and began checking the numbers closely, one by one, against the scribbles on the scrap paper. He rubbed his eyes, thinking he'd misread them. *No way.* He checked again.

"I won," he whispered. "I can't believe it." He sat down, stunned. Then the reality of winning swept over him.

"Wow."

He needed to tell someone—who better than his best friend? He grabbed the phone and dialed George, not realizing how late it was.

George groped for the phone, not wanting to open his eyes, but checked the caller ID anyway. As he picked up, he heard, "GEORGE!"

"Phil! What's going on? Are you okay?" George asked, alarmed by the frantic tone.

"Will you do me a favor?"

"Yeah, sure, ol' buddy. What's up?"

"Could you and Marge come over here?"

"When—right now?"

"Yes, right now. I've got something fantastic to tell you, and you ain't gonna believe it."

"Can't it wait until morning?"

"No, it's got to be tonight—as soon as you can get here, okay?"

"Boy, sounds like you must have won the lottery or something," George joked. "Okay, we'll be there as soon as I can roust Marge."

By this time Marge was awake, listening to the one-sided conversation. "This better be good, or someone is going to pay for this. I need my beauty sleep." With an *ugh*, she got up.

They tapped on Phil's door and came in. "This better be good," George said testily. "I could still be asleep."

"Yeah, humph," muttered Marge. "You're always asleep."

"Look on the table," said Phil.

"What?"

"Look on the table."

George walked over slowly, eyeing Phil all the way. "So what am I supposed to be looking at? These?" He picked up the ticket and the scrap paper.

"What do you think now?" Phil asked.

"Is this for real?"

"Yeah."

"Let me see," Marge snapped, snatching the ticket from George. "Oh, my word—how much did you win?"

"Well, I won one hundred seventy-nine million in payments, or sixty-eight million in a lump sum, as close as I can figure," Phil said. "Let's go celebrate! What do you say?"

"Where? Everything around here is closed. Man, what are you going to do with all that money?" asked George.

"I don't know. It's an awful lot, huh? I haven't even thought about that yet."

"We could go to Lewis Town," suggested Marge. "There's bound to be something open there." Her face had a look Phil hadn't seen before. Her whole attitude shifted; she was suddenly acting like his best friend. Even George couldn't distract her gaze from Phil.

"Okay with me. How about you, George?" said Phil.

"Let's go."

They hurried out to George and Marge's 2000 Chevy Impala. "Why don't you two sit up front, and I'll get in back," Marge said. "That way I can nap on the way. All this excitement has worn me out. Wake me when we get there, okay?" She settled into a corner and closed her eyes.

Her real reason wasn't sleep. She needed to think. With her eyes closed, she wasn't drifting off at all. Far from it—she was working on a plan. A plan to get the money. *She* was going to be rich, not Phil. She would see to that.

CHAPTER 2

MIDNIGHT FEAST, QUIET CON

Just before leaving Kamish, Phil realized he'd need some cash in his pocket. They drove over to the local bank ATM, and he withdrew what he thought he'd need.

The ride to Lewis Town seemed long, but with all the excitement, time wasn't an issue. The men swapped ideas about how to spend the money.

Marge, meanwhile, was putting together a plan to steal it. In her mind, Phil would never get to spend a dime if she had her way. She'd dreamed up a conniving scheme and deemed it perfect. All she needed was to convince George that it was the only thing to do—and she would.

By this time it was about three-thirty in the morning, and as they drove through Lewis Town, they saw that nothing was open at that hour. They considered what to do and decided to head for the town of Moscow, approximately another hour away. Surely something would be open by the time they got there. They knew of the American Inn and Restaurant, and if that was all there was, that would have to do. With all the excitement, they were getting hungry.

"I have an idea, Phil," said Marge.

"What's that?" asked Phil.

"Well, let's not tell anyone else about the money until after you get it."

"Hey, that would be a surprise to a lot of people," Phil said.

"Yeah. I mean, they'll probably know the ticket was bought at Klonger's in Kamish, but everyone will be kept in suspense. By the way, how do you get the money?" asked Marge.

"I've got to go to Boise. I read the instructions, and they say you have to go to the lottery headquarters to pick it up," Phil replied.

"You know that George and I can drive you there and keep you company, if you like," Marge said.

"What about work?" George asked.

"Just take the night off," Marge said.

"Hey, George, we both have vacation time coming. Why don't we just take off a couple of days now?" Phil added.

"Yeah, okay. Sounds good to me."

All the way to Moscow, George and Phil teased each other with jokes about all the different kinds of businesses Phil could get into—everything from making roller skates to putting hats on fat weenie dogs to belly stands for pregnant women.

By the time they reached Moscow, they'd worked up quite an appetite—and so had Marge. She had her plan worked out to the minute. She'd gone over it time and again in her head until she felt she had perfected it. She was surely thankful for that forensic medicine show a few months back; she felt she'd learned enough to take care of this little problem.

Driving into the inn's parking lot, they saw the sign that said the restaurant was open twenty-four hours. Once inside, the giddiness—from being tired and from the surreal sensation of actually coming into possession of that money—got hold of Phil and George. Marge was excited too, but her determination to relieve Phil of the money kept her emotions in check. She didn't want to let her secret out, so she played along.

After they were seated and given menus, the waitress came back and asked if she could take their orders. She was quite jolly for that time of day, they thought.

"Okay," said Phil. "What will you guys have?"

"I'll take a... number five," said George.

"Give me a three," replied Marge.

"Let's see... I'll have—everything on this side of the menu," announced Phil with a chuckle as he waved the card in the air.

"Are you serious?" the waitress asked, laughing skeptically.

"Yep," replied Phil. "And a large milk, and orange juices around the table."

By now George and Marge were laughing too.

"How are you going to eat all that?" asked George, a tear running down his face from laughing.

"Well, if we can't eat it all, we can give it away," said Phil.

"Maybe we can take it with us for lunch," added Marge.

"Okay then, will that be all I can get you?" said the waitress—somewhat annoyed, but laughing along. She wasn't sure whether to believe them. She brought their drinks while the food was being prepared, and the three continued to laugh and joke. Even so, Phil noticed that look in Marge's eyes again. He brushed it off and raised his drink of choice to make a toast.

"What better way to celebrate than with friends? To the best of friends."

About that time the manager of the restaurant came over to the table. "Pardon me, but you do plan to pay for all this food, don't you? I mean, this just doesn't happen very often."

"Yes, sir," answered Phil firmly, handing him two one-hundred-dollar bills. "If it's more than this, just let me know."

"Ye... yes, yes, sir, I surely will. You must be celebrating something special to go all out, huh?" he stammered.

"You might say that," joked Marge. "Let's just say that from now on things will be different." The gleam in her eyes left Phil unsettled for a moment, but he let the feeling pass.

The food began to arrive, and the manager had to pull in another table to hold it all. Phil's, George's, and Marge's eyes got bigger and bigger as the dishes kept coming. No doubt it was a lot of food.

"Not to worry," said the waitress. "We're ready and willing to put whatever's left in to-go boxes for you."

"Yeah, but what do we do then?" asked George.

"May I make a suggestion?" the waitress said.

"Sure," said Phil.

"If you go down to the A Street Apartments—number eleven—you'll find a family that's truly hurting right now and could really use the food. I know because I do volunteer work at the mission here."

"Excellent!" cried Phil, and they began to eat.

They ate quietly, though a few chuckles came when Phil and George started tossing whipped cream at each other, and every once in a while a blueberry or two went through the air. A red-faced Marge looked on, trying to pretend she didn't know either of them.

After they were stuffed and could hardly move, Phil paid the bill and left the waitress a big tip.

He got directions to A Street Apartments. They found the place and searched for number eleven. Even though it was early morning, surely someone would be up. Phil knocked, and a little old lady answered. He told her what they had done and said they wished to share the remainder of the food. He and his friends were traveling and couldn't take it with them.

She looked excited and said, "Come in."

They brought in the food, and the family was more than thrilled to receive it. The little old lady gave Phil such a big hug and thanked him. For a minute there, he wondered where the strength came from—he thought he was in the grip of a bear. Some children came out from behind her and thanked him. At that moment, it tore at Phil's heart, so he made out a check for fifty dollars—knowing it wasn't much, but that it might still help them in some way. He gave it to the old lady and, at the same time, wondered where the children's parents were.

Finally, it was time to head home.

"I'll drive to Lewis Town," Phil said. "Then maybe one of you can take over from there."

"Yeah, I'll sleep until then," said George. "With a little shut-eye, I should be okay and can get us the rest of the way home."

Marge sat up eagerly. "Why don't we get a good sleep today and head out for Boise tonight?"

"That's an idea," said Phil, "but we'll need to let our bosses know we won't be in for the rest of the week. In fact, I'm going to tell mine I quit."

"We can do that from Lewis Town," said George.

"Okay, then. It's Boise-bound tonight," said Phil.

When they reached Lewis Town, Phil pulled into the nearest gas station, eased up to the pumps, and turned off the motor. He got out, stretched, then reached into the car to wake George and Marge.

"Hey, if you two want to wake up and freshen up, I'll pump the gas," Phil said.

"Okay, okay," said George.

"While we're in here, we'll call your boss too," said Marge. "Will that be all right?"

"Yeah... uh... Just tell him I'll see him Monday, and I'll talk to him then," replied Phil.

"Okay," said Marge.

She knew the mill's number by heart. As she and George walked into the station, she said, "I'll call the mill for you guys. You go ahead and get freshened up and then grab us some coffee, okay?"

"Yeah, I suppose that'll be all right," said George as he shuffled off.

Marge heard two rings on the other end of the phone before, "Hello, this is Kamish Lumber. May I help you?"

"Hi, this is Marge Wetzel. I'm calling for my husband, George. He has some very important business out of state today, so he won't be back until Monday."

"Okay, thank you for calling—and tell George that we hope all is all right," came the voice on the line.

"Okay, will do. Thank you. Bye," said Marge.

With the call made, she went to the restroom, then caught up with George as he was paying for the coffee.

When George finished, they went back to where Phil was waiting. As George climbed behind the wheel, he said, "Phil, I think I hear my mattress calling. Next stop is your house—then mine."

"Sounds good. Take me home, James, and don't spare the horses," Phil said with a chuckle as he leaned back and closed his eyes.

CHAPTER 3

THE DEVIL'S WHISPER

Phil spent the rest of the day sleeping, but George and Marge never slept. Later, as they were finally preparing for bed, Marge said, "George, I hate to tell you this, but at the restaurant—remember when Phil went to the restroom and I said I had to go too?"

"Yeah," answered George.

"Well, the reason we came back together is because Phil was waiting for me when I came out. He said, 'Why be with a loser when you could be with me? After all, I've got money now and can give you everything you've ever wanted.' Then he tried to kiss me!"

"What? I don't believe it! Was he joking?" asked George.

"He was serious," she replied.

"That does it—I'm going over there right now and—" snapped George.

"No. What would hurt him more—your beating him up, or him losing his money?" Marge sneered.

"What do you mean?" asked George.

"I've got a plan..." She snickered.

At first, her plan didn't include getting rid of Phil. But the more she thought about it—and the more she told George about it—the more certain she became that it would be necessary. Soon she had George eating out of her hand more than ever. All she had to do was remind him of the "incident" at the restaurant. She knew she could do no wrong when it came to George and could get what she wanted.

The phone rang several times before Phil was awake enough to answer. "Hello?" he said.

"Phil," said George.

"Yeah," Phil replied.

"Say, let's use your car to go to Boise. After we dropped you off, something didn't sound right with Marge's car. I think it might be the transmission. Also, you can get a new car while you're there and surprise your mom. What ya say, ol' buddy?"

"Okay, sounds great. Now can I get some sleep?" mumbled Phil.

"Yeah, sure. Catch you later, buddy," said George.

Phil was up around 8:00 p.m. He showered quickly, then packed what he thought he'd need. He decided to call his mom. No one answered, so he left a message.

"Hi, Mom. Where did you go this time? You know it's getting harder to catch up with you these days. Are you sure you don't have a boyfriend you're not telling me about? Look, I've got to go to Boise for a couple of days, and when I get back, I'll tell you all about it. I've got a big surprise for you."

He hung up, then phoned George and Marge to say he was ready. After leaving food and water for Sparky, he headed for the door, locked it behind him, and went to the car. Halfway there he felt like he'd forgotten something. Thinking it was just nerves, he started for George's place.

He pulled into George's driveway, and they came scrambling out. "You got everything?" he asked.

"Yep. How about you?" said George.

"I don't know. Man, this millionaire stuff is making me crazy." Laughing, Phil said, "But it feels so-o-o good. Let's see—got my bag, cat's taken care of, thermostat's down, lights out, door locked... Can't think of anything else."

Marge piped up. "Do you have the ticket?"

"Oh my! Oh my! How nuts is that? That's it!" cried Phil.

"Figures," Marge muttered under her breath.

"Oh, for Pete's sake, Phil!" George was exasperated.

"Look, I've never had this happen before, so give me a break, will ya? You don't have to come with me—I can do this on my own."

"It'll be okay," said Marge. "We're all a little strung out and hyped up over this."

They drove back to Phil's. He rushed inside, grabbed the ticket—still on the table where he'd left it—slipped it into his pocket, and headed out the door.

While Phil was inside, George turned to his wife. "Are you sure you want to do this?"

"Yes, George, I'm sure. This is our only chance to have what we want. And sixty-eight million dollars can make us happy for a long time." She paused. "You're sure he hasn't told anyone?"

"I'm positive," George said, as Phil came back to the car.

"Now we're ready," said Phil.

They pulled away in silence, each sunk in private thoughts.

Out on the highway, passing the sign that read *Leaving Kamish*, Phil said aloud, "Just think—if I come back here in a few days, I'll be rich."

"Wha... what d-do you m-mean *if* you come back?" George stammered, wondering, *Does he know what's going to happen?*

"Well, what if I decide to go somewhere else and then send for my mom? There are a lot of other places to live besides Kamish, you know."

Relieved a little, George said, "Yeah, I guess you're right."

Silence fell again, making the car feel closed in—like a tomb.

Halfway to Main Ville, Marge couldn't take the quiet any longer and turned on the radio. Not liking the Christian station, she asked, "Mind if I change it?"

"Sure, but no hard rock," said Phil. "I can't stand that."

Smiling, she tuned in a country station. "Could we stop in Main Ville to top off the fuel and grab a bite? Then we can make it to Boise without stopping again."

"Sounds good to me," said George.

"Sure. I could use a Coke," said Phil.

Except for the radio, it was quiet again.

George was at war with himself. He and Phil had worked together for more than six years and had grown close. Now jealousy and greed were pushing him toward something terrible against the one person who truly cared for him. *How can I do this to my best friend?* Then anger took over. *If Phil hadn't bought that ticket, none of this would be happening. And he wouldn't have tried to make a move on my wife, either. He's not the good Christian he pretends to be. He deserves what's coming.* Shame crept in: *He's even made me feel like a worthless bum. Yeah, I gotta teach him a lesson.*

George had walked into Satan's trap. He was hooked and being played for the little fish he had become.

At Main Ville, George and Marge went into the store for drinks while Phil pumped gas.

"Marge," George whispered, "you got the stuff?"

"Of course, you idiot. What do you think? And keep it down. You want the whole world to know what we're doing?"

"Of course not. I just want to do this and get it over with," he shot back.

"So come over here so we're not in plain sight," she snarled.

She handed him a small medicine bottle. He twisted off the cap and dumped the equivalent of two tablespoons of powder into Phil's drink.

"My word—how many sleeping pills did you crush?" asked George.

"Enough to do the job," she said with a wink and a sinister smile. "I want to make sure he doesn't know what we're doing until it's done. Don't forget to leave your wallet on the counter so you can have Phil look for it when he goes inside to pay for the gas. That'll give this stuff plenty of time to dissolve. We need to stall for about thirty minutes. After that—it'll be sleepy time."

"How are we going to stall?" George whispered.

"For crying out loud, George—do I have to do all the thinking? Don't answer that. We'll just say, 'Hey, Phil, since we're here, let's get those burgers we talked about on the way.' He won't suspect a thing."

"I hope it works," George said flatly.

"You got any better ideas, Mr. Brainchild?" Marge sneered.

"No."

"Okay, then. Let's pay and get out of here."

Kind of gung-ho, isn't she, George thought. *Has she done anything like this before? Maybe I should keep a closer eye on her from now on.*

Back at the car, George called out, "Hey, Phil, I think I left my wallet on the counter. Can you check when you go in?"

"Sure," Phil yelled. He finished fueling, washed the windshield, and headed inside.

"Okay, keep an eye on him and tell me when he's almost done," Marge said, opening her door. She walked to the rear of the car, opened the fuel door, took off the gas cap, and set it on top of the pump—making it look as if Phil had forgotten to put it back.

Back in the car, she asked, "What time is it?"

"10:30," said George.

"Good. We'll stall another half hour before we take off. By then the traffic will be light—hardly anyone drives that road after ten."

"Why did you take the gas cap off?" asked George.

"Shhh—here he comes," she hissed. "I'll tell you later."

Phil got in and pulled away from the pumps to park by the curb. "Let's go in and get a bite," he said.

"Is this Coke mine?" he asked, nodding toward the cup.

"Yep—sure is," Marge chirped, handing him the tampered soda.

George watched her. She reminded him of a black widow spider snaring her prey—slowly winding Phil into a web while he waited helplessly for the final strike. Afterward, Phil would be relieved of his money, and *we* would be the rich ones. Another thought chilled him: *If she's this manipulative before she gets the money, what will she be like after?*

He shivered as cold ran down his spine.

"What do you think, George?" asked Phil.

"Huh? About what?"

"About eating a bite and saving the snacks for the road."

"Oh—yeah. Sounds good. I was daydreaming. Sorry."

They headed inside to see what they could find for dinner.

"Oh yeah—here's your wallet, George," Phil said. "It was on the counter where you left it. Not much in it, though." He grinned.

They all laughed—George, a bit nervously.

Phil drank half his Coke without stopping. "Man, this tastes kind of strange. Must not be enough carbonation or something." He turned to the cashier. "Excuse me, miss. This Coke tastes funny. Is it okay if I fill my cup with something else?"

"Yes, sir, go right ahead," she said.

Her name tag read *Jill*. The first thing Phil noticed was her smile, and he liked her right away.

"Looks like I'm going to have to come over here a little more often," he teased.

Jill blushed and smiled back.

"We'd like to get some burgers and stuff before we take off. What do you have that's hot?" asked Marge.

While they ordered, George held his breath. With his luck, this whole scheme was bound to unravel. Phil had already suspected something was wrong with his drink. Could George actually go through with it?

"What's the matter, George?" asked Phil.

"Oh, just a slight headache. I'll be all right once I eat," George said.

"So, what are you going to do with all that money?" asked Marge.

George shot her a sideways glance.

"Oh, I don't know. I'll probably come back to Kamish," Phil said. "There's a house about six miles downriver that Mom really likes. Actually two homes—both for sale. One's a log home; that's the one I like best. The other is the one my mom was talking about yesterday. It's a bit secluded, but what a view. Mom doesn't mind that it's back a ways—she likes the quiet."

"Is it real nice inside?" asked Marge.

"I guess—it depends on what you call nice. My mom sure thinks so," Phil said.

"Wow. Sounds just right for your mom," said George.

"Yeah—Mom really loves the place. She's been looking at it for a long time. The driveway needs work, but with what I'm about to get, I can afford it."

George ate nervously, looking back and forth between Phil and Marge. *How can she be so calm knowing what we're about to do to this poor, unsuspecting man? She's enjoying this.* He swallowed. *I'd better watch her after this is over. She might set a trap for me—especially if she thinks I'll double-cross her. One thing's for sure: she's ruthless. A true black widow.*

"Boy, Phil, that really sounds nice. I'll bet your mother will enjoy it," Marge said, snapping him from his thoughts.

"For sure! Man, is she going to be surprised. I haven't even told her I won yet." He laughed, giddy.

"You're right about that," Marge said smugly. "She *will* be surprised."

George cringed, hoping Phil missed the edge in her voice. *She'd better be careful or she'll let the cat out of the bag.*

"Whew," said Phil. "I didn't know I was this tired. Must not have slept as well as I thought. Do you mind driving when we head out, George? With the rain starting, I'm not sure I can keep my mind on the road instead of the wipers."

"Yeah, I can drive for a while. We'll switch down the road," George replied.

"Good. I'll get a little shut-eye, and then I'll be all right. Wake me when you're ready to swap," Phil said, yawning.

"Sure—I can do that," said George, wishing it were true but knowing it was too late to change course. He'd have to deal with Marge if he backed out now, and one look into those cold blue eyes convinced him he didn't want to tangle with her. He had no doubt he'd lose. From now on, he'd have to watch her closely and figure out this *new* person. He'd never seen this side of sweet little Marge.

He studied her from the corner of his eye. This was not the woman he'd fallen in love with four years ago and married a year later. In the single day since they'd found out about the ticket, she had completely changed. She'd put this scheme together in a few hours. He'd gone along without really thinking. In his jealous anger—hearing what Phil supposedly said and did—her idea had sounded good.

Now that he'd calmed down, he had doubts. Not just because Phil was his friend—but because of what *she* was becoming. She was beginning to frighten him.

CHAPTER 4

FIRE IN THE RAVINE

"I hope you don't mind if I snore, but I'm going to hurry up and lie down. Man, I'm really tired—must be all the excitement. Oh, by the way, I'm going to give you guys a couple of mil just for going with me. I mean, it's not like I won't be able to afford it and all," Phil laughed. "Anyway, I believe that's what God would want me to do, even though it was wrong to buy the ticket."

George shuddered. This man not only showed he was a Christian in his daily walk, but even now, in this very moment, he was still teaching them how to live. *If only I could tell him: Hey, Phil, we're going to rid you of your money—what do you think of that? Or even: Run, Phil! Get out of here! It's a trap!* If only he had enough guts to say *something.*

"George, are you ready to go?" asked Marge. "It's getting late, and Phil's really sleepy."

"Yeah," he said. His feelings and emotions were drained. He was struggling with all of it. He realized he wanted no part of this but couldn't muster the courage to tell Marge no. He knew he was in too far and couldn't turn back now, so he got behind the wheel and drove off.

As they pulled onto the highway, George looked over at Marge. She seemed to be gloating over her intended victim. She sat there, smiling and nodding to herself while she watched Phil, who was stretched out in the back seat. It looked like she was carrying on a conversation with herself—and maybe she was. He wondered if she had sold her soul for the money. There was nothing beautiful about her anymore, he decided—just a cynical, predatory animal about to eat its prey.

About a mile out of town, Marge reached up, took apart the interior light, and broke the bulb.

Phil watched, but he was so far gone he thought it might be a dream. He couldn't move, anyway. He had already tried. Then he realized he wasn't dreaming.

"What did you do that for?" asked George.

"Well, dummy, when we stop to take care of everything, no one can see us open the doors," Marge said, her voice so hoarse he could barely recognize it. "They won't think much of headlights coming to a stop, but if the interior light comes on, they might get nosy. If they get nosy and take a good look, they might get suspicious and call the police. So this is protection. Get it now?"

Marge turned back and looked at Phil. He was so still. She reached out and checked his pulse and barely found one at all. As she reached in and grabbed the ticket, Phil opened his eyes. For the first time, a flicker of knowing came into them. He managed to whisper, "Oh Lord, help me. I don't know what's happening." Then sleep overtook him once more.

Marge giggled like a schoolgirl, kissed the ticket, and slipped it into her purse. "You're mine now, baby."

"Do you really think we should do this? I mean, are we really going to get away with it?" asked George.

"Oh, are we getting cold feet, Mr. Chicken? It's a little late to go back now," Marge chided.

"I just don't want to do this to my friend. This isn't right. But now I don't have a choice," whimpered George.

"You've got that right, George—you *have* to do it. Because if you don't, something could possibly happen to you. You *do* have an insurance policy, you know... maybe not as much as this, but it would do in a pinch," Marge said in an icy voice.

George shuddered again. "I never thought... I never knew... how money could mean so much..." He drifted off into thought. The cold realization of what she had just said began to sink in, and sweat broke out across his back. *She truly is a psycho. I thought I knew her, but I don't think I ever did.*

"You see, George," Marge started again, "I'm going to have money one way or the other. Remember that night we went to Coeur d'Alene four years ago? You told me you had a five-hun-dred-thousand-dollar policy on yourself. You told me because you thought it would impress me. Well, I waited long enough to find out if it was true—then I married you. You ought to thank Phil back there. When he bought that winning ticket, he probably saved your neck. Because now I can have the money *and* you. You can quit right now—just pull over and get out—but remember, George, *you* put the powder in his drink, not me. And who are they going to believe? You—or a hysterical housewife who can't believe her husband just destroyed his best friend for money?"

George reluctantly stayed on the highway as they started up the mountain toward the pass. No matter how he looked at it, he was guilty. She had made sure of that. The powder alone was probably enough to take him down. *How could I have been so stupid and blind to buy into this scheme? I just wish I was somewhere else... anywhere else but here,* George thought remorsefully.

By the time they reached the pass, George was visibly shak-ing—not from excitement, but from the pure fear of what lay ahead.

Earlier that day, Marge had driven her car up to the top, and George had followed in his pickup. They found a place where a car would fit between two boulders about halfway down the other side. Beyond the boulders, the ground dropped in a long, steep fall to the ravine below. They left Marge's car uphill about thirty yards from the spot she had picked for the would-be accident.

Then they drove back to Kamish in George's pickup. Everything was still going according to Marge's plan. After tonight, Kamish—with all the people they knew and everything they had left—would be a thing of the past. Their lives were about to change with no way of turning back. George tried to swallow the lump in his throat as loneliness, deceit, and greed sank into his soul. He knew for the first time in his life that he was lost. But he was going to go through with it—come what may.

As they reached the top of the hill and started down the other side, nearing where they'd left Marge's car, George was in deep thought, trying to figure out a way out—knowing there wasn't one. He could feel Marge's eyes on him like knives.

"Wake up, George, from wherever you are. We're almost there."

Too soon, they were pulling into the spot they had chosen. George stopped between the boulders.

"Be ready," Marge said as she got out of the passenger side. She opened the back of the wagon and grabbed their bags.

"What are you going to do?" asked George.

"You just get him behind the wheel. Don't worry about me," snapped Marge. "And don't put it in drive until I tell you."

Slowly, George opened his door, then the back door where Phil lay. *He looks dead,* George thought as he reached for him. *No, he's still breathing.* He lifted Phil and half dragged him to the driver's door. It took a little doing to get him in; he had to tuck Phil's legs last. *I didn't realize he was so tall—or that a sleeping body could weigh so much.*

The engine was already running. George grabbed the brick he'd stored beside one of the boulders earlier and pressed it onto the gas pedal. The engine roared.

"Okay," said Marge. "Let her go."

Reluctantly, George reached over and pulled the shift lever into *Drive.* He barely made it out of the car before it lurched forward.

A flash flared near the rear. George realized Marge had jammed a strip of cloth into the fuel spout and lit it. "What's that?" he shouted, stunned. Marge didn't answer; she had already shouldered their bags and started up the road toward her car.

It was raining, so the tires spun before they found traction. George stood there, horrified, as the wagon slid and then disappeared over the embankment.

He ran to the edge and looked down in utter despair as the car tumbled end over end down the steep hillside. It exploded, caught fire, then exploded again as it slammed into the bottom of the ravine.

While he stood there, tangled in his thoughts, he heard a car approaching and froze as the headlights washed over him. He glanced around for a place to hide, wondering who would be up here on a night like this. Instead of running, he stood immobilized—like a deer in the headlights—staring at the oncoming car. Only when it drew close did he recognize Marge. He let out a long breath of relief. In all the chaos, he had forgotten that she'd gone to get their car.

She pulled alongside. George opened the door and got in, tears streaking his face. He was already sorry.

"Is it over?" asked Marge. "I mean, is it on fire and all?"

"Yes," mumbled George.

"Good. What are you crying for? We're rich now," Marge snapped. "It's not like he felt anything. He didn't even know what was happening. He was too far gone. Straighten up and act like a man, for crying out loud. If I'd known you were going to bawl and carry on, I would've done the job myself."

"Yeah, but he was still alive—I could tell he was breathing."

George ignored her rant and stared out the side window into the darkness and the flicker of firelight below as they drove away. No insult in the world could make him stop crying or feel less low. He had done the worst thing imaginable. He had killed his best friend—for money. He wished he had never been born.

Mike Patterson woke early that morning. He climbed out of bed and crossed the cold wooden floor to where his pants and shirt hung over the back of an old rocking chair. After dressing, he sat on the bed and pulled on his work boots. He stood, stretched this way and that to work out the kinks, then headed for the bathroom to get ready for the day.

A few minutes later, Mike stepped into the kitchen and took a seat at the table. "Morning, darlin'. How's my little helper this morning?"

"Fine, Papa," said Annie, already at the stove. It was five o'clock, but she looked like she'd been up for hours. She'd been calling him "Papa" since their wedding day fifty-four years earlier.

"Annie, did you hear anything strange last night?" asked Mike.

"No, dear. Why?"

"Well, I could have sworn I heard a blast or something loud. Not too close, though. Had to be around midnight, I reckon. I think I'll take a drive up the canyon after breakfast and see what I can find."

"Mind if I tag along? I'd sure like to get some morning air for a change," said Annie.

"You're always welcome to come along with me, little darlin'," Mike said, winking as he gave her a gentle pat.

Annie smiled as she set breakfast on the table.

They talked about the farm, the cows, and the garden. "Oh, Papa, I need some more canning supplies. I've got plenty of jars, but I need lids, rings, and some pectin. Uh... yes, some sugar and vinegar, too."

"Okay. We'll run over to Main Ville and see what we can pick up. We can do that after we run up the canyon. I'm puzzled about that noise, though. Maybe someone was getting some beef at a discount," he chuckled, "but it sounded more like a blast than anything—lot heavier than any of my shooters."

"I guess I should have checked it out when I heard it, but I was too doggone tired to crawl out of bed."

"Now, Papa, don't you fret about it. Things will work out. They always do."

Mike pushed back from the table with a sigh, feeling a little older than he was. "I tell you, Annie, these old bones hurt more after a full night's rest than if I just kept working twenty-four hours a day." He grabbed his jacket from the peg by the back door.

"Oh, my poor Papa," she cooed. "Come here and let me help you with your jacket. It's bound to be chilly out there at this hour."

After a bit of small talk, Annie slipped on her jacket and they headed out to their old Ford pickup.

"You know, Papa, if you made some steps for me, you wouldn't have to lift me up like this," Annie said.

"You're probably right, but that would take all the fun out of it." He snickered, lifted her as gently as a baby bird, and set her on the seat.

As Mike started the truck, daylight was just enough to see by.

"What a beautiful morning, Papa—and it's still early," Annie said.

"Well, sit back and enjoy the ride, little darlin'." He frowned. "I don't know—I feel something's wrong, but I can't quite put my finger on it. I've got a bad feeling about this, deep in my gut."

"I hate it when you get those premonitions. Your feelings haven't been wrong yet, and something bad always seems to turn up," Annie said softly.

Mike pulled onto what the locals called Old Speckled Bird Road. About midway up the grade, they noticed smoke hanging in the air.

"That's strange," he muttered. "Not many people use this part of the road anymore."

"Is that smoke up ahead, Papa?" asked Annie.

"I believe it is. Looks like something might be on fire. We'd better pull over and check it out when we get closer," Mike said, his brow furrowed.

When they rounded a bend, he thought he saw something but couldn't quite tell what. Smoke was curling up from near the valley floor, not far from their property.

"Annie, you stay here. I'll be right back. I'm going to take a peek."

He closed the door and walked to the edge of the hill. He peered down. Something that might have been a mangled piece of burning metal flickered through the haze. His eyes weren't what they used to be. He headed back to the truck.

"I think the trip to Main Ville will have to wait," he said as he climbed in. "There's something smoldering on the back of our property."

He turned the truck around and drove back down Old Speckled Bird Road toward their house. Nearing the drive, he turned off onto a narrow dirt road that led up the valley floor toward the rear acreage. At the gate at the mouth of the ravine, Mike hopped out, swung it open, then drove through. They rode in silence. His gut told him this was going to be bad—and not a pretty sight. It was a long drop from the highway above.

As they rounded a hillside, the wreckage came into view—charred and jumbled, an unrecognizable tangle of smoldering metal.

"Annie," Mike said, "you'd better get on the radio and raise the sheriff. Looks like there's been a wreck."

"Yes... I think you're right. Oh my word, Papa—oh my," she gasped, turning the CB to channel nine.

CHAPTER 5

ECHOES FROM THE RAVINE

M ike sat quietly, holding Annie as they stared blankly at the wreckage. Burned patches dotted the slope where the vehicle had tumbled end over end down the steep hillside. Fortunately, last night's rain kept the fires from spreading more than a few feet in any one spot. The exception was at the bottom of the ravine where the vehicle had stopped and exploded; there, flames had spread around the jangled mass of molten metal and glass.

Officers from Main Ville arrived in response to Annie's CB call. Instead of going directly to Mike and Annie, the county sheriff and his deputy first searched the area where the vehicle had gone over the embankment. After peering down into the ravine, the sheriff whistled. "Man, this vehicle took one heck of a ride. We'd better get some help up here."

As the deputy called for backup, the sheriff began a slow, methodical survey. He looked for skid marks on the highway, any sign of braking near the turnout, and disturbance at the edge where the vehicle had left the road. He found no evidence of braking. Studying the path just before the drop, he spotted two parallel tracks in the wet gravel—marks of spinning tires that led straight to the edge and ended abruptly. He also noticed smaller footprints that appeared to start on the passenger side and loop around to the driver's side, along with a larger set on the driver's side. What he didn't register were the faint drag marks beside the prints.

The sheriff began issuing orders. "Rope off the entire area. I want at least four people working the hillside, searching for remains and anything out of place. Bring extra ribbon in case we need it."

"I figured we might," the deputy said. "Already taken care of."

"Good. I've got a feeling this is going to be a mess," the sheriff said.

They had just finished stringing ribbon along the top of the embankment when the backup team arrived. After a quick briefing, the sheriff motioned for his deputy to come with him. "Let's get down to the bottom and see what's left."

They drove around to the back side of the Patterson property, following Annie's directions. Mike eased out of his truck and met them halfway.

The sheriff extended a hand. "Are you Mr. Patterson?"

"Yes, I am," Mike replied.

"I'm Sheriff Gage; this is Deputy Pipcorn, out of the Main Ville office. We'll need to talk to you and your wife, so if you don't mind, please stick around while we take a quick look."

"We'll be here," Mike said.

The officers approached the burned-out shell.

"What a mess," Deputy Pipcorn muttered.

"You can say that again," Sheriff Gage said. "Can you see anything inside?"

"Not much left... but it was a car," the deputy said, leaning through the opening where the windshield had been. "If that's a body, I only see one."

"Yeah, I think you're right," the sheriff said, looking past him. "I noticed something strange up top: no braking—no skid marks on the highway or the turnout. And those huge boulders... how did he miss them? I *did* find two parallel tracks in the gravel, like a car stopped and then spun its tires before going over. Maybe he wanted to take a quick ride out." He paused. "But what troubles me is the two different sizes of footprints on the driver's side."

"You think it might not be an accident?" the deputy asked.

"I don't know yet," Gage said. "If not, it's either suicide or homicide. I can't see a man dozing off and threading that gap between the rocks without touching either. I checked—no scrapes on those boulders at all. Nearly impossible, given how close they are. I've got a bad feeling, but nothing to substantiate it. We'll wait for the investigation. Maybe the coroner can tell us something."

"Either way, we've got our hands full," the deputy said.

"No doubt. Get the lab boys out here. I want plaster casts of the tracks up top—and the footprints."

The coroner arrived, taking in the scene with a grim shake of his head. He looked up the path where the car had tumbled before coming to rest in a twisted heap.

"Hope you boys haven't touched anything," he said.

"No, sir," the sheriff replied. "Just a look to see if anyone was inside."

"We'll need the fire department to cut this metal away from my victim," the coroner said.

"That's an understatement," the sheriff murmured. He hated accidents—especially the ones that ended like this. He had never grown used to death.

"What's your call?" the deputy asked.

"Officially, let's log it as an accident for now," Gage said. "But a lot doesn't add up. We'll know more once the evidence is in and the autopsy's done. Did they get everything cordoned off up there?"

"Yes," Deputy Pipcorn said. Seeing the sheriff's frown, he asked, "What are you thinking?"

"I'm going back up top for another look. Something's being overlooked," Gage said. "Stick here and assist with recovery." As he spoke, Investigators Cahill and Jones arrived.

"What've we got?" Cahill asked.

"A mess," Gage said. "Deputy, give Jones a rundown and take statements from Mike and Annie so they can head home. I'll take Cahill back up and walk him through what we've seen. And the wrecker and fire truck?"

"On the way," the deputy said.

"Make sure the wrecker brings a flatbed," Gage added.

"Already requested."

Gage and Cahill returned to the turnout. "We'll look at this from every angle. On the surface, it mimics a suicide," Gage said, "but it doesn't fit: no skid marks, and if he'd been at or near the limit, he'd have landed farther out. Plus these burned patches—looks like the car caught fire *before* it went over. How does that happen?"

"I agree," Cahill said. "It's suspicious."

"Exactly—and that's just the start," Gage said, filling him in as they parked behind a patrol unit. Several deputies were combing the turnout and sighting down the slope for missed clues.

"Sir, you'll want to see this," an officer called.

"What've you got?" Gage asked.

"There's a burned area about forty feet down the hill from that patch there," the officer said, pointing. "Found this in the middle—looks like a rag. Burned."

"Let me see," Gage said, studying the charred cloth. "Cahill, hold the scene. Nobody moves anything." He jogged to the car and radioed the deputy.

After a minute, a breathless voice answered. "Yeah—go ahead, Sheriff. Sorry—was interviewing the Pattersons when the lab guys started waving like they'd found another body. I hustled over. I gotta lay off Betty's doughnuts and—"

"We'll discuss your fitness later," Gage cut in. "Check the vehicle for a gas cap. Tell me what you find."

"Hold on." The deputy hurried to the left side of the wreck. The fuel door was twisted; the tank had ruptured. The only recognizable piece was the open spout.

"Sheriff, you still there?"

"Ten-four. Go ahead."

"No gas cap on the vehicle—or anywhere near it," the deputy reported. "You find one up there?"

"No," Gage said. He glanced at the scorched rag again. "Looks like someone stopped, stuffed a rag into the tank, lit it, and then drove off the edge. One heck of a way to go."

The coroner's sedan rolled up. He joined them at the shoulder. "Victim's male," he reported.

"I wonder what drives a man to choose *this* way out," Gage said quietly. "From what I've seen, he probably suffered before he died."

"No argument," the coroner said. "Something new every day."

Gage keyed the radio again. "Let's start wrapping. Have you run the plates?"

"Ten-four," Deputy Pipcorn replied. "Registered to Phillip Allen Gunn—white male, DOB eleven-twenty-six–sixty-eight—two hundred ten pounds, brown eyes. Address: Boyd's Mobile Home Park, number eleven, Kamish."

"Thanks," Gage said. "We'll wait for your next-of-kin update and the coroner's findings. State investigators can take it from here. Head back to the station and start the paperwork. I'll finish here and come pick you up."

"Ten-four," the deputy said.

The coroner glanced down-slope at the twisted metal. "He must've had serious problems to end himself like this. There are easier ways. I guess there's no end to what people will do."

CHAPTER 6

THE FACES THEY WEAR

G eorge stewed all the way to Boise without saying a word. His mind was back on Speckled Bird Road. *How could I have ever let this happen? Where do I go from here? What am I supposed to feel like now? Oh, God—what have I done?* He began weeping again.

Marge was deep in thought too, but hers ran to the things money could buy—homes, cars, clothes. Her mind reveled in the prospect of finally living in the lap of luxury.

Just outside Horseshoe Bend, she said, "I want a home on the beach in California, George. Oh—forgot to tell you. I've got a friend in Boise who's going to help us get new IDs. We can't be George and Marge Wetzel anymore. We'll go by Terrance and Jody Weinburger. What do you think?"

George only nodded.

"You know," she went on, "you'll have to beef up a bit—get in shape, look more respectable. You can't go around looking like a down-and-out bum, especially when we pick up the check. And cheer up, for crying out loud. We can't show up for the money all long-faced, can we? Besides, there isn't anything we can do for poor old Phil now—except thank him for the ticket."

When she laughed at that, George exploded. "You conniving little wench! Haven't you got any feelings? What in the heck are you made of—stone? We just killed my best friend! And for what? Money? Do you know what this means, Marge?" he seethed.

"Yes—that we're millionaires. And the name isn't Marge; it's *Jody* now, remember?" she shot back. "Anyway, you'd better get it together, Mr. High-and-Mighty. *You* put the sleeping powder in his drink, not me. And *you* sent him over the edge. Or did you forget already?"

"Yeah—and I'm sorry I ever let you talk me into this," he yelled.

"Don't get sanctimonious on me. You wanted him dead as much as I did. Stop your yelling and crying and pull yourself together. When are you going to start acting like a real man?" Marge spat. "Move on, George. What's done is done. It's over. End of story."

That ended the shouting. Silence swallowed the miles. George fumed. This was a nightmare, disaster written all over it. But she was right: *I put the powder in Phil's drink. I sent him over the embankment. Man, did I play into her hands. I've never been such a fool in all my life.*

About five miles before they reached the small town of Banks, roughly thirty miles from Boise, Marge said, "Let's stop in Banks so I can call Jerry—the friend who'll set us up with new IDs and different appearances."

"Whatever," George said flatly. "Why did you set Phil's car on fire?"

"If you'd paid attention to those crime-lab shows, you'd know," she said proudly. "Once a body's burned, it's very hard—almost impossible—to find anything in the bloodstream or stomach because of the heat."

George stared straight ahead.

"Anyway, I'll call Jerry and see if he can meet us after nine."

"How do you know he'll do it?"

"He owes me a favor," Marge said bluntly.

"Sounds like you two have worked together before," George prodded.

"Stop prying," she snapped. "All you need to know is he owes me. If you're smart, you'll leave it at that."

She paused. "You know what—forget calling from Banks. I'll call when we get into Boise. Then we'll get the show on the road."

When they arrived in Boise, Marge asked, "Want to get something to eat?"

"I'm not hungry," George muttered.

"Look, you've got to pull yourself together. It's 6:30 now—so you've only got a couple more hours to do it. You're starting to make me *mad*. I'm warning you, George: if you don't act normal, I'll get the makeover and the money myself. And trust me—you don't want that to happen," she said, menacing.

"I'll be okay," he said. He gave her a cold look that made her shiver; maybe she'd underestimated him.

"Maybe call Jerry now and see what he wants us to do," George suggested, half-heartedly.

"That's a good idea," she said quickly. "There's the George I fell for—George the thinker."

George flashed a false smile. *Might as well play along. Too late to turn back now, no matter how sick she makes me feel about all this.* "I'll try to eat something," he added. "Maybe it'll help."

"Good boy. Let's hit that truck stop at the next exit. We'll eat, and I'll call Jerry from there," Marge said, suddenly cheerful. Maybe George was coming around.

Inside the café, they stopped at the pay phones by the door.

"Stand over there and make sure nobody gets too close while I'm on the phone," Marge ordered. "I don't want busybodies eavesdropping."

"I can't tell people they can't use the phone. Take the end phone; I'll 'use' the one next to you so no one can get close," George said.

"Great idea," she said brightly, giving him a chilly peck on the cheek. She lifted the receiver; George did the same beside her. The other line rang eight or nine times before answering.

"Hello, Jerry?... Margie—yes, Calderman. Who did you think?... I'm fine. Look, I'm in a hurry—save the small talk. Remember the favor you owe me? The *big* favor? Can you talk now? Good. Here's the deal..."

When she finished, Marge hung up and winked. "All finished. Ready to eat?"

"That was quick," George scoffed.

"When you need something done, you don't beat around the bush. He owes me big-time, so he didn't have much choice but to listen. He'll do it. He knew he'd have to pay up one day. It's nice when people owe you favors. And believe me—I've got plenty owed to me," she smirked.

"Jerry says we need a hotel room. Stay inside and out of sight until after dark. Makes sense. He'll meet us at 9:30 at Seventeenth and Ustick. And what are you doing in those muddy shoes? For Pete's sake—that's why I packed your boots! I took mine off hours ago. What's the matter with you?"

"Whatever, Marge," he said, rolling his eyes.

They ate mostly in silence. George thought about the night before—and about his best friend, now dead by his hands. He thought of all the times he'd relied on Phil. Day or night, the man was always there—always willing to help, always smiling, always lifting people up. That smile would haunt George for the rest of his life.

Marge's thoughts were elsewhere. Phil was the last thing on her mind. She was thinking about Jerry. *Jerry, old buddy, you came in handy at just the right time. Glad you're still around.* Her mind drifted back to the night she earned his favor. *Six years already?* It seemed so long ago when she heard that desperate knock at her apartment door.

Marge had gotten up from the sofa and checked the peephole. Jerry stood on the stoop, looking around nervously, hands jammed in his pockets, stamping his feet against the cold.

She unlocked the door. Jerry pushed past her into the living room.

"Close the door and get in here, Margie," he whispered hoarsely. "Hurry—help me get these lights off."

"Why? What the—" Marge began.

"Just do it," he snapped. "I'll explain later."

She locked the door and killed the remaining lights. In the bedroom, the neighbor's porch light striped the room through the venetian blinds. Jerry sat on the edge of the bed, kicking off his shoes.

"Why all the sneaking in the dark, Jerry?" she hissed. "You're going to tell me what's going on, or your little behind is right back out that door."

"Not now, Margie. We don't have time. Get your PJs on and hop into bed. If anyone comes to the door, tell them I've been here all night—and we've been in bed since eight-thirty, okay?"

"Why? What happened?" She gave him a cool, appraising look.

"Just do this for me—cover for me—and I'll owe you one. Anything you want. Please," he pleaded.

She studied him a long moment. "Okay, Jerry. But you'd better come through when I need it. And later, I want the truth—not your usual line of garbage."

"You got it, babe. You won't regret it," he said, relief flooding his voice as he slid under the covers, clothes and all.

"Whether I'll regret it is yet to be seen," she said, slipping into her pajamas.

Ten minutes later, a hard knock rattled the door.

"Just a minute," Marge called in her best sleepy voice. The knocks came again, more insistent. "I'm coming, I'm coming—for crying out loud, hold your pants on!"

Through the peephole she saw two uniformed officers.

Time to earn that favor, she thought, steadying her breath. She opened the door. "Hi, officers. Can I help you?"

"Good evening, miss," the taller one said. "There's been a shooting nearby. The perpetrator was last seen entering this complex. Have you heard anything strange or suspicious in the past half hour?"

"No, not that I'm aware of," she said with feigned concern. "I've been sleeping, so I'm afraid I won't be much help."

"Are you alone?" the officer asked.

"No, my boyfriend's here. He's a heavy sleeper—didn't even hear you knocking. He's been out cold since about eight-thirty. But if I see or hear anything, I'll tell you right away," Marge lied smoothly.

"That'll be fine. Keep your doors and windows locked; don't open to strangers. The suspect is armed and dangerous and on the run."

"Yes, I'm sure there's no telling what he'd do," she said wryly. "I hope you catch him, officers. I know I won't feel safe until you do." She closed the door, smiling to herself.

Marge, you deserve an Oscar for this one. She glanced toward the bedroom. *Yes, Jerry—you definitely owe me. Who knew one of your drug deals gone bad would pay off years later? Good old Jerry shoots a man and needs an alibi. Little Margie is in the right place at the right time—and gives him one. And now, Jerry pays it back with new IDs for Marge and George. Ah, the wheels of fate. Isn't life grand?*

CHAPTER 7

NIGHT OF NO RETURN

George and Marge spent the rest of the day in a motel room at the inn within walking distance of the truck stop where they'd eaten earlier. They were both tuckered out; neither had slept for almost forty-eight hours and they were ready for hot showers and bed.

After they cleaned up, Marge asked, "When do you think we ought to get up?"

"Well," George said, thinking it through, "it's 10:45 a.m. now. We should get at least five or six hours."

"Why don't you just set it for eight p.m.? That will give us plenty of time to get where we're supposed to be," Marge said. Sleep was all she wanted.

"I've got a better idea. Set it for 6:00 p.m., we'll walk over and get something to eat, then call a cab from the truck stop so the driver won't know where we came from," George suggested.

That gave Marge pause; she hadn't expected George to produce a smart plan. "Well... I guess that's better after all. What made you think of that? I'm impressed."

George just stared and said nothing, then reached over and set the alarm for six. They rolled over and soon were asleep.

Four hours later George sat bolt upright in bed, startling Marge awake. "What's the matter?" she mumbled.

"Oh—nothing. Just a nightmare," George said, trying to wave it off.

"Oh, oh—did you see a dead man floating in front of your eyes?" she taunted.

"You're a demented she-devil, Marge! You have no regrets at all about what we've done, do you?" He was boiling again.

"Of course not. Why should I?" she smirked. "It gets easier as you go."

"You're telling me you've done this before?" George was aghast.

"What if I have? You can't prove anything—no one can." She lifted her chin. "But to answer your question—yes. Twice. Once when I was in grade school. Another girl and I were on the slide; I pushed her off. No one was around, so I said she fell. She died. I got away with it. The second time was my ex-boyfriend. Everyone knew he was a drug addict. When they found him with a syringe in his hand, they called it an overdose. I was at work when he was found—perfect alibi. Best part? He left his money to me. Not much, but it helped. Can you believe he *gave himself* the overdose? Ha! I got away with that too."

"You're more evil than I thought," George growled.

"Hey, you married me for better or worse. Remember?" She laughed. "Guess what—it got worse. Oh, and start calling me *Jody*, okay? Now—what was that nightmare about?" she added, dripping sarcasm.

"Nothing," he said, rolling over and turning his back.

"Hmph." She settled and drifted off. George stayed awake, the dream replaying. He was in Phil's kitchen again, staring at the table: a lottery ticket, and a scrap of paper with the winning numbers and *I WON* scrawled beside them. Then another memory kept repeating: *Okay, Mom, gotta run. Bye.*

Two grave mistakes, he thought. *Mistakes that can catch up with us.* Should he tell Marge? *Not on your life.* Whatever came, at least this part would soon be over.

It took a long time for sleep to return, and when it did it was fitful. He saw Phil lying there, then the ball of fire rolling down the mountainside—over and over. At last another dream came: this time, a dove chased him. *Why am I afraid of a little bird?* He ran down a slick, wide path—well traveled by many feet. Just before he dove into oblivion, the dove flashed in front of him. He veered onto another trail climbing back up the mountain—rough, narrow, steep, hardly used. He wanted to turn around, but the dove pressed him on. At the top, the path ended in a Bright Light. He looked back. The dove came again—so he stepped into the light and woke, drenched in sweat, breath ragged. *What does it mean?* He wanted to tell someone, but not Marge. *The less she knows, the better.*

About then the alarm blared. George didn't feel rested, but it was time. He reached up and shut it off. "Marge—time to get up."

"M-m-m—not yet. I'm still sleepy. Can't we sleep a little longer?" she asked. "We've got until nine, don't we?"

"Remember the money—and what we've got to do to get it, okay? This gives us time to eat before we call the cab. You don't want to be late, do you?" He felt like he was scolding a grade-schooler.

"All right, if you insist," she groaned. She sat up, rubbed her eyes, yawned wide enough to swallow a basketball, then headed to the bathroom.

They dressed and walked the two or three hundred feet to the truck-stop café. As they stepped inside, Marge broke the silence. "Do you feel any better about the money?"

"The way I see it, I don't have much choice," George said. "Phil's dead; I can't change that. I might as well enjoy it while it lasts." It was blunt, but true. He knew they'd pay for what they'd done—somehow, somewhere.

"That's one way to look at it," Marge said thoughtfully. "Can you smile for me, or am I reaching too soon?"

George took her hand. *Might as well act like everything's fine—and keep my eye on her. Maybe this makes it easier.* "How's this?" He kissed her. He wished he could fake it; the truth was, he still loved her. That made everything worse.

"Wow—coming around!" Marge beamed. *I've won,* she told herself. "I'll follow you anywhere, mister. Where do you want to sit?"

"Let's sit at the counter. I don't like these booths—too many ears. Up here we can see who's trying to listen." Thinking out loud, he still managed to pacify her.

"Okay by me," Marge said.

"May I help you?" asked the waitress.

"Coffee, and some menus, please," George said. He clocked the woman's rough hands and lined face—someone who'd worked hard and probably taken pride in it. Not that she couldn't use more money; she just liked earning it.

Menus in hand, George scanned the choices. Marge murmured, "We ought to get you some clothes tomorrow. You look pretty rough. Too rough for someone who just won sixty-eight million."

"You're probably right. I wasn't thinking when we left," George said.

"You *weren't thinking* is right. You had too much pity for somebody who thought he was better than you," she sneered.

"I don't think Phil ever thought he was better than anyone! Where do you get that?" George snapped.

"He made a pass at me, and he called you a loser. What else could it mean? Figure it out," she sniffed.

"Oh, it's over now. And your blouse is wrinkled. You could use new clothes too, Mrs. Perfect," George shot back.

"Ready to order?" the waitress asked, refilling their coffee.

"I'll have biscuits and gravy," Marge said.

"Make it two," George added. "Side of bacon and a large milk."

"Be right out," the waitress said, scooping up the menus.

"What's the first thing you want to buy?" Marge asked. "It's not like we can't afford anything we want."

"I haven't let myself think about it," George said. "Maybe I should."

"I'd say so! You can have anything—the world at your fingertips. Snap, and it's yours. Ever had that before?"

George shook his head. Of course not, and she knew it. What ate at him was *how* they'd gotten the money. There would never be enough to wash his hands clean. He'd carry it to his grave—a monkey on his back.

They finished their meal making small talk about what might be nice to have.

Around 7:30—after George paid—then they called for a cab. It arrived in plenty of time to drop them near the meeting place, at Twelfth and Ustick. They paid the driver and watched until his taillights vanished, then walked to Seventeenth and Ustick.

"What's Jerry drive?" George asked.

"I wouldn't know anymore. I doubt I'd even recognize him. Last time I saw him was six years ago. Long, almost yellow hair; beard and mustache to match. Tall and skinny then. I wouldn't venture a guess now," Marge said.

"Thank God it's not raining," George muttered.

"Thank *who*? You don't really believe in Him, do you?" she asked, surprised.

"Let's just say I've got to believe there's *something*. Look at everything—we didn't just *happen*. There's more to it. Besides, I remember a song where the man says, 'I hope there ain't no heaven, and I pray there ain't no hell.' Maybe I'll go with that." *I must sound like an idiot,* he thought. *I don't believe. I could be forgiven anyway.*

"If that's all it takes, George, *I'll* forgive you. How's that? Now forget it, get over it, and get on with your life," Marge said.

"I suppose you're right," George said.

"I am—as usual," Marge gloated.

A black Mercury Town Car glided to the curb. The window whirred down.

Marge bent low and squealed, "Jerry!" Then she lunged halfway through the window, trying to hug him.

"Hurry, Margie. You two need to get in—we don't want to draw attention," Jerry urged.

Marge slid back out, opened the door for herself and George, and they climbed in. As quickly as they arrived, they vanished into the night.

Chapter 8

Paper Souls

"Margie, Margie, *Margie*! You haven't changed a bit—well, maybe a pound or two," Jerry teased.

She swatted his arm. He snickered. "Seriously, I'm glad you called from a pay phone. I'm keeping a low profile these days. Not that I'm in trouble, but the neighborhood's getting too crowded for me. I'm thinking of selling—getting uncomfortable. Good thing you called when you did. Another week and who knows?"

"Okay," he continued, businesslike. "We'll start your IDs tonight. By tomorrow you'll have your bearings. I'm going to tell you what I'd do and how to do it. First—this money: legit or tainted? I have to ask. If it's legit and you just want makeovers, that's one thing. If not, whole different route."

"Well, it's legit... but it's not. You know what I mean?" Marge said.

"Margie, nobody knows what you mean—sometimes I'm not sure *you* do." He grinned. "Don't pout—I'm kidding."

He grew crisp again. "All right, then we go the other way. The cops can probably trace you to the motel. If they're good, they'll trace the taxi drop—but no further. From now on, wear gloves in public. Fewer fingerprints, the better. At least until you're out of state."

Jerry drove about half an hour, turning into a well-to-do neighborhood. He pulled into the fifth driveway on the right—an elegant, oversized home.

"My, Jerry! Doing well for yourself," Marge said, awed.

"Oh, I do all right. You know me, Margie—always got an iron in the fire."

"Any of them legal yet?" she quipped.

Jerry shot her a warning glance.

"Oh, George is fine," Marge went on breezily. "He won't say a word. He just killed his best friend for his money."

George nearly crumpled. *What is she doing?* It had been her idea, and now she was hanging it on him. A blade of pain slid through his chest at the thought of Phil. He almost cried out, but swallowed it.

Okay, lady. If that's how you want to play it—two can play this game.

"That's my kind of guy!" Jerry barked, killing the engine and opening his door. "Come in, get comfortable. We'll get started soon enough."

George noted how rake-thin Jerry was, but said little. This was Marge's friend; better to keep quiet—and he was afraid, wondering how long before Marge turned on him entirely.

At the front walk Jerry detoured behind tall shrubs and up a side stair to the door. Inside, a beautifully appointed entry opened onto a luxurious living room—rich hardwood, a massive fireplace.

"Wow. You're going to sell this?" Marge asked.

"I'm afraid so. Too many eyes, ears, and mouths around here. You know me—I don't like people close. Too many things can go wrong."

"Make yourselves at home while I make a couple calls," he said, pointing at a cabinet. "Booze in there. Other stuff too, if you know what I mean. Help yourselves."

"Yeah, I know you, Jerry. Got a girlfriend?" Marge winked. "I'll have a drink. You, George?"

"Yes, please," George said, stunned by how openly she flirted—as if he weren't there. *Is she trying to needle me—or play this guy?*

Jerry reentered. "You two eaten?"

"Yes," Marge said. "George's idea—walked to the truck stop, ate there, called a cab."

"Smart," Jerry said, nodding at George. "Good call. You done anything like this before?"

"Uh... no," George said.

"That's okay. You'll get used to it." Jerry grinned. "I could use another hand, if you're interested."

"Honestly, we're thinking California," Marge said. "It won't take long for someone to start connecting us. We figured we'd better leave the state."

"Good long-term play. Want advice?"

"Of course," George blurted.

"Leave the country. As soon as you can. With the makeovers and new IDs, nobody will connect you to that guy's death. By Monday you'll be comfortable enough with the new looks to buy clothes and gear for the trip—wherever you're headed. By the way, how much—and where is it? Maybe I can help you get it."

"About sixty-eight million," Marge said, smug.

"Are you kidding?" Jerry stared at George.

"Nope," George said.

"Man, George—I would've done my friend in, too!" Jerry crowed.

"Yeah, well, he made a pass at Marge—that made me mad enough to do... anything, I guess. I mean—" George faltered. He disliked this man, and here he was trying to justify the unjustifiable. The truth was guilt. Remorse. What he'd done was wicked. He wished he could take it all back.

"Guess the excitement's got me twisted," he finished weakly.

"Don't worry about it. Another drink?" Jerry asked.

"I'll have a bourbon," Marge said.

"Sure. George?"

"Fine, thanks."

They settled on the plush couch facing the hearth. Jerry returned with the drinks; small talk drifted between old times and new until the glasses were empty.

"Tell me the whole story while I start your IDs," Jerry said at last. "This has got to be one of the best I've heard—hopefully." He reached behind a framed painting and pressed a sequence of buttons. "Come with me."

A section of floor swung up—a trapdoor revealing a narrow stairway.

"Wow," Marge breathed. "I didn't even see that."

"The other houses don't have basements. This one didn't either. But for what I do, I needed one—so I put one in. Quietly. Tough job, worth it," Jerry said.

"I wouldn't have thought it possible," George said.

The basement wasn't as large as the house but crammed with gear: cameras, printers for documents, laminators, and, farther back, a compact beauty salon.

"Oh—forgot to mention," Jerry said. "Another couple's coming to help with everything. Don't worry if you hear footsteps overhead. And my old lady will be back from the store in ten minutes—she'll be down to help. She's young, but she knows what she's doing. Makes me feel younger, too." He winked at George.

"So—George, for the record—ha, *for the record*, bad choice of words—how'd you end up with the money? I like to know my clients."

"My friend Phil won the lottery," George said.

"You mean someone you *know* actually won that thing?" Jerry was surprised.

"Yeah," George said, hollow.

"That's a switch. Usually takes money to win money. He didn't have much, I take it?"

"Not really," George said. "Maybe a few thousand saved."

"No, Jerry," Marge cut in. "This man was more common than you or me."

The rest of the night—most of it, anyway—went to makeovers, new identifications, and the story of how they ended up with the winning ticket. Once the telling was done, the talk turned to Marge and Jerry, rekindling old times and catching up.

Jerry's wife—a redhead who clearly thought the sun rose and set on him—was pleasant, if treated like a servant. Between her and the other couple, George and Marge became different people.

George was no longer thinning on top, nor brown-haired. He now had a full head of black hair; thanks to Jerry's stash of contacts, his eyes were green. Marge became a brunette with brown eyes.

"Wow," she said, admiring herself in the mirror. "I look stunning. I didn't know lenses worked like this!"

"Hush," Jerry said. "Long way to go."

They worked through the night into early morning, transforming. Exhaustion finally won; they called it a night. The next couple of days were spent mostly lying low in the house, practicing new looks and names.

"Remember," Jerry said, drilling it in, "you two must use these names with *each other* or they won't stick. You've got to learn them and respond to them, automatically. Okay?"

They both nodded.

CHAPTER 9

THE KNOCK AT THE DOOR

Laura Gunn woke at five o'clock on the nose. She'd been waking at that hour without an alarm for as long as she could remember. As always, she reached for John's pillow. A small whimper escaped as she thought of her husband. It had been a little over six years since his heart attack, and she still missed him so much it ached. His passing had left her a heartbroken, lonely woman. She tried not to show it, but she suspected Phillip noticed—by the way she did certain things. He loved her enough to play along. *If only I could do something special for him,* she thought. *Something to show how much he means to me.* One of these days she'd find a way to surprise him.

She lifted John's photo from the nightstand and kissed it. "Someday, honey, I'll be there with you," she whispered.

After a shower and dressing, she headed to the kitchen. The automatic coffeemaker had a fresh pot ready—one of those thoughtful gadgets Phillip kept buying to make her life easier. She smiled and poured a cup.

Through the open window she spotted her neighbor June, across the courtyard, stepping out for her newspaper.

"Good morning, June!" Laura called, waving. June waved back. Next to Phillip, June was Laura's best friend.

Thinking of Phillip, Laura hoped he'd stop by today. She considered calling him now, but he'd likely still be asleep. She'd wait.

She had just started breakfast when June poked her head through the back door nearest the kitchen. "Knock knock."

"Come on in, June," Laura sang. "Want some eggs? You know where the coffee is—help yourself."

"Sounds good to me, kiddo," June said with a smile. "Whatcha got going today?"

"Oh, I don't know," Laura said. "Maybe work on my flowers a little."

"Well, me and a couple of the girls are going for a walk. You might as well join us—exercise those old bones. Those flowers aren't going anywhere," June teased.

"I don't know..." Laura hedged. "Where are you going?"

"To the river. It's a ways, but we can sit in the park and rest before walking back. Haven't been down there for a week or so. Figure it's about time while the weather's still nice."

"Maybe I will," Laura said. "Sounds fun. Okay—count me in."

"Boy, you gave in quick *this* time. I thought I'd have to twist your arm like always," June laughed.

"Going to the park reminds me of John," Laura said softly. "We used to walk there all the time when we lived on Beach Street. He was always saying things like you just did." She smiled as the memories washed over her.

They chatted through the morning. June was about to leave when a knock sounded at the front door.

"Come in!" Laura called from the kitchen.

The door opened and a deputy from the Lewis County Sheriff's Office stepped into the living room. "Hello?"

"We're in the kitchen," Laura said.

"I'm looking for Laura Gunn," he said, appearing in the doorway.

"That's me," Laura answered, rising. "How can I help you?"

"Is your son named Phillip Allen Gunn?"

"Yes," Laura said. "Why do you ask?"

"I think we should sit down in the living room," he replied.

They moved to the living room. The deputy took the old over-stuffed chair. Laura and June sat close together on the sofa, hands entwined.

"There's been an accident out on Speckled Bird Road," he began. "I'm very, very sorry to tell you this, but your son, Phillip, didn't make it."

"No—you're wrong," she said flatly. "He's at home. I'll call him right now and you can talk to him yourself."

"Ma'am, please understand—" he started, but she was already dialing.

"Pick up, Phillip," Laura pleaded into the phone. "He's only sleeping," she told the deputy. "Come on, Phillip... answer the phone... Phillip, I know you're there. Pick it up." The ringing droned on. Tears streamed as she cried into the receiver, "Phil-lip, wake up! Why aren't you answering me?"

Realization landed like a blow. The receiver slipped from her hand and thumped to the floor. She swayed. June leapt up, caught her, and eased them both to their knees, Laura sobbing uncontrollably, rocking, moaning, "Oh, my son, my son, my son."

The deputy twisted his hat in his hands, rose, and hovered, helpless. After a moment he said softly, "I'm so sorry for your loss. If there's anything I can do—if there's any way I can help—please let me know. I'll leave my card here on the coffee table. Feel free to call anytime, okay?"

He wasn't sure she heard, but June looked up, nodded, mouthed *thank you*, then turned back to Laura. The deputy let himself out, closing the door quietly. He stood on the stoop a moment, blinking back tears. He knew Phil too, which made this worse than telling a stranger. It always tore his heart out. This was the part of the job he hated most.

He slid into his squad car and stared through the windshield at nothing. As far as he was concerned, the day was already shot—and it would get worse. He'd spend the morning running into friends of Phillip Gunn's. Phil had been his friend, but he hadn't realized how many lives the man had touched. Today would be a very sad day. One he'd never forget.

Ted—one of Phil's church brothers and a coworker at the mill—was also close to the sheriff. That morning, they crossed paths at the Stop and Go.

"Hey, Sheriff, how's it going?" Ted called cheerfully. "You don't look happy. Something you want to talk about?"

"Ted, sometimes I really hate this job." The sheriff's voice roughened. "I can handle drunks, insults, fights, abuse—just about anything. But telling someone a family member has died? Especially the mothers?" He shook his head. "That tears my heart out. Worse when you know the person."

"Yeah, I get it. I couldn't do it. I don't envy you," Ted said.

"You know Phil Gunn?" the sheriff asked.

"Yes. He's a good friend—goes to my church. Why?"

"I just left his mother's. Phil died last night in an automobile accident," the sheriff said, choking up.

"*What?*" Ted gasped. "You've got to be kidding!"

"I wish I were. It was his car. Only one body in the wreckage. No one's seen him since yesterday morning and he wasn't at home or work. Far as we know, no one else drove his car."

Ted's eyes reddened. "Are you sure? It doesn't seem real. Do they know how it happened?"

"They aren't saying yet. Nothing will be released until the investigation is complete," the sheriff said, fighting his own emotion.

"Excuse me, Sheriff," Ted blurted, backing away. "I've got to go. This is devastating. What a shame—he was such a good man. I need to call our pastor. Thank you—I'll talk to you later, okay?" He jumped in his car and tore off.

The sheriff watched him disappear, then went inside. As the door swung shut, Betty said, "I was going to have you holler at Ted—he drove off without paying for gas."

"Don't worry about it, Betty. I'll take care of it," the sheriff said. "A good friend of ours was killed up on Speckled Bird Road last night. We're all pretty shaken."

"Oh, no. That's awful. Anyone Mac and I know?" she asked, voice tight.

"Do you know Phil Gunn?"

"Oh, n-o-o-o-o, not him," Betty gasped, fumbling for the stool. Tears flooded her eyes. "Not Phil. Tell me it isn't so."

"I wish it wasn't," he said. "It was his car, he wasn't home or at work, and no one's seen him since yesterday morning."

"Are you sure it was his car?" she asked between sobs.

"The plates were his. The ID was his. That's what I've got from Sheriff Gage," he said.

"What's up?" Mac asked, stepping in and catching the tail end. Concern etched his face.

Betty rounded the counter and collapsed into his arms. "Phil Gunn was killed last night," she managed before the sobs took her.

Mac held her, forcing back his own tears. He needed to be strong for both of them—at least for now. There would be time to grieve later, alone.

"Has anyone identified the body?" Mac asked quietly. "Do they need someone to go to the morgue?"

"I'll let you know if we need that," the sheriff said. "Mac, can I speak with you a minute?" They stepped aside. "Idaho County asked me to check with the local dentist for Phil's records. Do you know who he saw?"

"Dr. Fields, here in Kamish—down at the clinic," Mac said.

"You sure?"

"Positive. I've taken him there more than once. He's been going for years."

"That'll speed things up for the coroner," the sheriff said. "I'd better get moving. You two take care. I'll get what we need right away. Thanks, Mac."

He grabbed his coffee and headed out.

Mac turned to Betty, took her by the shoulders, and eased her back to look into her face. "Let's call someone to cover for us. We need to pull ourselves together and go see Phil's mother—make sure she's all right. Have a good cry now and let it out." He drew her close again. "We'll have to be strong for Laura. She's going to need someone to lean on now that Phil's gone."

"Okay," she sobbed, melting into his arms.

Chapter 10

The Ball of Fire and the Dove

Pastor Stan Kiely awoke with a pounding headache. No doubt the evil one was behind the migraine, punishing him for interceding most of the night for his church members. He also felt the dread certainty that something was wrong, though he couldn't name it. He prayed a brief prayer for relief, strength, and guidance for the day—and rose in faith. In all these years, God had never let him down. By the time he finished showering and dressing, the headache was gone.

As he descended the stairs, he glanced upward with a smile, gave a small thumbs-up, and murmured, "Thanks for Your healing touch, Lord."

In the kitchen, his wife, Gwen, handed him a hot cup of coffee and finished setting breakfast. She rubbed his shoulders, bent to hug him, and sat beside him. He began describing the nightmare.

"All I know is this," he said. "I saw a ball of fire rolling down a mountainside. When it hit bottom, it erupted into a huge column of flames and smoke—and a dove rose out of the smoke and flew heavenward. I can't help believing it was a sign from God. I've got an empty feeling deep down."

"No," Gwen said softly, "I don't know what it means. But I *do* know God will be with you, whatever it turns out to be."

They ate in silence for a time, each turning the dream over in their minds.

Halfway through breakfast, the phone rang. Gwen answered. "Hello... Oh—hi, Brother Dickerson. How are—" Her face tightened as she listened, then she covered the receiver. "It's Carl Dickerson," she whispered. "He sounds like he's crying." She passed the phone to her husband.

"Good morning, Brother Carl," Pastor Kiely said, mustering warmth he didn't feel. "How can I help you?"

After he heard the news about Phillip Gunn, Stan and Gwen sat together, absorbing their own grief before they could help Phil's family. Then they rose to go to Laura Gunn at once.

At Laura's apartment door, Gwen at his side, Stan exhaled. "This is the hardest thing a pastor has to do."

"God will give you strength," Gwen said, squeezing his arm. "He is with us always. He will not leave us or forsake us."

He knocked. The doorbell bore a taped note: *broken.* He lingered on the word—*broken*—and thought of how often he had seen lives in pieces. How many more had God seen, waiting for mercy they wouldn't ask for?

June opened the door. "Come in. You must be Pastor Kiely—I spoke to you on the phone."

He'd taken many calls since Carl's; he simply nodded. "Yes, ma'am. This is my wife, Gwen. As I mentioned, Phil was a member of our church."

"Thank you for coming," June said with a sad smile. "Laura really needs the Lord—and you—right now."

"How is she?" he asked.

"Holding her own, I suppose," June said. "She's had a couple of bad spells, but friends have stopped by with condolences and what little comfort they can. I'm afraid it isn't enough. What she needs is the love and peace only God can give."

"Amen," he said.

"I'll see if she's up to visitors." June slipped down the hall and murmured, "Laura, Phil's pastor is here. His wife is with him, too."

Laura looked up, eyes red and puffy. "Okay. Let me freshen up. I'll be out in a few minutes."

June returned. "She'll be out shortly."

"Do you attend a church nearby?" Pastor Kiely asked gently.

"I used to," June said. "Stopped going. Too many self-righteous people—no room for the rest of us, you know, the poor folks. If you didn't have money, or wouldn't pretend you did, you didn't belong. My husband and I walked out one day and never went back. God rest his soul—he passed a few years ago."

"If you ever want to try ours, we'd be honored to have you," he said. "Not many rich folks in our little flock—poor in worldly terms, maybe, but wealthy beyond measure in heavenly riches."

Laura made her way in, trying to smile. "Hello, Pastor Kiely." Tears trembled in her eyes.

"Hello, Mrs. Gunn. I've wanted to meet you for some time," he said softly, "but the timing was never right."

"That was my fault. Phillip kept wanting me to meet you and your wife, but I was afraid. When I was a girl, our preacher shouted fire and brimstone—always telling us we were damned and going to hell. I was convinced nobody was going to heaven. He acted like a judge on a high throne, pointing a finger and listing all we'd done wrong. Phillip told me you weren't like that, but I wasn't willing to chance it. Oh, how Phillip loved you and your church..." Her voice broke and the tears spilled over.

Gwen and June drew her between them, and Pastor Kiely laid a hand on Laura's brow and prayed:

"Dear Heavenly Father, reach down with Your mighty hand of comfort and love. Fill this house with the peace that passeth all understanding. Though we do not know why this terrible scene has unfolded, let Your assurance that You are still in control wash over Laura and comfort her. Let something good come of this sorrow, as Your Word says: *And we know that all things work together for good to them that love God, to them who are the called according to His purpose.* Lord, we know Phil loved You and was a godly man. Why You called him home, we may never know on this side of glory—but we do know he is with You and will be there when You come in majesty. For this we rejoice."

"Father, the sorrow of his passing weighs heavy on family, friends, and church—more than we can bear alone. Send Your angels to comfort and strengthen Phil's family for the road ahead. Grant wisdom and courage to walk on with You. Give mercy and grace as lives are changed by this loss."

"Now, a special blessing for Laura Gunn: fill her with the comfort and peace only You can bring. Give her strength, wisdom, and insight to seek and find Your path. Bless her spiritually, physically, emotionally, and mentally. In Jesus' name, amen."

By the time he finished, tears were coursing down every face—Pastor Kiely's included.

CHAPTER 11

GRACE ON THE ROAD

Jeannie Gunn was stepping out of her apartment when the phone rang. She set her purse on the coffee table, sprinted to the kitchen, and snatched up the receiver on the fifth ring.

"Hello," she said, breathless.

"Hi, Jeannie," Laura answered without enthusiasm.

"Hi, Momma! How are you?"

Silence. Uncomfortable, heavy.

"What's the matter, Momma?"

"Jeannie—" was all Laura could manage before she broke into tears. June gently took the receiver.

"Jeannie, honey?"

"Yes. What's wrong with my mother?"

"Honey, listen to me," June said softly, groping for the words. She chose the direct way. "Phil was in an auto accident last night and... sweetie, he didn't make it. He was killed. I'm so sorry."

"What? Oh, no. It can't be. Are you sure? I mean—" Jeannie gulped air, fighting hysteria. "Is my mother all right?"

"She's having a hard time, as you'd expect. But she needs you. I'll stay with her until you get here," June said.

"I'll be there as quickly as I can. Thank you for being with her, June. You're a good friend."

"Not a problem. You be careful getting here. If you need anything, let me know, okay?"

"I will. Thanks again."

"I'll tell your mother you're on your way. We'll see you soon," June said.

Jeannie hung up and stared out the window, stunned. *This can't be real.*

"Jeannie? What's wrong?" asked Valerie, her roommate, entering the room.

"My brother was killed in an accident. I've got to go home. How am I going to do that? I don't have a car, or even enough money to get there—and I've got classes—" She unraveled into sobs.

Valerie slipped her arms around her. "Shh. Don't worry about a thing. I'll make sure you get home."

After long minutes of keening and tears, they turned to practicalities.

"Valerie, should I take this? I don't have much to wear for the services, but I supp—" Jeannie choked on the word *funeral* and fell silent.

"Like I said—don't worry about a thing. You're like my sister; sisters look out for each other. Stop worrying."

"I don't see how I'll pay for everything. I live on a shoestring now. That's the part you keep skipping," Jeannie said, accusing and afraid.

"Not a problem," Valerie said. "But since you'll feel better if you *see* it..." She picked up her purse. "Voila." She fanned her credit cards. "My mom adores you and told me to do whatever's needed to get you home—she'll handle it later."

"Why would she do that for me? She barely knows me."

"She knows you well enough to claim you as a second daughter. She loves you almost as much as me," Valerie teased, grinning.

"Well, Sis," Jeannie said, returning the smile faintly, "I appreciate it—both of you."

"Glad to do it. And so is my mom."

They packed in quiet spurts. After a while, Jeannie asked, "Your mother's a Christian, isn't she?"

"Yes—why?"

"Because that's what Phil would have done," Jeannie said, affection and ache in her voice.

Bags ready, they loaded the car and drove to the school to report the emergency and miss classes.

"Before I forget," Jeannie said, "we need to stop at the post office to get our mail."

"Then that's next," Valerie said. "School—check. Susie will pick up the newspapers so they don't pile up. Am I missing anything?"

"I don't think so. I'm sorry I haven't been much help. It's just—"

"Don't," Valerie said, cutting gently. "You'd do the same for me."

She smiled warmly. "Okay—post office, then fuel up and hit the road. Sound like a plan?"

"Sounds good," Jeannie said. *I just need to be with Mom.*

At the post office, Jeannie took longer than expected. After a few more minutes, Valerie went in and found her huddled in a corner, sobbing. Jeannie clutched a money order for $250 in one hand and a letter in the other.

"Come on, Jeannie—let's get out of here," Valerie said, guiding her outside. In the car, Valerie gently slid the money order, envelope, and note from Jeannie's hands. She read the short message: *Don't even say it—I know you can use the little bit extra. Take care and God bless. Love you lots, Sis. —Phil*

"Oh, honey," Valerie whispered. She opened the glove box. "Let's put this away for now—out of sight. Try not to think about it, all right?"

Jeannie nodded through fresh tears, knowing the ache would linger a long time.

A little later, Pastor Kiely and Gwen returned to stay with Laura—she didn't want to be alone, and June needed to run errands and fill a prescription to help Laura rest. By then, Valerie and Jeannie were arriving in Kamish and went straight to Laura's apartment. Seeing them up the walk, Pastor Kiely opened the door.

Jeannie, red-eyed and puffy, said, "I'm Jeannie—Laura's daughter," and shook their hands. "Is my mother here?"

"She's lying down," Pastor Kiely said. "She was very upset this morning, so June called her doctor. He gave her a mild sedative and left a prescription; June is out getting it filled. She'll be back shortly. We're very sorry about Phil. We'll miss him."

"I know. It feels like a bad dream." Jeannie studied them. "You both look familiar. Have we met?"

"I'm not sure," Pastor Kiely said. "We meet so many people that it's hard to keep track."

Jeannie thought, then snapped her fingers. "I know—you're the pastor at Phil's church. I went to a service with him once, before med school, about four years ago. I wondered why you said you'd miss him—now I know."

"Oh, yes, I remember," Gwen said. "It *has* been a long time."

"It sure has," Jeannie said. "Has Mom said anything about my brother, Jonathon? How we're going to reach him?"

"No," Pastor Kiely said. "Do you have any idea where he might be?"

"The only one who knew how to reach him was Phil," she said. "Last I heard, he was somewhere around Oakland."

"Was he working then?"

"No. Not for years. He lives on the streets," she said. "Phil and Jonathon were inseparable as kids. After Vietnam, Jonathon was completely different. He came home, picked fights—especially with Phil. It was like they turned into opposites overnight. Phil became a Christian and served God every way he could; Jonathon fell into drugs, alcohol, and petty crime. We tried to get him help; it got worse. Then he left without saying goodbye. We haven't heard from him since."

"Oh—this is my roommate, Valerie," Jeannie added. "She and her mother made it possible for me to get home. Without them, I'd still be in Spokane trying to figure it out."

Pastor Kiely and Gwen shook Valerie's hand. "Hello."

"Hi," she said softly, flushing.

"You may think it's odd," Jeannie said, voice trembling, "but Phil told me once that when he died, he wanted a sermon about sinners finding God—so his going out would bring others in, as he put it. As his pastor, I think he'd have wanted you to do that for him. Would you?"

"I'd be honored," the pastor said, blinking back tears.

"Do you have any ideas about finding Jonathon?" Jeannie asked.

"We can start with the sheriff's office," he said. "See what help they can provide."

"All right. Could you make the call? I don't think I can—" She broke down again.

"Of course," he said. "You focus on your mother. If you need anything, call me or Gwen." He handed her a card. "We're glad to help in any way we can. If you lose the card, we're in the phone book."

Jeannie nodded and shook his hand. Gwen hugged her; Jeannie clung, wept a few seconds, then wiped her eyes.

"Thank you for staying with my mother," she said.

"Surely," Gwen replied. "We're here."

Jeannie stood in the doorway and waved as they pulled away, then went back inside.

After dropping Gwen at the grocery store—"I'll be right back," he told her—Pastor Kiely drove to the sheriff's office to ask for help finding Jonathon.

CHAPTER 12

THE YELLOW GAS CAP

Jill had just come on duty. She was tired, but in two days her weekend would start.

"Did you see this?" asked Bernice, the day-shift attendant, as Jill came behind the counter.

"What's that?" Jill said.

"This guy—killed on Speckled Bird Road. They say it happened between eleven and midnight. Might be a suicide."

"Let me see." Jill scanned the item and blanched. "Oh my word, Bernice—he was in here *earlier* than that window!"

"Are you sure?"

"Yes. He told me he was going to come back more often." She flushed. "I think he liked me a little."

"Did they say anything about other people?" Bernice asked.

"What other people?" she added, bewildered.

"There was another man and a woman with him. And the *other* guy was driving when they left," Jill said.

"That's crazy. Are you sure that's what you saw?"

"I swear. I watched him—closely." Jill's voice softened. "He said he was really tired and got into the back seat."

"I'm not sure, Jill, but maybe you should call the police. That doesn't sound right," Bernice said.

"Do you think so? I mean..."

"Look, we have to be good citizens. If we know something that could matter, we should tell them. Right?"

"Okay, you're right," Jill said, reaching for the phone. "If there are repercussions, I'm looking you up—you hear me?"

"Yeah, yeah. And hurry—it's your shift now," Bernice teased.

"Main Ville Sheriff's Office. How may I help you?" the dispatcher answered.

"Hello, I'm... I'm Jill Bennett. I work at the Quik Mart."

"Yes, ma'am. Please go on."

"The man from the paper—the one killed on Speckled Bird—was here just before the wreck time. And there should be *two more people* with him."

"Why do you think two more people, Miss... Bennett?" the dispatcher asked, waving an officer to the other phone.

"He came in with a man and a woman. When they left, the other man drove because the deceased said he was too tired and got in the back."

"You're certain?"

"Yes."

"What time?"

"They got here around 10:30 p.m. The deceased bought gas and food. The other two bought the drinks—he left his wallet on the counter, and the deceased took it out to him when he paid for gas. They ate burgers at the table and left about 11:30."

"Are you positive?"

"Yes, ma'am."

"Okay, I'm sending an officer to take your statement. You'll be there?"

"All night."

"Thank you, Miss Bennett."

The dispatcher hung up and turned to the deputy. "Did you hear that?"

"I sure did."

"Get the sheriff. He'll want this right away."

The deputy stepped outside, spotted Sheriff Gage and Deputy Pipcorn still talking. "Hey, Sheriff! You and Pipcorn need to come inside—Dispatch has something big."

"We're on our way," Gage called.

At the desk, Gage asked, "What've you got?"

"Go to the Quik Mart. Miss Bennett says your victim was there with another man and a woman just before he went over the side."

"You're kidding." Gage stared.

"Nope. I told her we'd send an officer. Figured you two would want it."

"We're out of here," Gage said.

They made the short drive, donned their hats, and headed inside.

"We're looking for Miss Bennett," Gage said.

"I'm Jill Bennett. Is this about my call?"

"Yes, ma'am," Pipcorn said. "What can you tell us about last night?"

Jill led them to a small customer table. "Like I told the dispatcher—he and the other couple came in around 10:30. The deceased bought gas and food. The other two paid for drinks—he'd left his wallet on the counter and the deceased carried it out when he paid. They sat *right here* and ate burgers before they left."

"Are you sure they were together?" Gage asked.

"Yes. They arrived together, sat together, and left together."

"What else makes you believe it?" Pipcorn asked.

"He was... well, good-looking. I kept an eye on him," Jill admitted. "When they left, he got in the back seat and said he was extra tired."

"So you're saying they arrived and left in the same car?" Gage said.

"Yes."

"Can you describe the other two?"

"The man—mid-thirties. Balding on top, brown hair around the sides to his shoulders. I *think* blue eyes. The woman—very pretty, mid-twenties, blonde hair, blue eyes."

"Could you identify them again— in person or from photos?" Gage asked.

"Oh, no doubt."

"Anything else?" Pipcorn asked.

Jill hesitated. "One thing seemed strange. I watched the deceased put his gas cap back on and close the flap. Later, when I read the pump meters at closing, I found a yellow gas cap sitting on top of the pump."

"Are you sure it was his?" Pipcorn asked.

"Yes—it was the same yellow as his car."

"And you're certain you saw him put it back on? Could you swear to it in court?"

"Yes."

"Do you still have it?"

"Yes." She went behind the counter, lifted a small box of stray caps, and handed them a yellow one. Gage took it carefully.

"Thank you, Miss Bennett. If we need you again, where can we find you?" Pipcorn asked.

"Here—or at my apartment over Oscar's. Number 112."

"Thank you," Gage said.

"You're welcome. I hope it helps. There *should* have been three people in that crash, not just one. He got in the back seat when they left—I'm sure of it."

Gage met Pipcorn's eyes. "You're sure about that last part, Miss Bennett?"

"I watched almost every move he made. Such a waste," she said quietly.

"It sure was. Thank you again," Gage said. Outside, he asked, "You get all that, Pipcorn?"

"Every word," the deputy said, letting out a low whistle.

"My gut was right," Gage murmured. "Now we prove it. We may need to talk to her again—but first, I want to do a little checking on my own."

Pipcorn looked across the street, thinking. "This could be the break we needed. Like you say—now we put it all together."

CHAPTER 13

THE FAX FROM IDAHO

It was 8:30 Saturday morning when Sergeant Wilson tapped on the window of the door to his captain's office. Captain Steele motioned for him to come in.

Wilson opened the door slightly and poked his head inside. "Captain Steele, I've got a strange fax from a Lewis County Sheriff's Office up in a town called Kamish, Idaho," he said, pronouncing the town's name "Kamish."

"Come in and close the door, Sergeant," ordered Steele. "Kamish? Where in the world is that?"

"Sir, I've checked the maps, and as far as I can figure—because I can't seem to find it—I think it must be somewhere southeast of Lewiston," declared Wilson.

"Well, I'd say that helps me a whole lot," Captain Steele said sarcastically. "Now, Sergeant, where the heck is Lewiston?"

"Sorry, Captain," he replied. "It's about halfway between Boise and Spokane, Washington. Looks to be about a four-hour drive either way. Anyway, Kamish is a little spot in the road, probably no bigger than the neighborhood I live in," he continued with a chuckle. "A man by the name of Phillip Gunn died in an auto accident up there recently. According to them, he has a brother living down here in the Oakland area by the name of Jonathon, and they're asking us to locate him and notify him of his brother's death."

"Sounds pretty cut-and-dried, Wilson. Why are you bothering me with all this?" Captain Steele said, obviously annoyed. "What could be so difficult—or, as you put it, strange—about a simple request to locate someone?"

"Well, sir, the fax says he's a drug addict and lives on the streets with no known address. According to them, the guy doesn't even believe in carrying any ID and has essentially dropped out of society," Wilson replied. "When I saw all of this, I was going to file it, but I thought I'd clear it with you first. We really don't have time to be chasing down phantom street people for other jurisdictions. We've got our hands full as it is."

The captain ignored Wilson's complaints about being overburdened and asked, "Did the fax contain any other information that might give us an idea where he could be found? What you've told me so far doesn't give us much to go on."

"I don't know, Captain. I didn't read much more after I got to the addict part. Let's see... yadda, yadda, yadda," Wilson mumbled as he scanned the fax from Idaho. "Okay, here's something interesting. Looks like Phillip Gunn—the one that died—frequently sent money to an officer in our department down here to give to his brother."

"Well, that might help us some. It's a start, anyway," said Captain Steele. "Put the word out and see if you can track down this officer. Then check and see if we have a sheet on this guy. If he's a homeless addict, we've probably had him in here at least once."

"And Wilson," the captain added as Sergeant Wilson was about to open the door to leave, "put a little effort into this. Don't just file it away like I know you're still tempted to do. This must be important enough for them to go through all this trouble to locate him—and you never know when we might need a little favor from those boys in Idaho."

"Okay, Captain. I'll get right on it," Wilson said as he stepped out of the office.

"Riley!" Wilson shouted.

"Yeah, Sarge," a tall and slender but very muscular detective hollered back from across the busy room, his voice muffled by a mouthful of doughnut.

"Do you know of a Jonathon Gunn? Homeless, alcoholic, druggie, a bum?" shouted back Sergeant Wilson.

Riley shook his head no and finally managed, "I don't think so," as he swallowed the last of the doughnut.

"Well, whether you do or not, I want you to see if you can pull a file on this guy," ordered Wilson. "Captain wants us to find him for some sheriff up in Idaho and notify him that his brother died in an automobile accident."

"Okay, Sarge. I'll get right on it," Riley shot back. Then he and his partner Simmons, who had been listening to the entire exchange, sat back down in unison at their desks.

"Well, you heard the Sarge. Let's see what we can come up with," said Riley.

"Don't look at me, Riley. You're the computer whiz around here. Besides, you're the lucky guy who got selected for the honor of filling *His Highness's* latest request," quipped Simmons.

"Some help you are," Riley said sarcastically as he began typing his request on the keyboard. "Okay, Mr. Bum, let's see if we can find you."

"Nothing so far," Riley said to no one in particular as he continued typing commands. "Nothing under Jonathon Gunn. Let's see... uh-huh, now we're getting somewhere," he murmured as he began scrolling down through the alphabet listing of Gunns. "Okay... Brad, Jacob, Jeff, Jeremy, Nathan, Rachel—nope. Salley—wrong again. Samuel... Scar? I wonder."

Riley hit a few more keys to bring up the file on "Scar." The full name read: *Scar Gunn, a.k.a. John Gunn.* The address listed for him was *unknown.*

"Bingo!" he chirped happily, giving his partner a wink and a nod. "Am I good or what?"

"I'm taking the Fifth on that one," Simmons said, smiling as he got up and stood next to Riley, who was leaning back in his chair with his hands folded behind his head, staring at the screen in front of him.

"Hey, Sarge!" Simmons shouted across the room. "You might want to take a look at this!"

"What you got?" Wilson said as he ambled up to Riley's desk.

"Well, for starters—twelve separate convictions for trespassing, fourteen drunk and disorderly, a couple of indecent exposures—seems he likes to urinate in public—and six vagrancies," replied Riley. "If that's not enough, it gets even better. Looks like he threw in a few misdemeanor assaults just to spice things up."

"Any active warrants?" the sergeant asked.

"None listed," replied Riley.

"Got an address?" inquired the sergeant.

"Nope. Just says here that he frequents the missions on Third and Fifth Streets."

"That's no surprise," interjected Simmons.

"Got a picture?" asked Wilson.

"Yeah. And it goes on to say he's had some kind of military training at one time, but it doesn't go into any detail," said Riley.

"All right, Riley. Thanks for getting right on it. You did good," complimented Wilson. "While we're trying to find the officer that knows him, why don't you two get down to the mission district and see if you can locate him. Maybe we can get this thing wrapped up today and move on to bigger and better things."

"Here's a copy of the fax request we got from Idaho. Read it on the way," Wilson said, handing it to Simmons. "He's not wanted for anything, so if you find him, just inform him of his brother's death and give him the telephone numbers listed there to contact his mother or the sheriff's office in Idaho. Then I want you two to get your little tails right back here. We've got more important matters to take care of than tracking down homeless bums for the dearly departed."

"You got it, Sarge," said Riley. "Come on, Simmons. Let's get going. You heard the Sarge—we've got ourselves a real whodunit here," he said, flashing the sergeant a sarcastic grin.

"Just don't get lost, you two," Sergeant Wilson shot back as Riley and Simmons grabbed their mugs of coffee and left the building.

CHAPTER 14

MAKING ARRANGEMENTS

By this time, it had been over a week since the accident that took Phil's life, and Jeannie was thinking about all the arrangements that needed to be made—especially now that they were looking for Jonathon. Everything had been put on hold up to that point, waiting to see if they could find him. Now they could start making a few plans, though the final ones were yet to come.

"Mama, do you think we should maybe pack up some of Phil's things tomorrow?" she asked.

"Valerie and I can do most of it. You wouldn't need to do much."

"Yes," said Laura. "I guess the sooner the better."

She was getting over the shock now, and though the pain was still there, it was easier to talk about. She was even sleeping better.

"In fact, Jeannie, I was thinking about moving into his trailer. I believe it would save me some money, and—oh, I forgot about Sparky, Phillip's cat! I'd better call Phillip's neighbor, Mr. Addison, and find out about that little guy!"

"Phil had a cat? I thought he didn't like cats," Jeannie piped.

"Well, this one was special," said Laura. "It wormed its way into Phillip's heart, and Sparky could do no wrong after that. What do you think about me moving into the trailer, honey?"

"I think it would be great! That would give me a place to live also.

See, I'm thinking about asking for my internship early. I can take it at Cottontree or Oroville. That way I can work and be with you both at the same time," said Jeannie.

"Do you think they'll let you?" asked Valerie.

"I don't know, but it won't hurt to ask," Jeannie replied.

"If they don't, it'll be all right," said Laura.

"If they don't, I'll become a nurse here in the clinic. I'm not leaving you here by yourself, Mama. It was different when Phil was... when Phil was here. But I won't leave you alone now, and that's final."

"Well, if you've made up your mind, dear, I won't try to change it. I sure wish I knew if Jonathon was going to be here," said Laura.

"I know. Me too," sighed Jeannie.

"Yes, that would take a load off. Valerie dear, would you like some coffee?" asked Laura.

"No thank you, Mother Gunn. I'm still trying to find this word to finish my crossword puzzle," said Valerie with a chuckle. "My mother always told me I wasn't the sharpest tool in the shed, and at times I believed her."

"Let me help you, dear," said Laura, leaning over Valerie's shoulder. "Let's see... a figure of speech in which a part is used for the whole, as in 'ten sails' for 'ten ships.' Oh, that would be hard if I hadn't heard it on TV the other day. The word is synecdoche."

"Amazing! Your mother is fantastic!" praised Valerie.

"I know it," Jeannie smiled. "Oh Mom, I've already asked Pastor Kiely to officiate at the funeral. You knew Phil wanted him to—"

"To preach on repentance and turning your life over to God and all? Yes, I knew. That's what I wanted to ask him also. Did he say he would?" asked Laura.

"Yes," Jeannie replied. "He said that he promised to do that—for Phil's sake."

"Good. That's possibly the last thing we can do for Phillip."

As she said this, tears started to fill Laura's eyes again, so Jeannie and Valerie both stepped close and hugged her.

"We still have some things to take care of, though," Jeannie said gently. "Who would you like to handle the funeral—Tom's Funeral Home or Jacobs and Sons?"

"Well, Jacobs and Sons has been a friend of the family ever since I can remember, so let's go to them," offered Laura.

"Flowers?" asked Jeannie.

"Let's let the local florist take care of that. I'm sure glad you girls are here to help me with these things. I could never think of them all," said Laura.

Valerie smiled a little. "What about music?"

"That's one thing I didn't think of," admitted Laura.

"Boy, I didn't either," said Jeannie. "What do you think about letting the church handle that?"

"You know," said Valerie, "that's not a bad idea. They know the songs he liked—and not only that, I'm sure the men there would be honored to be pallbearers, too."

"That's a good idea," said Laura. "I'll call Pastor Kiely right now."

As she picked up the phone and started dialing, it seemed as if a renewed strength had come from somewhere—perhaps an inner peace whispering that things were going to be all right after all.

"Hello, this is Pastor Kiely. How can I help you?" he asked.

"Hello, Pastor Kiely. This is Laura Gunn—Phillip's mother. I'm kind of lost right now and not quite up to making the arrangements for Phillip's service. I know we need pallbearers and a lot more, but this is what we've come up with so far, if it's okay with the church."

"Sure, Mrs. Gunn," said Pastor Kiely. "We'll do our best to fulfill your wishes."

"Okay, so far we thought Jacobs and Sons would do the funeral, and we'll contact the local florist for the flowers—but we're kind of lost from there."

"Mrs. Gunn, why don't you let us handle everything? We can have Jacobs and Sons bring Phil over the morning of the funeral—whenever it's convenient for you. We'll supply the pallbearers and the music," offered Pastor Kiely.

"That's what we thought—if it isn't too much to ask," said Laura.

"Absolutely not," said Pastor Kiely. "In fact, the church would be happy to do the whole thing—even the dinner afterward—if that's okay with you."

"That would sure ease our minds, sir," said Laura. "I hope it's not too expensive though, 'cause we haven't got much. Please, call me Laura. I'm not used to 'Mrs. Gunn.' I feel we're all part of Phillip's family anyway."

"All right, Laura. If you'll take care of the mortuary, we—the church—will take care of the rest. It's the least we can do for our friend and brother," Pastor Kiely said.

"Oh, that would be wonderful, Pastor. We'll start thinking about what the meal should be, then," said Laura, relieved.

"Well, Laura, why don't you let the women of the church figure that out? We have some marvelous cooks here, you know," Pastor Kiely told her.

"Well, that won't leave us much to do here—but if you think it best," replied Laura gratefully.

"Believe me, Laura, you'll have plenty going on there, so don't worry about a thing. We've got it, okay?" asked Pastor Kiely.

"Okay—and thank you, Pastor. Your church members truly are servants of God," said Laura. "I guess I'll hang up and tell the girls. God bless you, Pastor."

"And you also—and your family. May the blessings, grace, and strength of the Lord be with you."

With that, Pastor Kiely hung up the phone. Laura told the girls what he had said, and they smiled with tears in their eyes.

CHAPTER 15

THE LEAD FROM THIRD STREET

Detectives Riley and Simmons had been working together for over eight years. They were about as opposite in looks and style as any two people could be, but they'd become extremely close friends over the years. Riley planned on retiring with Simmons at his side. Until then he wouldn't want any other officer covering his back. Simmons had saved him from certain death or injury more times than he cared to remember.

"I hope this guy is peaceful," said Simmons. "I really don't feel like dealing with some crazy addict today."

"What do you mean? He's homeless, drunk, and on drugs. If we find him, he'll be a pussycat. Believe me, I know how these guys are. He'll be lucky if he can even stand up straight," Riley said with confidence. "Besides, when he takes one look at your good-lookin' mug, he'll melt."

Simmons ignored this last comment and asked, "Hey, did you see that movie on Channel 7 last night?"

"Which one?" asked Riley.

"I think it was called *Thinner*," said Simmons.

"*Thinner*?" asked Riley.

"Yeah. Stephen King wrote the book, and the movie was based on it. It was a real good flick," added Simmons.

"No, I didn't see it. Haven't read the book either. What was it about?" asked Riley.

"Well, it started out with this fat guy and his family... let's see. I think he was a lawyer. Anyway, he runs over this gypsy's daughter. The daughter, by the way, looked like she was as old as her father, who had to be in his nineties. But anyway, he got a curse put on him by this gypsy, and no matter how much he ate he just kept getting skinnier and skinnier and—"

"Is there a point to all this, Simmons," Riley interrupted, "or are you just talking to hear yourself talk again? Make this long story of yours short and just tell me how it ended."

"That's just it. I don't know. I fell asleep before it ended, and I was hoping you could tell me what happened," Simmons said flatly.

"You know, Simmons, sometimes I really worry about you," Riley said, shaking his head.

"Interesting you should say that—so does my mom," replied Simmons seriously. "She never knew what I was going to say when I was a kid. She really hated it when company came over. Said she couldn't even trust me to say hi." They both laughed.

Twenty minutes later they were parking in front of the Third Street Mission. Once inside, they approached two nuns standing at the end of the main serving line. They looked like they were supervising the whole operation.

Riley pulled a copy of Jonathon's most recent mug shot out of his pocket and said, "Pardon us, Sisters. We don't mean to intrude at dinnertime, but have you seen this man?" He showed them the picture.

"Why, yes. That's Scar," the short, stocky nun bubbled enthusiastically as the other sister shot her a disapproving glance.

"Is he in trouble again?" asked the disapproving nun. "He promised he would be good and has been, as far as I know, for quite some time. Although we haven't seen him in a couple of days, so there's no telling what mischief he might have gotten himself into."

"He's not in any trouble, Sister. We just need to find him. It's a family matter," said Riley.

"Family matter?" she asked. "I didn't know he had any family from around here."

"He doesn't. His family in Idaho is looking for him," replied Simmons. "Any idea where he might be?"

"No. He comes in here quite regularly, though," she answered.

"I tell you what, Sister," said Simmons, handing each of them his business card, "if you happen to see him, call us at this number, okay?"

"Okay, Officer," she replied.

"Hey," came a gruff voice from behind the two nuns. "You say it's a family matter and that he's not in any kind of trouble?" He stepped around the nuns and came within inches of the two detectives, who were standing fairly close to each other.

"Yeah, that's what we've been telling the Sisters here," said Simmons as they both took a couple of steps backward, appalled at the sight and smell of the apparition before them.

"I ain't no rat, you understand, but if it's family..." He paused, pulling at his beard nervously. "Well, if it's family, then family is family, I always say." He was old and stooped, with long, thin white hair and a white, matted beard that hung down to the middle of his chest. The beard was yellowed by tobacco from the corners of his mouth all the way to its tip. The only part of him free of filth was the palms of his hands, and he smelled like the city landfill.

"Do you know where he is?" asked Riley bluntly.

"Well, I ain't sayin' I do, and I ain't sayin' I don't. Like I said, I ain't no rat. If it weren't for family and all, I wouldn't be tryin' to remember. Ya see, when a feller gets to my age, his memory needs a little boost every now and again, if ya know what I'm gettin' at," he said, giving them a sly look with one raised eyebrow.

"Yeah, we know what you mean there, old-timer," Simmons said, giving the old man the most innocent look he could muster—knowing exactly where this was heading but refusing to give in so easily. "You think you can stir up your memory and help us out? Maybe you should lie down over there on the sofa for a minute if you think that will help. This is real important, so take your time."

"Well, since it appears yer partner's still wet behind the ears"—he gave a nod toward Simmons—"and it don't look like he's learned the ropes yet, I'll give it to ya real plain. Anything in it fer me if I can get my memory back in order?"

"Will a fiver do?" asked Riley.

"I hear my memory stirrin' already," the old man said with a twinkle in his eye.

"Simmons, give Methuselah here a five," said Riley.

"I don't think so. I paid last time," Simmons said.

"I'll pay you back later," replied Riley.

"That's the problem, Riley," said Simmons. "You said that last time, and I haven't seen a dime yet."

"Will you just give him the money, for Pete's sake, so we can let these folks get back to their dinner?" Riley said through gritted teeth. He turned to the nuns, who were watching with rapt attention, and gave them a shrug and his best winning smile.

"Okay, okay!" Simmons said as he reached into his pocket and dug out his wallet. After thumbing through several bills to locate a five, he handed it to Methuselah with a flourish and said, "Try not to spend it all in one spot, you old codger."

"My name's Nate," he said as he took the money. Then he began examining the bill very carefully, holding it up to the light and tugging on the corners, turning it this way and that.

"Come on, old codger," Simmons said impatiently, purposely avoiding the newly revealed name. "We ain't got all day to stand here waiting for you to get acquainted with that five-dollar bill.

You'd think you'd never seen one before. You gonna tell us where he is, or do I have to repossess that five?" he said sarcastically.

"Hold yer horses there, youngster," Nate said, examining the bill with slower deliberation than before. "Can't trust nobody these days."

Simmons looked at Riley, rolled his eyes, and stared at the ceiling in sheer exasperation.

"Okay, I guess it's the real McCoy," Nate said, stuffing the five quickly into his pocket.

"Do you think we'd give you phony money?" asked Riley.

"Never can tell these days," Nate replied matter-of-factly.

"I'm about out of patience, old man," Simmons said menacingly. "You've got about two seconds to stop fooling around and revive that memory of yours, or we're hauling your rear back to the station."

"Out with it, N-A-T-E," he continued, spelling the name slowly. "Where is he?"

"Take it easy there, youngster," Nate returned, oozing politeness. "No need goin' and gettin' yer feathers all ruffled. Now, let's see... last time I see'd him, he was at Old Man's Park. That was around 10:00 yesterday mornin'. Said he was headin' back to the Fifth Street Mission tonight."

"The Fifth Street Mission?" clarified Riley.

"Yep," said the old man. "But if ya can't find him there, he usually sleeps in the alley between Fifth and Sixth, behind Charley's Pool Hall."

No one thanked Nate for this bit of information. Simmons was staring at him with the same look a pit bull gives just before devouring a fresh steak being held aloft by its master.

"Thank you, Sisters," Riley said to the nuns, giving Simmons a nudge with his elbow. "Have a pleasant day."

"Don't tell him I told ya nothin'," Nate interjected. "Got my reputation to look after, ya know. But bein's it's family and—"

"Yeah, yeah, we know. Family is family," Simmons interrupted mockingly, "especially when five bucks is involved."

"A man's got to earn his livin' somehow, ya know. Besides, it ain't often a man can do a good turn for his friend and earn a livin' at the same time," the old man cackled, then went into a fit of hacking and coughing as Riley and Simmons turned their backs on him and hurried out of the mission to follow up on their newest hot lead.

Simmons was fuming when they got back to the car. "Family is family," he mocked. "Just give me some money and I'll spill my guts."

"It's not the family thing that has you upset—it's the money, isn't it?" asked Riley.

"Maybe it is," he replied. "I just want to know why it's always me doing the paying. Something just doesn't seem right about that. Why don't you pay sometime?"

"I tell you what, I'll spring for lunch today. Will that make you feel any better?" asked Riley.

"Maybe. But it better be at least five bucks' worth," Simmons said with a smile.

CHAPTER 16

FIFTH STREET AND FALLOUT

Ten minutes later, they were in front of the Fifth Street Mission. Every eye was on them as soon as they walked through the front door. It was a much warier crowd than the one at the Third Street Mission. Everyone was seated at four long rows of tables, in various stages of eating their lunch.

"Must be the bad boys of the Mission District," Simmons whispered to his partner as they stepped up to the head of one of the tables.

"Let me have your attention," Riley said loudly, addressing the motley group of men assembled before him. "We're looking for John Gunn. Can anyone help us out?"

"I can," a big, burly man called out. "The door's behind you."

Everyone in the room broke out in laughter.

"That's real funny there, Mr. Comedian," said Simmons, giving everyone in the room his nastiest look. "Hopefully one of you fine, upstanding citizens can come through with his whereabouts pronto, or it's going to be a long afternoon for all of us—if you know what I mean. Now let's try it again. We're looking for a guy named John Gunn. You probably know him by his street name—Scar."

The whole place went deathly quiet as everyone started looking at one another. After a few moments, they erupted in laughter again.

"What's the matter with you nuts?" Simmons shouted over the bedlam. "I say something funny?"

The man who had offered them the door spoke again. "Quiet, everybody!" he ordered, silencing the crowd. Then he turned back to the detectives. "You two hotshots going to take him in?"

"No. He's not in any trouble," said Riley. "It's a family matter. That's it. You think you could help us out so we can get on with our jobs and let you guys get back to your meal?"

"Sorry to hear that," the man said innocently, giving the man on his left a wink. "Well, in that case, he's in the alley two blocks down on your left. Can't miss him. He's big, he's ugly, and he's got a scar across his nose. If you look real close, the scar goes all the way across his cheek, too. That's why they call him Scar."

A nun appeared in the doorway at the back of the room that led to the kitchen. "What's going on here, officers?" she said as she shuffled across the room toward them. When she was about ten feet away, she asked, "Is there something I can help you with?"

"We were just looking for Scar, ma'am," said Simmons.

"Oh, my word," she said dejectedly, shaking her head. "Is he in trouble again?"

"No, ma'am. We're trying to locate him. It's a family matter," said Riley, taking over.

"Oh, thank God for that," she said. "Although I didn't know he had any family."

"Yes, ma'am, in Idaho," Riley replied.

"He just left here about forty-five minutes ago. Said he was going to go lie down for a while," she said, trying to be helpful. "These gentlemen ought to know where he is."

"Yes, ma'am, they've already been a lot of help to us. I believe we know right where to find him now," said Simmons.

"Gentlemen, really?" Simmons scoffed as soon as they got out of earshot of the sister. "That nun must be as blind as a bat."

Once outside, Simmons looked across the roof of the car and commented, "Thought I'd never say it, Riley, but this smog-laden air I'm breathing right now sure smells good. Know what I mean?" He took a long, deep breath and let it out slowly.

"Yep. Sure do," replied Riley.

It only took a couple of minutes in light traffic to reach the entrance to the alley. They pulled into the nearest empty parking space on the main street, got out, and walked the rest of the way. About a third of the way down the alley, they saw a man wrapped from head to toe in a filthy green and red Indian blanket with two empty bottles of wine by his side. The hand poking out from under the blanket held another empty bottle.

Simmons leaned down and gently pulled the corner of the blanket back from covering the man's head. The man stirred and mumbled something but didn't wake up.

"Looks like that's our man," said Riley.

"Scar!" Simmons said loudly as he nudged him with the toe of his shoe.

Scar immediately jumped to his feet, his red, bloodshot eyes wild with fear. The second he was off the ground, he gave Simmons a vicious roundhouse kick that caught him on the side of the head and sent him flying into four nearby garbage cans, then into a wall, knocking him unconscious.

Before Riley could respond, Scar hit him with three quick blows to the face, followed by one wicked strike to the sternum, knocking the wind completely out of him and putting him down for the count. Then Scar took off running down the alley, screaming, "Snakes, Mama! Snakes! Help me, Mama! Snakes!" Then he turned the corner and was gone.

It took Riley and Simmons a few minutes to get back on their feet and regain their composure.

"What in the world did he hit me with?" groaned Simmons, trying to nurse his wounds. He looked like he'd just been run over by a truck. His clothes were in total disarray, one side of his face was lacerated and bleeding, and he had a knot the size of a grapefruit where Scar's boot had caught him just above his right ear.

"A roundhouse kick," fumed Riley, working his jaw back and forth with his hand. "Get on the radio and tell them what just happened—and while you're at it, find out exactly what kind of military training this guy had. And get us some backup down here. It's going to take a lot more than the two of us to bring him in."

"You gonna be all right?" Riley asked as they slowly limped back to the car. "Your face is lookin' a whole lot worse than it usually does."

"I will be—in about two weeks," said Simmons. "That's gotta be the hardest I've ever been hit in my whole life."

"You can say that again," replied Riley.

When they reached the car, Riley opened the trunk to retrieve the first-aid kit, then tossed the keys to Simmons, who opened the passenger-side door and got in, leaving it open. He took a deep breath to gather himself, then reached over and picked up the mic.

"Unit Forty-four to Central Control, come in."

When the dispatcher came on, he explained their situation, requesting backup and an immediate APB. As he was about to sign off, he added, "Oh, and can you check to see what kind of military training this John Gunn, a.k.a. Scar, has had? I'm looking for specifics if you've got them, okay?"

"Ten-four, Unit Forty-four. I'm checking... The computer's only showing military enlistment, but nothing specific. Let me do a little digging, and I'll get back to you as soon as I can. Dispatch out."

A few minutes later they heard, "Central Control to Unit Forty-four, come in."

Simmons picked up the mic. "Unit Forty-four, go ahead."

"Unit Forty-four, I've got his records just coming in... Let's see, says here: Sergeant, Army Special Forces. Looks like he was a Ranger—Commando. Purple Heart and Bronze Star. Served from 1967 to 1980. Desert Storm vet. Honorable discharge. He's also a fifth-degree black belt in karate. Looks like that's about it. Hope that helps you out."

"Thanks, Reynolds. That was quick work," said Simmons.

"Anytime. Dispatch out," she replied.

Simmons looked over at Riley and gave him a sarcastic look. "Some pussycat," he muttered, angrily forcing the mic back onto its hook.

CHAPTER 17

THE NOTE IN THE TRAILER

Laura, Jeannie, and Valerie were at Phillip's trailer late Monday afternoon. They had decided to go and pack things up. Laura had her own key, so she unlocked the door, and as soon as she did, Sparky—Phil's cat—ran between her legs. He started to meow; he was hungry and wanted something to eat. Now.

"I'm so sorry I forgot about you, Sparky. Jeannie, will you find the food and give him something to eat?"

The cat didn't stop meowing until she had his bowl full. Then, as he began to eat, he started to growl at the same time. All three women laughed at him and tried teasing him a little with their feet.

Finally, Jeannie said, "Mama, Valerie and I will start the packing. Why don't you just make some coffee? I know that will be better for you right now, okay?"

"That would probably be easier, I guess," remarked Laura.

As the girls started packing Phil's things, Laura began searching for all the essentials to make coffee. "Boy, Phillip, you weren't very organized," she mumbled.

He had a Mr. Coffee, so all she had to do was put the coffee in the filter—after she found it, of course—then pour water in the tank, put the pot under the drip, and let the machine do the rest.

While waiting for the coffee, she decided to sit down at the kitchen table. As she did, she became lost in thought about Phillip and slid the paper back. The girls were in the back trying to make heads or tails of things.

"Man, I hate to say this, but my brother sure couldn't take care of a house, could he?" remarked Jeannie.

"Well, Jeannie, I wasn't going to say anything, but that's true," agreed Valerie.

There were clothes all over the floor, dishes left from snacks, and shoes scattered in disarray. The carpet was mauve—and you could actually see it in places! The bed sat in the middle of the room under the window, blankets every which way. The closet door hung open, and hangers were everywhere—some with clothing, some without.

"I'd hate to see the bathroom," sighed Jeannie.

"Well, may I make a suggestion?" asked Valerie.

"Sure, Val, shoot!"

"Why don't we just start washing all these clothes now? That way we can pack clean clothes from here and have the work part done and over with."

"Sounds all right with me. Let's go ask Mom."

With that, the girls walked out of the bedroom and down the hallway past the bathroom door. Jeannie grabbed the handle, wrinkled her nose at Valerie, and opened it to peek in—but that was as far as they got, for Laura yelled, "Girls!"

The scream came from the kitchen. Both girls turned white.

As they rushed down the hallway past the second bedroom, they heard her yell again.

It only took seconds to get there, but it seemed like hours. Everything got in the way—the couch, the coffee table, even Mr. Sparky.

When they entered the kitchen, Laura had backed up against the counter beside the range. She was holding her hands on each side of her face and was just about to yell again when Jeannie grabbed her.

"Mama! What's the matter?" asked Jeannie.

Laura had a look of disbelief on her face. All she could say was, "Look! Phillip won the lottery! Phillip won the lottery!"

"What do you mean, Phillip won the lottery?" asked Jeannie.

Finally, Laura gained a little composure and pointed to the table. "Phillip bought a lottery ticket and won. That's why he went to Boise." Then she started to wail.

Jeannie and Valerie went to the table and looked at the papers lying there. In Phil's handwriting it said, *Lottery numbers*, and beside that, in big letters: *I won! I WON!*

The numbers read 10–22–14–54–06–10.

In disbelief, tears welled up in Jeannie's eyes. "Mama, we don't know for sure. I think we need to call someone who knows the ticket numbers for sure. What do you think?"

Valerie was standing next to Laura with her arm around her. "Mother Gunn, I think that would be best. That way we'll all know for sure, okay?"

Laura slowly nodded. As Valerie comforted her, Jeannie looked for Phil's phone. She found it in the living room by the couch. As she pressed the numbers for Klongers there in Kameish, she tried to hold back her hope. What if her mother was right? Then what were they going to do?

"Hello, this is Jeannie Gunn. I'm calling to find out if I could get the winning numbers of the lottery last week—and could you tell me who had the winning ticket? I have a piece of paper here that says my brother Phil, who was killed last week, says he won. So, I'm trying to find any information I can."

The clerk at Klongers said, "We're so sorry to hear about your brother. I can give you the lottery numbers, though. They were 10–22–14–54–06–10. The ticket was bought here, but the name is a privacy matter. I hope this helps you, Jeannie, and again we're very sorry for your loss."

"Thank you," said Jeannie as she hung up. She stood there for a moment, then said, "These numbers that Phil wrote down are the correct ones. I think, Mama, we'd better call the sheriff. I'm not sure what's going on here, but something isn't right."

Laura agreed, so Jeannie dialed the sheriff's department.

"Hello, this is the Lewis County Sheriff's Department. How may I help you?"

"This is Jeannie Gunn. My brother, Phillip Gunn, was killed in a wreck a few days ago—"

"Yes, Miss Gunn. We're very sorry. Is there anything we can do to help with arrangements?"

"No, sir, not that I know of." She started to cry. "I... we think he might have been killed for money."

"What money would that be? We were under the impression that he didn't have much."

"We're at his trailer now, and there's a note in his handwriting that says, 'Lottery numbers,' then in big writing, 'I won! I WON!' We think he won the lottery and someone might've killed him. I called the store, and these numbers are the right ones, but they couldn't give me the person's name."

"Miss Gunn, the Lewis County sheriff is here with me right now. Would you mind if we come over and take a look? We just ask that you don't move or touch anything else until we get there."

"Please do," Jeannie said. "We need to get my mother home as soon as possible."

It wasn't long before the sheriff's car drove up. Officer Hasselblat knocked on the door.

"Come in," said Jeannie, as she opened it. She had dried her eyes, but they were still red. Laura, however, was still sniffling.

"Miss Gunn?"

"Yes, the note is in here." She led him to the kitchen.

"Mrs. Gunn," he said with a nod. "I'm Officer Hasselblat from the sheriff's office."

Laura nodded back, trying to stay strong, though her tears betrayed her.

"Here's the note. We haven't touched it or anything," sniffled Laura.

Officer Hasselblat's face stiffened as he read the note. "You know we can't jump to conclusions, but there may be a possibility you're right. May I take this with me?"

"Yes," said Laura.

"Are you sure this is your son's writing?" asked Officer Hasselblat.

"Look at the letters here and here. See—they're the same." Her voice was as shaky as her hands. "See this envelope here? This is his writing, too. Compare them and see what you think."

"Mrs. Gunn, may I keep these for a little while?"

"Yes! Take it. Find out what really happened to my son."

As she turned to Jeannie, a tear slipped down her cheek. "Jeannie, I can't stay here any longer. Please take me home."

Jeannie reached for her hand. She had never seen her mother look so old before; the sight almost made her look twice.

"Sure. We can do this later, Mom. Maybe by then Jonathon will be found and come home, and we'll take care of Phil's things together. Would you like that better?"

"Yes—yes, I think that would be much better."

So with that, they all left the trailer—the officer, the women, and Sparky the cat. The cat didn't mind the car ride; Phil had taken him on many rides since he was a little kitten.

Valerie kept glancing in the rearview mirror. "That's strange," she said, looking at Jeannie.

"Do you have any warrants on you?" Then she laughed.

"No, why?" asked Jeannie.

"I'm just teasing you. But that officer is following us all the way home. I wonder what he wants now?" remarked Valerie.

As Valerie pulled into the parking lot of Mother Gunn's apartment, she turned off the engine and waited for the officer, who was approaching. She lowered her window.

"Is there something else, Officer?" she asked.

Officer Hasselblat bent down. "I'm sorry to bother you ladies again, but did your son leave any kind of message or anything else that would tell you where he was going?"

Laura thought for a moment. "Well, no, not that I can think of. Wait a minute! I don't believe I've checked my phone messages since the night of the accident. I haven't needed to because the girls have been here."

"Do you mind if we check it while I'm here?" asked Officer Hasselblat.

"I suppose we could," Laura said, leading the way to her apartment. "Oh! I forgot to lock this door again. I swear my mind isn't getting any better lately."

She opened the door and led the little group over to the answering machine.

As she hit the play button, the machine began cycling through messages.

Finally, on the seventh call, they heard— "Hi, Mom. It's me again. Where have you gone this time?"

Jeannie and Valerie both took Laura's hands in theirs.

"You know, it's getting hard to catch up with you these days. Are you sure you haven't got a boyfriend somewhere? Say, Mom, I've got to run to Boise for a couple of days, and... oh... I'm going to quit my job. Anyway, when I get back, I've got a big surprise for you."

In the background they heard: "Hey, Phil, you ready?"

"Yeah, George, I'll be right there." Then back on the phone: "Okay, Mom, gotta run. Love ya. Bye."

Valerie had to do double duty, as Laura and Jeannie were both crying now. The sound of Phil's voice was too much for either of them to endure.

"Do you want me to turn it off?" she asked.

Laura shook her head. "No, he might have called back again. I don't want to miss it if he did."

So they listened to the rest of the tape.

The last message was from Pastor Kiely. "Mrs. Gunn—uh, I mean Laura—this is Pastor Kiely. I just got off the phone with the sheriff's office, and they've located Jonathon. You can pick him up Tuesday evening at the Spokane airport. My wife and I will be glad to take you up there if you like. Please let us know; you know how to reach us."

Then the recorder went quiet.

After a couple of minutes, Officer Hasselblat asked, "Ma'am, do you know who this George is? Do you know his last name and where I might find him?"

Laura looked very tired, but she took a deep breath. "His last name is Wetzel, and he lives somewhere on the Old Nez Perce Road. I think they have two cars—no, one car and a pickup."

"Okay. If we have any more questions, we'll get back with you. We're very sorry to intrude at this time. Thank you for your cooperation."

"Yes, that'll be fine. Either the girls or I will be here," replied Laura.

"One more thing—may I take this tape with me, too?" asked Officer Hasselblat.

As tears welled up in Laura's eyes again, she said, "Please, don't erase it. It's the only thing I have left."

And with that, all the pent-up tears could no longer be held back.

As Officer Hasselblat excused himself and walked out the door, a wave of grief swept over him like a bad breeze. "We're going to have to talk with Mr. Wetzel," he said aloud. "See if he can shed some light on this whole thing."

Jeannie had followed him outside and told him where George lived, so he decided he would drive by there on his way back to the office. "I really don't think we're going to find anyone home here," he muttered.

The other officer, waiting in the car, finally spoke up. "I believe you're right," he said, "but I really hope you're wrong."

CHAPTER 18

NEIGHBORS AND LEADS

I t turned out that Officer Hasselblat's hunch was right. As he pulled up the driveway, he found a neighbor feeding an Australian shepherd.

"Hello, are you Mrs. Wetzel?"

"No, I'm just the neighbor. I can't stand people who take off and leave their animals to fend for themselves—especially the ones who leave them tied on a chain with no food and water. There ought to be a law against that."

"Yes, ma'am. I know the feeling—and there is a law against that. What's your name?" asked Officer Hasselblat.

"Prudence. Prudence Westfall." She was mid-fifties, medium build, graying hair streaked with brown. She spoke matter-of-factly.

"Well, Miss Westfall—" began Officer Hasselblat.

"Please call me Prudence. I answer better to that."

"Okay, Prudence, do you know where the Wetzels are?"

"No, I don't," she snapped.

Hasselblat watched her closely. He knew she had more to say, so he waited.

"Let me see... They haven't been here since a week ago last Wednesday. I take that back—they left late Wednesday night, came back a little late Thursday morning, then left again."

"Did they return after that?" asked Officer Hasselblat.

"Well, they must have, because when they left that morning they took both the car and the pickup. When I got back from going into Kamish, the truck was here and there was no sign of life. But around 8:15 p.m. I looked out and the truck was gone, and about 9:00 they were back. Only this time there was a man with a yellow station wagon with them. They parked the truck, got in the station wagon, and took off."

"Do you know the approximate year of the car?" asked Hasselblat.

"Mid- to late-'70s. I had one similar," she said.

"Thank you, Prudence Westfall. You've been a great help. If we need to talk again, can we call you for an appointment?" asked Officer Hasselblat.

"Yeah, I'll be here. Husband's been gone eight years. The number's in the phone book. Yeah, he just took off one day. Don't know where he went either. Just like these people. Must be something in the water."

Prudence laughed at her little joke, and Hasselblat smiled.

"You know, there just could be. Thanks again, Prudence," he said. "Oh—you mentioned another car. Do you know the make and color?"

"Chevy. Impala, I think. Light-colored."

"I'm going to look around a bit and then I'll be gone. Thank you again for your help."

"That's what I'm here for—to help," said Prudence.

Hasselblat looked around the Wetzels' place. He didn't find anything from the outside and decided to wait for developments before seeking a search warrant. Then he headed back toward the sheriff's department.

On the way, he called dispatch. "Central, this is Unit Three, over."

"Unit Three, this is Central. Go ahead."

"Central, pull up everything on a George Wetzel. Try to find his wife's name and check her out too. Something's fishy here, and it might have something to do with the Gunn accident. I'm on my way in."

"Ten-four, Unit Three. I'll get on that now and should have it for you by the time you get here. Oh—there's a message from the Idaho County Sheriff's Office. Sheriff Gage wants you to call him at your convenience."

"Okay, put the message on my desk, Central. I'll be there soon enough. And I want a unit out at the Wetzels' house on the Old Nez Perce Road as soon as possible. Stake it out in case someone comes home. Send Danielson—he can handle it. Make sure he understands to stay there until he's relieved."

"Ten-four, Sheriff."

"Oh—one more thing. Call Prudence Westfall and tell her if anything happens around the house before Danielson gets there, to call the sheriff's office."

"Ten-four. You got a number?"

"She said it's in the phone book."

"Ten-four. Out."

In the pit of his stomach, Hasselblat knew they weren't coming back. Not now, not ever.

He pulled into the office about twenty minutes later. As he walked in, he wore a look of pure business—enough to make everyone gun-shy.

"Here's what we found on the Wetzels," an officer said, handing him the reports. "Her name is Marge. No arrests, no warrants—clean as a whistle."

Hasselblat scanned the file as he dialed the Idaho County Sheriff.

"Sheriff Gage," came the answer.

"Hello, Gage—Hasselblat. Got your message. What's up?"

"Hey, Hasselblat. How are you?"

"I'm fine. Can't complain."

"Yeah, I know the feeling. Say—you know I'm investigating that Gunn accident, right?"

"No, I wasn't aware of that. Why?" asked Hasselblat.

"I've got a gut feeling there's more to it than accident or suicide or whatever you want to call it. Wondering what you might know—who he worked for, who with. Friends, enemies. Places he hung around. Whether he was alone the night he left town. You're closer over there—anything helps," Gage said.

"Tell you what, Gage—can we meet for coffee? I've got some stuff that'll blow your mind—just found it out this morning."

"Can you come over to Oscar's? Say around 2:00?"

"2:00 it is," said Hasselblat.

He hung up, stuffed the file into its folder, scratched his head—an old habit he never quite broke—and headed out. To dispatch, he called, "I'm headed to Main Ville. I'll be at Oscar's with the sheriff there. Unless it's critical, let Baker handle anything that comes in."

It was just before 2:00 when he got to Oscar's. Since he was early, he asked for a semi-private table.

"Will there be just one?" the hostess asked.

"No—one, possibly two more. Do you have a table where we can talk without interruption?"

"Yes—please follow me. If you tell me who they are, I'll send them back when they arrive."

"Sheriff Gage. He might bring another officer—Officer Pipcorn."

"Oh sure, I know him. He's a regular," she said with a smile. "Coffee while you wait?"

"That'll be fine."

She returned with his coffee just as Sheriff Gage and Officer Pipcorn came through the door.

"Been waiting long, Hasselblat?" Gage asked, extending a hand. Pipcorn did the same.

"No, not really. Figured I'd wait to order so we can eat while we talk," said Hasselblat.

"Sounds great. The chicken-fried steak is excellent—done to perfection," Gage said.

"My favorite," replied Hasselblat.

They ordered, then got to business.

"Hasselblat, you said you had some things about the Gunn case," Gage began.

"Yes. I was on my way to the office in Kamish this morning when dispatch sent me to Phil Gunn's house. His sister claims he won the lottery. When she and her mother went to start packing, the mother saw a piece of paper on the table with the lottery numbers and, in his handwriting, *I won. I WON!* They called the store—the numbers match—but the store wouldn't release the winner's name."

"Do you have the paper?" asked Gage.

"Yes. I found it just as they said. I also grabbed an envelope with the deceased's handwriting—looks like a match. Here." He handed the paper over.

"Could there be two winning tickets?" Gage asked.

"Not according to the station. I checked. I looked around but didn't find anything else, so I left. Mrs. Gunn was really shaken. I followed them back to her place in Kameish to ask another question. She hadn't checked her answering machine since the accident. We played it. Phil left a message—said he'd be in Boise a couple of days and had a big surprise when he got back. In the background, a George called to him. A George and Marge Wetzel might have been with him. I went to their place—found the neighbor, Prudence Westfall, feeding their dog. The Wetzels haven't been home since the time of the accident."

"That's interesting. We have a woman who can put a couple with the victim at an all-night station here in Main Ville just before the accident," Gage said. "Do you have the tape?"

"Yes—right here. Sorry—I should've handed it over with the other." He passed it across. "Prudence says they left Wednesday night, came back Thursday morning, took both car and pickup, then left again. If that's the case, there might've been another vehicle involved."

"We need their vehicle info. We'll run them through DMV," Gage said. "Anything else?"

"Yes—the most important thing. Westfall says she saw them getting into a yellow Ford station wagon, seventies model, around 9:00 the night of the accident. They never returned."

"That ties with what we've got," Gage said. "Now we need a car with tires that match our plaster casts—and two suspects. If we can put this together with the car, we can pick them up on suspicion. Then we'll get answers."

Lunch wrapped up, and the waitress brought the check.

"Hasselblat, since you brought us this wealth of information, lunch is on me," Gage offered.

"I knew I should've ordered a T-bone," Hasselblat said, and they laughed.

Outside, Gage turned to him. "I mean it—I owe you for this. If you hear anything else, keep me posted."

"You got it, Gage. Let me know what you put together. I knew Phil Gunn."

"You'll know when I do. Thanks again. All we need now is a photo of the Wetzels."

"I'll see what I can find," Hasselblat said.

They went their separate ways.

As Riley and Simmons finally caught their breath and climbed back into their cruiser across town, the weight of what had happened settled on them. Scar wasn't just desperate—he was dangerous, trained, unpredictable. This wasn't going to be a simple missing-persons pickup. Somewhere beneath the chaos was a tangled web. And now, with the lottery ticket in play, everything had just gotten a lot more complicated. For the first time, they knew this case wasn't just about Scar—it was about much more. The real story was only beginning.

CHAPTER 19

TRACKS AND WARRANTS

The day after having lunch with the sheriff of Lewis County, Sheriff Gage and Officer Pipcorn were back up at the site of the accident.

"Sheriff, has it rained since the night of the accident?" asked Officer Pipcorn, squatting about fifty feet from where Sheriff Gage was peering over the edge to make sure nothing had been missed.

"Not that you'd notice. What are you getting at?" Gage called back as he stepped away from the rim and walked toward Pipcorn.

"Well, I don't remember any rain since then. And if it hasn't rained, I think we might have some more tracks to check out," Pipcorn said, pointing at a row of impressions leading toward where the crash had happened.

"Let me see. Where are you looking?" Gage asked, stopping beside him.

"Right here. See?"

The tracks continued up the slope where Pipcorn pointed. "There's nothing right where the car was, but say this was one of the passengers. If they got out on the other side, where there was no mud, they wouldn't leave prints at the car. They'd cross over here to get into the other car and drive down to pick up the remaining person. How's that sound so far, Sheriff?" He hoped for a nod.

"Weak. Can you give me something else?" Gage wanted to buy it, but he needed more than theory.

"Okay, look. You can trace the prints all the way up—except where there wasn't mud. And look here: this car was sitting before it rained." Pipcorn pointed to a clean set of tire impressions. "Then it left after it rained, and those footprints lead right to this second car."

Gage scratched his head, studying the scene. "Yeah. It does look like the car left after the rain. And if it had been driven through here during the rain, there'd be tire tracks cut through that mud back there." He pointed at a wide patch of now semi-hard mire. "I admit it looks strange—but maybe strange enough to be true."

He stared off, piecing it together. "Mmm. Let me run this by you. We'll have to check weather reports to make it stick, but—" he paused, thinking. "Let's say the Wetzels brought a car up here the day of the accident and left it, knowing they'd be back that evening after they sent this guy over the edge. They could've used a different car to get home. They probably never gave the rain a second thought. They thought they were safe—until my supersleuth partner uncovered their tracks."

Pipcorn followed the logic, brow furrowed. "Yeah, but wouldn't the victim know the car? Especially if they were friendly enough to go to Boise together?"

Gage lifted his hands. "Of course—if he was awake. But remember what the cashier said? He got in the back seat because he was sleepy."

"So that means he either moved to the front seat under protest or he was put there," Pipcorn said. "And if he was put there, why didn't he wake up?"

Gage smiled. "Exactly. Now are you thinking what I'm thinking?"

"I sure am!" Pipcorn said, suddenly animated. "We get the coroner to test Gunn's body for drugs—anything he can find."

"Let's go," Gage said, heading for the unit.

On the way back to Main Ville he asked, "Got plans for dinner?"

"I think it's spaghetti night—just the wife, the kids, and me. No, nothing else."

"Good. This won't take long. I want to talk to that night-shift cashier again—make sure of the descriptions and that she can ID them from photos."

Pipcorn hesitated. "Should we call the coroner before he leaves for the day?"

"You call the coroner when we get back. I'm going to talk to the lab boys about plaster casts of the other set of tracks."

"In the next couple of days, after we check the weather reports and such, I want to see the sheriff in Lewis County and get warrants for the Gunn residence and the Wetzels' place," Gage added, eagerness creeping into his voice.

"Okay. I'll do that," Pipcorn said as he pulled into their spot.

It took a few minutes to gather what they needed from the unit and walk in. Pipcorn set his things on his desk and dialed the coroner.

"Hello—this is Officer Pipcorn, Main Ville Sheriff's Office. We met at the Speckled Bird accident... Yeah, that was me. Do you still have Phillip Gunn's body? The victim in that crash?... Right. I need a favor—complete toxicology, Sheriff's orders. We know the condition, but do your best. Call me or the Sheriff if you find anything. I know he was badly burned, but anything helps. Thanks—we owe you one. Bye."

"Pipcorn, does the coroner still have Gunn's body, and will he check for us?" Gage asked.

"Yes—and yes," Pipcorn said.

"Good. I'm sending the lab to cast the other footprints and tire marks. Maybe we get lucky."

Gage glanced at the reports in his hands and breathed a quick prayer: *God, please let this come together.*

After Jill Bennett—the cashier—confirmed she could ID the people with Phillip that night, Gage and Pipcorn prepared to head to Nez Perce. Gage had just reached his desk when the phone rang.

"This is Sheriff Gage... Yes—hey there, Coroner. We've been waiting for your call... Yeah, he's here. What do you have?... How do you spell that? S-E-A-N-A-L—Seonal?... What is it—sleeping pills?... Self-induced, you think?... Depends on the person, huh?... Could that much be put in a drink?... Only if crushed to powder... Is that a lot for an overdose victim?... Okay. Thank you. Bye."

Gage's eyes sparked as he hung up. He clapped a hand on Pipcorn's shoulder and steered him toward the door.

"What's up? You look like the cat that ate the canary," Pipcorn said.

"Curiosity killed the cat, you know," Gage chuckled. "I'll tell you on the way to Nezperce."

On his way out, Gage asked another deputy to pull weather for the last week. "Sure thing, Sheriff. Anything you say," she replied—he sounded upbeat again, which usually meant good news.

"Let's run, Pipcorn. I want to look at the Wetzels' house. But first I'm going to make sure there's nothing that points to Gunn committing suicide."

The thirty-five–minute drive passed mostly in silence after Gage filled Pipcorn in on the toxicology lead. Both men were turning over the same questions: what they might find at the houses, whether the Wetzels were capable of murder, and—after a week and a half—where they might be now.

At the Nez Perce Sheriff's Office they parked out front. No court day meant plenty of space. Inside, Gage asked the dispatcher, "Is Sheriff Hasselblat around?"

"You just missed him—he'll be right back. He walked to the store for a snack," she said.

"That's the next block, isn't it?" Pipcorn asked.

"Yes."

"I think we'll meet him there," Gage said as they turned to go. "Tell me, Pipcorn—how'd you know where the store was?"

"I've been here a time or two," he said.

"I thought you said you didn't come over this way."

"Well, it was a while ago. And there isn't much here—hard to forget."

"Pipcorn, Pipcorn, Pipcorn... what am I going to do with you?" Gage lifted his eyes and spotted Hasselblat exiting the store. "Hey, Hasselblat! How you doing today?"

"Sheriff Gage! What brings you to this neck of the woods?" Hasselblat asked.

"We've come to ask a favor. Think we could look at both the Gunn house and the Wetzels' house?" Gage said.

"I think we can convince the judge to give us search warrants. Why?"

"I want to make sure Gunn didn't commit suicide. And you said the neighbor mentioned a second car. I want pictures of the Wetzels, plus anything useful—bank records, loans, the usual."

"Let's see the judge," Hasselblat said. "For what it's worth, I don't buy suicide either. He was a friend, and I'm a decent judge of character. I'm willing to do whatever it takes to put the perpetrators behind bars—if there are any."

"That's what I hoped you'd say."

At the courthouse it didn't take long to secure the warrants. Soon all three were in Hasselblat's cruiser headed for Kamish.

Entering town, Hasselblat radioed his office so they'd know to expect activity.

"Officer Pipcorn, I want you looking for anything unusual," Gage said. "Don't leave anything unturned. We can do a lot without tearing the place apart—be careful."

"Yes, sir," Pipcorn replied.

"I'm going by Mrs. Gunn's first," Hasselblat said. "Phil's sister has a key. Best to have someone from the family with us."

"Good idea," Gage said.

They pulled up beside Valerie's Mustang. As they got out, the apartment door opened—Jeannie and Valerie.

"Hello, Sheriff. What can we do for you? Any news about Phil?" Jeannie asked.

"Miss Gunn, we need to see the inside of your brother's trailer," Hasselblat said.

"Sure. We were just headed there to try packing again. You can follow us."

"Thank you for your cooperation. How's your mother?" Hasselblat asked.

"She's coping better. She and Phil were close. This has been a blow."

"Before I forget—this is Sheriff Gage and Officer Pipcorn from Main Ville. They're investigating the accident," Hasselblat added. "We have a warrant to search for clues. I didn't think we'd need one for your brother's place, but we got one just in case."

"No, you wouldn't need one," Jeannie said.

Valerie ducked back inside. "Mother Gunn, the sheriff wants to look at Phil's trailer. We'll let them in while we're there."

"Okay, dear. Who are the other officers?" Laura asked.

"They're from Main Ville."

"Oh—have they found anything?"

"Not yet—that's why they're here."

"Let them do whatever they need," Laura said. "And don't touch anything until they say it's okay."

"Okay—we'll be back after a while. Love you," Valerie said.

"All right, dear."

"Oh—Mother Gunn," Valerie added, "don't forget to tell Pastor Kiely we'll accept his offer to take us to meet Jonathon. He's supposed to arrive at 6:45 tomorrow night at Spokane Airport."

"I'll let him know. You two take your time—I'll be fine," Laura said.

"Okay."

At the trailer, they filed in.

"Would it be too much to ask that you don't move anything for a few minutes?" Gage asked. "We need to see things as they are."

"That's absolutely okay with us," Jeannie said. "Anything we can do to help."

"Miss Gunn," Gage said gently, "I'm sorry about your brother. I hate to ask this, but if—worst case—he did commit suicide, is there anything you can think of that would've pushed him over the edge?"

"I can't think of anything. He was good-looking, muscular, he had money, he liked his job and his co-workers. He always said if his smile lifted someone's spirits in a day, his day was well spent. That's how he lived—helping others."

"Nothing else bothered him?" Gage asked.

"The only thing, maybe, was not being able to buy a new double-wide. But that's not a reason, is it?"

"No," Gage said. "I don't think so either."

"I can't find anything out of the ordinary," Pipcorn reported. "No note, nothing staged. Doesn't look like a man planning to die. Looks like an eligible bachelor with everything going for him."

"How do you know he was a bachelor?" Valerie asked.

"Well, Miss Valerie, any woman worth her salt wouldn't let a man throw clothes all over the floor or leave dirty dishes around," Pipcorn said, laughing. "I was a bachelor not too long ago—that's how my place looked. My wife would kill me now if I did that. She gets mad if I leave my coffee cup in the living room."

"So, in your opinion there are no signs of suicide?" Gage asked. "Sheriff Hasselblat—do you concur?"

"Absolutely," Hasselblat said. "We've checked everything we can find—no notes, no overdue bills, nothing out of the norm."

"Okay, I'm satisfied," Gage said. "Thank you, ladies, for your cooperation. We're sorry to trouble you at a time like this. If we need anything else, we'll be in touch. Have a good day."

"Ready?" he asked Hasselblat and Pipcorn.

"Yeah—let's see what we find at the other place."

Jeannie walked them to the door, puzzled by "the other place," but let it go. If they wanted her to know, they'd tell her. For now, it was enough to pack Phil's things and get back to the only place that made sense—home with Mom.

CHAPTER 20

THE WETZELS' HOUSE

The officers felt a twinge of guilt over the inconvenience they'd put Jeannie and Valerie through—especially leaving them there after the women had been so helpful. But they were anxious to see what they might find at the Wetzels' house.

"You know, Gage, if these Wetzels are guilty, we're going to have a time finding them now," Hasselblat said, thinking aloud.

"Yeah, I've been thinking that too," Gage agreed. "They've had plenty of time to get far away."

"Think we'll be able to track them?" Officer Pipcorn asked.

"Depends on the paper trail," Hasselblat said. "If we can find enough people and evidence of their whereabouts, we can nab them—hopefully."

"Oh, I've got news," Gage said. "The coroner almost missed the most important clue in this case—mainly because we didn't know what to look for. He found Seonal in the victim's remains. A lot of it. He said if the body had been burned any worse, he wouldn't have caught it. There was enough in him to kill an elephant. They almost got away with it—and probably would have if it weren't for the Bennett girl in Main Ville."

"Who is she?" asked Hasselblat.

"She's the one who called us and told us there was someone else with him that night," Gage answered.

"So that's how you got the information about the other couple?" Hasselblat said.

"Exactly. Now, if we can find a picture of them—and she can make the match—we'll be in like Flynn," Gage said.

"Yeah—if we can find them," Pipcorn added.

"That's the hard part." Gage fell silent, weighing possibilities. No one spoke again until they turned into the Wetzels' driveway.

Prudence Westfall was there feeding the dog again. When she saw Hasselblat, she smiled and waved. "Howdy, Sheriff. Any news on these characters yet?"

"Not exactly," he said. "But if you want that dog, you might as well take him home. I don't believe the Wetzels will be back anytime soon."

"I think I'd like that—if you're sure. Jackel and I have become pretty good friends. Oh! I hope you don't mind, but I've been taking fresh doughnuts and coffee out to your deputy. He's not married, is he?"

Hasselblat chuckled, and the others joined him. "No, I believe he's very single—and I don't mind. If it weren't against the rules, I'd give you his number. I bet he'll give it to you if you ask, though."

Inside, he was laughing; Danielson had sworn off women years ago. *We'll see how confirmed a bachelor he is,* he thought.

"Prudence, we're going inside to look around. We have a warrant, so we'll say goodbye for now. We may need more information later—would that be all right?" Hasselblat asked.

"Absolutely."

"Fine. Let's go, Gage. Pipcorn." The three headed to the house. The door was unlocked, so they went in.

"Boy, they left in such a hurry they forgot to lock up," Pipcorn said.

"I'd say they knew they weren't coming back," Gage replied. "Right, Hasselblat?"

"Yeah—that's how it looks."

"Okay, Hasselblat, take the upstairs. Pipcorn, the basement. I'll work the main floor."

"Got it," they said together.

"I'm already downstairs," Pipcorn called.

It didn't take long to turn up incriminating evidence. Hasselblat came down with photographs in hand. "Gage—pictures you were looking for. Boy, this guy's wife was a looker."

"Let me see." Gage studied them. "Now I know what the Bennett girl meant. Why would a doll like that be married to the likes of him?"

"Let's see what Pipcorn has," Hasselblat said as they found the basement door.

"Pipcorn! You find anything?" Gage shouted.

"No. Nothing down here!"

"Okay—come up and help on the main floor."

"I'm on my way."

Back in the living room, Gage spotted a half-burned sheet of paper in the fireplace. He lifted it carefully. There were rough drawings labeled Speckled Bird Road; midway down, a line veered off the grade—right where the paper had burned away.

"Hey—look at this!"

Hasselblat joined him. "Let me see. Hmm. I wonder if there's more of this notebook somewhere, so we can see the whole page."

"It's worth a look. Pipcorn—check that room that looks like a study. Especially for a pad that matches this sheet. Hasselblat, you take the back bedrooms. I'll finish the front," Gage said.

"You got it." They split up.

Gage went to the corner table by the phone. Loose paper—nothing that matched the scribbled map. In the kitchen, the fridge was full and mostly spoiled. A bill rack held overdue notices: two months behind on the mortgage, three on the car, another pleading for a truck payment before repossession. Credit cards and other monthly bills overdue as well.

He whistled softly. *Deep in debt. That might be our motive.*

"Sheriff Gage!" Pipcorn called from the study. "You'll want to see this."

Gage crossed to the study. "What do you have?"

"Here's your writing pad. I did a little shading—this page matches your burned sheet. It even shows the pullout where they parked, an 'X,' and a car beside it. This arrow says, 'Bye-bye Phil.' Also found overdraft slips from their bank."

"Good work, Pipcorn. Exactly what I was looking for. Let's see what Hasselblat found."

They headed to the back bedrooms.

"Hey—we were starting to worry you got lost," Gage said with a grin. "Anything?"

"Yeah. They're not coming back," Hasselblat said. "They took a few clothes, but not all—looks like they sorted and discarded what they didn't want. The rest are on the floor, still on hangers. Suitcases are packed, but none here—maybe an overnight bag or two. Her makeup is still here; if she were coming back, most of it would be packed. The bed's unmade from the last sleep. From how immaculate she kept things, she'd have made it if she planned to return. I'm thinking they're gone for good."

"I think you're right," Gage said. "Pipcorn, get a lab crew over here. I want this place gone over with a fine-tooth comb—we may have missed something."

"On my way."

"What else do you need me to dig up?" Hasselblat asked.

"Everything on their finances—loans, defaults, bills—their general life picture, even mental status if we can get context," Gage said.

"I'll notify the banks and the credit union to release statements. If they need a court order—and they will—I'll handle it. Want me to hit DMV for vehicles?"

"I can run DMV from Main Ville," Gage said. "That's all for now. Let's cross our fingers and hope something pops. We're headed the right direction; I just hope the trail doesn't go cold. One more thing—contact the Lottery Office. I want the winner's name and address as soon as possible."

"I'll get on it and leave a message at your office if I miss you," Hasselblat said.

"Excellent. I'm taking these pictures to see if the Bennett girl can confirm them. If she IDs them, I'll talk to the prosecutor—see if it's enough for a warrant. If nothing else, we may bring them in for questioning. That might rattle them into a mistake," Gage said.

"Sheriff Gage, want me to stay until the crime lab gets here?" Pipcorn asked.

"No, I need you with me." He turned to Hasselblat. "Can you have a deputy hold the scene until the lab arrives?"

"Sure—I'll take care of it," Hasselblat said.

They rode back to Hasselblat's office, said their goodbyes, and Gage and Pipcorn headed for Main Ville to talk to the Bennett girl—right after grabbing a bite to eat.

CHAPTER 21

THE WITNESS

As they drove back to Main Ville, they were quiet, thinking about all they had learned and how the investigation would go from here. They pulled behind Oscar's and parked. Just before shutting off the engine, Sheriff Gage called in to his office.

"Main Ville Central, Sheriff Gage, over."

"Go ahead, Sheriff."

"Yeah, Central... Officer Pipcorn and I are at Oscar's. We're going to talk to the Bennett girl right afterward and then we'll be at the office. I need all information on George and Marge Wetzel on my desk as soon as I get there. Copy?"

"Ten-four, Sheriff. We'll contact DMV as well. Over."

"Good. I knew I could count on you. Sheriff out."

Gage got out and stretched. "Man. Sometimes I hate this job. I'm getting too old for most of these goose chases. I need a hot tub to soak in at night."

Pipcorn came around the car. "You know, those Swedish girls know how to work out the kinks. You being single, handsome, rich and all—Sheriff, I bet you could hook one easy."

"If you don't mind, I'm backing out of this conversation, old buddy. By the time we crack this case, it'll be vacation. Then I'll get my hot tub and be just fine."

They went in to eat. They tried small talk, but both kept circling the evidence and wondering whether the Wetzels would ever be found. As soon as they finished, they climbed the stairs to Jill Bennett's apartment. Pipcorn knocked. Footsteps, a latch—and the door opened.

"Oh—hello, Sheriff. And you, Officer Pipcorn. Would you like to come in?"

"Thank you, Miss Bennett," Gage said. "We hope we're not intruding on your time off. We won't take long."

"That's okay. I'm off tonight anyway."

"Miss Bennett, do you know these people?" He handed her a photo of the Wetzels. "Have you seen them before?"

"Yes. That's the couple who were with the man the night of the wreck."

"Are you absolutely sure, Miss Bennett?" Pipcorn asked.

"No doubt about it. That's them. Have you found their bodies?"

"No," Pipcorn said. "We just need them for questioning right now. If you see them again, please let us know. Will you?"

"Of course."

"I know I'm reaching," Gage said, "but did you notice anything strange about them that night?"

"Not really. They came in first while the other guy pumped gas. They stood by the Coke dispenser for a while before they paid for drinks and snacks." She hesitated. "I did notice one thing, though. I didn't think anything of it at the time. I saw her pull a vial out of her pocket and hand it to the man. He seemed reluctant to take it, but he finally did."

"Did you see what they did with it?" the sheriff asked.

"Yes, sir. He poured it into a cup. I thought it was some kind of medicine he needed. Then he handed the vial back to the woman, and she put it in her purse."

"Did they have another car around the station?"

"I didn't see any other cars parked nearby. If they'd stopped earlier, I couldn't tell you."

"Anything peculiar about the two people?" Pipcorn asked.

"Well, I wondered what a good-looking woman like her was doing with an overweight, balding guy like him. They weren't the most perfect couple—complete opposites. You know, like Mutt and Jeff. Or the Odd Couple."

"Would you testify to this?" Pipcorn said.

"I'd have to tell what I saw—and that's what I saw."

They thanked her for her time and headed downstairs to their car.

Inside, they looked at each other.

"Pipcorn, we're going to catch these people," Gage said. "I can feel it in my bones."

"Yeah. I hope we crack it. From what Hasselblat said, this Gunn guy was a pretty nice guy. I hate seeing the good ones fall. There aren't enough of them in this world."

They rode in silence until the office came into view.

"Sheriff, how long do you think it'll take?" Pipcorn asked.

"To what?"

"To catch them."

"I'm afraid we've got a long wait. We don't even know if they're still in the country, let alone the state. By now they could be in Timbuktu. We may be able to pin this on them and prove it, but finding them—only God knows when. Right now I'd just like to have them here to answer questions. Yep, we'll be on this one for a while. Let's get to the office, see what's come in, and try to fit the pieces."

Later, Gage glanced at the clock. "Well, we've put in a day's worth. You'd better get home before your wife hangs us both."

"What are you doing for dinner?" Pipcorn asked.

"Oh, probably chicken pot pie."

"Like spaghetti?" Pipcorn said.

"Thought you'd never ask," Gage answered.

They locked up and left the station for the night.

CHAPTER 22

FAREWELL AND WATCHFUL EYES

M arge woke at 6:00 a.m. feeling giddy as a school girl. She rolled over and kissed George and then jumped out of bed. "I want a house just like this one George, isn't it wonderful? In fact, I love everything about it! Even the beds! Don't you think it's wonderful?"

"Yes, I must admit, it is quite nice. If we can find something like this where we are going, it will be money well spent. Marge, while you were with the others last night, you know when Jerry took me out to make my identification, well he talked to me about our plans. He told me that I should start thinking on where we wanted to go and to start making arrangements for it. So, I'm asking you where you would like to go? Or what country sounds good to you?"

"Boy, George, I never really thought about it. What do you think? Do you have any place in mind?" asked Marge.

"I thought maybe south. You know Puerto Vallarta or in that area anyway. We could go there first then if we don't like it, we can go somewhere else," suggested George.

"Why don't we ask Jerry where he would go?" asked Marge.

"His main concern is that we don't tell him where we are going. He doesn't want to know. Not that he would tell, but the less people that know, he says, the better for us all," stated George.

"Well, that does make sense. Okay we'll go south."

"Now, another thing is this. After we pick up the check, we will contact this friend of Jerry's, a man named Bigalow. He is going to launder the money for us and it will end up in a bank in the South Pacific in our names. We will be notified by him when it is complete. In fact, we'll be in his office when the transaction is made. So, we'll know when and where before we leave his office. Of course he will take his cut out of it, but that will only be a small amount," George shared.

"Are we going to have any to use here?" asked Marge.

"We'll have some. Jerry is going to loan us ten grand that he'll collect from Bigalow. It seems he owes Jerry that much and more, so we won't have to worry about that. Anyway, that will leave us approximately 31 million left, but it will be almost untraceable then. With what we get from Jerry we'll have the money transferred to a bank there, buy the house we want and do what we want to do after that," said George.

"I hope we can find a nice one."

"I don't want one if it's not by the ocean. It seems to me that's where you wanted to be wasn't it? Right, Marge?" asked George.

"You really mean it, George, I can actually have my house on the beach?"

"Of course!" And for the first time since this whole escapade started, she kissed him like she really meant it. And for a minute he was almost fooled into believing that she would never do anything against him, but not quite. "So, Mrs. Jody Weinburger, today is the day we say goodbye to all we knew. Literally all. Are you ready for that?" asked George.

"Yes," confirmed Marge.

"Any regrets, like people you want to see first but can't?" asked George.

"No," replied Marge.

"Good. The sooner we get out of here the better," said George.

What George didn't tell Marge is that there was going to be a big profit by the transaction made by Bigalow. Most of that was going to Jerry and Bigalow, so she didn't need to know. What George liked was that it was going to be untraceable. So that's where he left it.

There was a slight knock on their bedroom door. "Breakfast will be ready in about an hour. You two should get up and get your things packed. It will be best for you to get a room at a hotel this morning sometime. We'll say our goodbyes and take you where you want to go. And then my friends, it's up to you and Bigalow," Jerry shared.

"You heard the man, Terrance. Let's go!" Marge said as she picked up a pillow and threw it at him. And as she bounced into the adjoining restroom said, "I get the shower first!"

George thought to himself, if this was any other time in my life, I'd be really happy. I truly hope things change when we are out of here and somewhere else. I know I'll never be able to let my guard down. She's too dangerous. I will always be watching. Not only that, but I believe somehow, somewhere we are going to pay for what we have done. It seems imminent.

Forty-five minutes later, the four of them, Jerry, Ally, George and Marge (the new Terrance and Jody Weinberger), were sitting around the small table in the kitchen having breakfast.

Jerry started talking, "First of all, I'd like to wish you both the best of luck. After you leave the states you should be safe. And oh, I've got another bit of good news for you George. I have reworked the figures and you will come out with about thirty-three million and a little change after the transaction. Now, getting back to you leaving though, I won't quit worrying until you're out of the states. So, when you get where you are going, call me person to person and I'll know then that you are safe." He looked at Marge and with a little grin, he said, "Looks like we're even, Margie."

"Yes, we are." She giggled a little. "You really came through when I needed you, Jerry. Thank you, my friend."

"You know we'll never see each other ever again after today so all I can say to you, both of you, but to you especially Margie, is spoil yourselves. But do the right thing when it comes around. Don't do what I did. I'm doomed. I sold my soul for what I got and someday I'll pay." Jerry had never looked more serious in his life and Marge knew it.

"It's too late," is all she could say. And they all seemed to know that this money was going to be her curse.

George gave her a sideways glance that told her he knew all along. So the rest of the meal was spent in silence. Their thoughts were all different, but yet, all alike. For they were all thinking on how this money was now going to change the lives of these people.

Jerry thought of the misery that lay ahead for them both. Marge was thinking of her new-found life of luxury. George was thinking on how to keep a better eye on Marge while trying to enjoy being rich at his best friend's expense. And Ally was thinking how this money was going to change these two as it had Jerry. She had become his slave and now was truly sorry for the man, for he had no real life. It was spent on making money to make more money and that was all.

"After we are at the hotel, I'm going to call the lottery office for an appointment," said George.

"Now you're thinking. I believe you will only have a week or two grace period to get out of town before the law will be looking for you. But I personally wouldn't wait that long." And after taking a sip of his coffee, he added, "I could call Bigalow and tell him to expect a call from you in the next couple of days if you like," offered Jerry.

"That would be great. I've got his number that you gave me, so tell him as soon as we get the check, he'll be the first one we call," confirmed George.

"Please remember to destroy his number when you are done with this whole transaction. Okay?" reminded Jerry.

"I promise," George said earnestly. "Were you going to drop us off at a hotel?"

"Yes, just remember to use your new names. For everything!"

Both George and Marge nodded their heads as they took in everything Jerry had said. And as soon as the breakfast dishes cleared the table, they were on their way.

It was time to go to the hotel. Time for the final goodbyes and the start of their new lives. Only fate was going to play a big role in all three lives; Jerry's, Marge's and George's. Never again would their lives be savored. In the end greed will take its toll.

Unknown to the little group that left Jerry's house, eyes were watching them. Ever so earnestly they were studied. An older woman across the street was peering at them through a set of closed drapes. She closed them ever so carefully to not let anyone know she was there. But she was! She had always had an eye peeled for the unusual or the strange activities that might be not quite visible to someone else and every time she saw something she would tell her husband of fifty-two years. But as usual, he didn't believe her either. She always told him, "Someday you'll see that I'm right." Today she slowly let the curtain go, very slowly so that no one could see them move. "Harry, it's happened again!"

"What's happened again, Hazel?" Harry didn't have much time for this. He had just sat down in his easy chair to read the paper. He always read the paper after breakfast and did not like to be disturbed. But here she was being her old self. His pet name for her was Toby Tobias Percival Snoop. And today just proved the name was true. For some reason she always thought the guy across the street was doing something illegal. It was all Harry could do to keep her off the phone to the police. He'd talked her out of it every time so far and he might have to do it again today.

"Do you remember those two people I told you came home with that man, over there, the other night?"

"Yes, what have they done now, thrown a car bomb at the cat?"

"No! Don't be silly! They are leaving though."

"So, what's so strange about that?" asked Harry.

"The thing that is so strange is they have made themselves look different!"

"Maybe it's two different people," Harry said, lowering his paper, "or maybe they just wanted to change their look for a while. Why can't you leave things alone?"

"Because something's wrong over there! I just know it. And they're the same people—I can tell by how they walk. She kind of sways side to side, and he's got a slight limp. No, it's them all right."

"Hazel, have you taken your pills today? You know—the ones that bring you back to earth. You're always seeing things."

"Pills, poo! One of these days, mister, you'll be sorry you've made fun of me. You just wait."

"Honestly, Hazel," he sighed. "You remind me of that Kravitz woman from that old witch show. She was always spying and stirring things up. All I want is to read my paper without you peeking out the window at people who don't concern us. Is that too much to ask?"

"You just mark my words, Harry. Someday you're going to eat those words!"

Hazel marched into the kitchen to finish the breakfast dishes. Her feelings were hurt that he didn't believe her—but someday, she told herself, he would see.

And she might just be right.

CHAPTER 23

CHECK, CAMERAS, CONSEQUENCES

Jerry pulled up to the side entrance of the Grand Hotel on Third and Main. "Well, Margie, here we are—saying goodbye again. This time, forever. What do I say? You might have done well this time. Let's see how it turns out, huh?"

"George, take care of yourself—Don't lose that number I gave you. If you ever need anything, call it. They'll get hold of me somehow. And always call from a pay phone. Okay?"

"You've got it. And thanks for everything. I mean that." George shook his hand.

Jerry waited while they got out. He popped the trunk with a button on the dash; they pulled their luggage free and stepped back. Jerry slipped the car into drive. As he rolled away, Marge and George gave a small, final wave.

Once he'd gone, they picked up their suitcases and climbed the steps. A bellhop opened the door.

"Thank you," George said, and they stepped inside.

"May I help with the bags?" the bellhop asked.

"Yes—take hers, will you?"

"Very good, sir."

"Thank you!" Marge said. "That was getting heavy."

"Yes, ma'am. Will you be with us long?" he asked.

"Oh, for a few days—maybe," George answered. "Depends on how a business call turns out."

"Very good, sir. The check-in desk is this way." He led them over.

"We'd like a room, please," Marge said—so sweetly it almost made George nauseous. He'd never heard that voice from her; he didn't like it.

"How long will you be staying, madam?" the clerk asked.

"A few days, as of now. It depends on my husband's business dealings."

"Smoking or non-smoking?"

"Non-smoking," George said.

"If you'll sign here, please, Russell—the bellhop—will show you to your room." He handed the key over. "Russell, Room 421."

"Would you follow me, please?" Russell scooped up not only Marge's bags but George's, too.

George realized how much they had spent on clothing—more than he'd wanted—but Marge had insisted. She'd said people would be less likely to wonder if they had more than one bag each.

In the elevator, Russell set the luggage down, pressed 4, and the bell dinged. "Right this way, sir." At Room 421, he set the bags down, unlocked the door, let them enter first, then carried the luggage into the bedroom before returning to the sitting room.

"If you need anything, dial 10 for the lobby—ask for me and I'll come up. For room service, press 62. For an outside line, press 901 and then your number." He handed George the key and extended his palm.

George put a ten-dollar bill in it. Russell smiled. "Remember—just ring the desk."

"We will," George said. "Thanks for your help."

While Marge unpacked, George dialed lottery headquarters.

"Good morning! Lottery and Sweepstakes Headquarters. How may I help you?"

"Hello, this is Terrance Weinberger. I'm the winner of last Wednesday's drawing. Do I need an appointment to claim the money, or do I just come down? This is new to me."

"Okay, Mr. Weinberger, you do need an appointment. How about 9:45 a.m. tomorrow?"

"Yes—that's fine."

"Will you be coming alone, or are you married?"

"I'm married, and my wife will be with me. That's all right, isn't it?"

"Of course. We just need a headcount for the meeting."

"Two of us," George said.

"Great. Tomorrow we'll verify the ticket, then have some documents and clearances for you to sign. The IRS will be present—they'll need their share. Finally, the press will be here for photos and a brief Q&A. Will that be all right?"

"As far as I know, yes."

"Fine. We'll see you at 9:45 a.m. Congratulations, Mr. Weinberger!"

"Thank you." He hung up.

"Marge," he called through the bedroom door, "I'm going to find a pay phone to call Bigalow."

"Okay—but hurry back. I want to know everything."

George walked two blocks and found a pay phone. He unfolded Jerry's paper and dialed.

"Bigalow here."

"Mr. Bigalow, I'm the man Jerry Kesselton told you about—the one with the money coming in."

. "You'd be Mr. Weinberger. Terrance Weinberger, right?"

"Y—yes, sir," George said.

"Settle down. No reason to be nervous. This is a simple business transaction."

"I've never had anything like this happen," George said.

"What can I do for you?"

"I called the lottery office. I have a 9:45 a.m. appointment to-morrow. What do you want me to do?"

"That's simple. After you get the merchandise, call me. I'll pick you up at your hotel and bring you to my office to start the trans-action. You do know that ten percent of the action is mine, right?"

"Yes, sir."

"I'll handle the merchandise, move it to a Cayman Islands bank in your name. The feds won't be able to trace it. How's that?"

"Sounds too good to be true. You'll hear from me tomor-row—as soon as we can get away."

"Until tomorrow. Goodbye, Mr. Weinberger." Click.

Back in the room, Marge looked up. "Did you make the calls?"

"Yes. Lottery at 9:45. Afterward we call Bigalow—he picks us up and we go to his office for the transaction."

"How long will that take?"

"I don't know. We'll see tomorrow. After that, plane tickets." He rubbed his temples. "I need a drink."

"I'll have one too," Marge said, dialing room service. "Want pizza with that?"

"Sure—why not?"

"Bourbon and Coke?"

"Make it a double."

"I can do that." Into the phone: "Two Bourbons and Cokes—one double—and a pepperoni and cheese pizza. Thank you."

"Now comes the hard part," George said. "Waiting. Marge—you didn't tell Jerry where we're planning to go, did you?"

"No. And please, Terrance—I'm Jody. Remember?"

"Yes. I need to remember that. Sorry."

They stayed in, ordering meals from room service. The day felt long; the night felt longer. Neither could sleep.

"George—I mean, Terrance?"

"Yes, Ma—Jody. This is going to be harder than I thought."

"What are we going to do when we get there?"

"I haven't thought about it. I don't have to work now, so... I don't know."

"I guess we'll do what rich people do," Jody said.

"Not me. I don't like rich people. Never have, never will."

"But you are one now. Can't you see? You're going to have to become one—or at least try."

"Let's try to sleep," he growled. "We've got a lot to do tomorrow. I want to be ready for anything."

"Okay, grouch."

They settled on their own sides of the bed, each lost in private thoughts. Neither slept before the wee hours.

From early morning to nine, everything blurred: hurried breakfast, quick shower, change of clothes, then a taxi to lottery headquarters.

"Hello—we're the Weinbergers. We're here to—"

"Hello, Mr. Weinberger! And Mrs. Weinberger." The receptionist beamed. "We've been waiting for you. One moment." Into her phone: "Mr. Beaufort, your 9:45 a.m. is here." Back to them, conspiratorially: "This must be so exciting."

"It's like a dream come true," Marge said. "Nothing like this has ever happened to us!"

"We're all thrilled for you," she said. "If everything checks out, we'll be congratulating you very soon."

Some luck, George thought. *First we kill a guy. Then we take his ticket. Dumb luck, maybe.*

A small, jolly man entered—a squeaky voice in a suit. "Ah—Mr. and Mrs. Weinberger! Wonderful to meet you. Please, this way."

"In a moment we'll attend to a few formalities," he squeaked. "We must make sure the ticket is valid and that the numbers correspond."

"Yes—we understand," George said.

"What most people don't realize," Mr. Beaufort went on, "is that we want to give them the money as badly as they want to get it. I'm sure we'll have no problems today."

Twenty minutes crawled by while they verified the ticket. For George, it felt like an hour; Marge remained cool and confident. Finally Beaufort returned.

"Let me be the first to bring glad tidings and congratulate you. Mr. and Mrs. Weinberger—you are last week's winners."

George exhaled audibly. Beaufort smiled. "A bit relieved now?"

George smiled back.

"If you'll follow me to the boardroom, we have a couple more items."

Down a corridor they went, doors lining either side, until they reached the Board Room. Inside was a long, polished black walnut table surrounded by leather chairs; wainscoting of dark oak paneling ran three feet up the walls, with ivy-patterned paper above. At the head hung a portrait of Mr. Bentwood.

Six men were seated. Beaufort introduced them as the attorneys.

"The attorneys have releases, disclosures, and a few other documents for you to sign. They'll also need the name of your bank to transfer funds to your account—or set up a new one, if you prefer. You may take a lump sum now, or payments over twenty years, which would be about $268,000 a month. Your choice."

"We've talked it over," George said. "We'll take the lump sum." Marge nodded.

"Very good. And our last two guests are from the IRS. They'll see to the government's share. You'll still have a very nice sum."

"Where do we sign?" Marge said.

Smiles all around, pens appeared, and the signing began. For twenty minutes the lawyers guided them through *this* page and *that* page until all were signed and dated. Finally, everyone rose, shook hands, and offered congratulations.

"Now," Beaufort said, "one more thing—the press." He led them to the next room. "This is for the publicity shots that accompany all winners. People are anxious to know what you'll do with all that money," he said, smiling.

"Yes—I've heard they like success stories," George said. He squeezed Marge's hand and mouthed, *Follow my lead.* She nodded.

At the podium, Beaufort announced, "Ladies and gentlemen—our winners from last Wednesday's drawing: Mr. and Mrs. Terrance Weinberger—that's W-E-I-N-B-E-R-G-E-R." Applause. Cameras everywhere. Marge soaked it in—smiling, posing, radiant. George tried not to bolt.

"I'm sure they'll answer a few questions before embarking on their new adventure," Beaufort said.

"Where did you buy the ticket?" a gravelly-voiced woman asked from the front row.

"In Kamish," George said. "We were passing through from up north and decided to buy one because the pot was so big. We've never bought one before. I guess we were lucky."

"What are you going to do with all that money?" a man in the middle row asked.

"My husband and I are starting a project for the homeless and for underprivileged children," Marge said. "This will go a long way toward that goal."

"Also, we're looking to go back East—around New York and Pennsylvania—to gather information on how to get started," George added.

"Did you take the lump sum?" another asked.

"Yes," George said.

"What about your children? How do they fit into this new life?"

"I can answer that," Marge said. "When we have some, they'll definitely go to college."

Ten more minutes of questions, and George felt he couldn't stand one more. Beaufort stepped in. "Okay, let's get a few more pictures and then let these good people go on their way. I'm sure they'd like to get on with their lives. Bring in the publicity check, please... thank you. Mr. and Mrs. Weinberger, if everything is correct, hold it up, smile, and I'll shake your hands. Okay?"

"Sounds good to me," George said.

Six more flashes—and it was done. They left the building with the money they'd killed for already transferred into the Bank of Boise. The lottery's final courtesy was a limo ride back to the hotel.

CHAPTER 24

THE FLIGHT OUT

"What do we do now?" Marge asked as they reentered the room.

"I've got to get to a pay phone and call Bigalow back. You can pack while I do that. As soon as he's here, we're gone."

"Sounds like a plan. Bye," Marge said.

It took George longer than he liked to get a phone—someone was already using it. He paced until the man scowled and left. George grabbed the receiver and dialed Bigalow.

"Hello. Bigalow here."

"Mr. Bigalow, this is Terrance Weinberger. The money is in the bank and we're ready to make the transaction."

"Where are you?"

"The Grand Hotel on Third and Main. And—"

"Yeah, I know it. I'll be there in twenty minutes. Can you be outside waiting?"

"Sure. My wife is packing now; it won't take long to check out and meet you."

"Good. Meet me on the south side."

"We'll be there," George said.

He hurried back. Marge had already packed.

"Okay, Mar—Jody. We've got to meet him on the south steps in about ten to fifteen minutes."

"I'll be right with you—I have to use the bathroom."

"Can't you do that at Bigalow's? We're in a hurry. I don't want to miss him," George snapped.

"No. I can't," she shot back.

George rang the desk to have the bill ready. Less than a minute later came a knock. Russell stood there.

"May I get your luggage, Mr. Weinberger?"

"Yes. My work called—we have to go right away. I was hoping to stay, but you know how business is."

"Yes, sir," Russell said.

Downstairs, George settled the bill and tipped Russell well. He and Marge took their bags and stepped out the south door to wait.

A deep, regal blue Cadillac glided to the curb. The passenger window lowered. "Mr. Weinberger?"

"Yes—we're the Weinbergers," George replied.

"Good. I'll pop the trunk. Load up and get in. We've got work to do—and if we get to it, it won't take long. Ready?"

"Sounds good." George stowed the bags, slid in beside Marge, and shook Bigalow's hand. "We'd like to be on our way as fast as we can."

"If it all goes well, you'll be on your way in a couple of hours," Bigalow said, smiling.

"Mr. Bigalow, any chance we could get a couple thousand in advance—for expenses?" Marge asked. "We've got some, but a little more won't hurt."

"No problem, Mrs. Weinberger. We'll get it back at the other end. It won't hurt to have a few grand. Let's say five Gs in travelers checks."

"That would be great. Enough, George?" Marge said.

"More than enough," he said—thinking they didn't need it after the ten grand from Jerry.

At Bigalow's office the last details fell into place. George told him where the money sat; from there Bigalow worked his magic—fake companies, laundering stops, a choreography of transfers. He pushed buttons for what seemed forever to Marge, then leaned back, hands laced behind his head.

"What now?" Marge asked.

"We wait. Drink?" Bigalow said.

"Bourbon?" George asked.

"Terrance—should you?" Marge said. "You going to be able to fly?"

"I'm about to fly now. I hate waiting. And besides—we'll have a pilot."

Marge gave him a look, shrugged, let it go.

Exactly two hours—and three drinks—later, the phone rang.

"Bigalow," he said. "...All taken care of? Great. I can send them on their way? Fine—thanks."

He hung up and turned to them. "Have a pleasant trip. You're good to go."

They stood and shook his hand. "Thank you for all your help," George said.

"My pleasure, Mr. Weinberger."

In less than forty-five minutes at the airport, they were airborne. First stop: Los Angeles, traveling as John and Angela Duke.

"This is the way Jerry told me," George said. "We have an hour and fifteen before the next plane to Puerto Vallarta. We ditch the first IDs, then buy the next tickets as Chester and Louise Gardener. That way, no one has a trail for Terrance and Jody Weinberger. The last place we used those names was the hotel."

"That makes sense," Marge said.

They booked the next flight under the new names. Three and a half hours later they touched down in Puerto Vallarta and went straight from the airport to the first hotel they found.

It took three days to open the bank account and another six to settle on a house.

George didn't like some—too small, wrong shape, too far from town. Marge didn't like others because they weren't "high-class" enough—or expensive enough. (She figured if it didn't cost a lot, something must be wrong.) At last they chose one by the ocean—on Lajon Drive, not far from town—in an elite district. Two acres, maid's quarters in a separate building about 100 yards from the main house. The main house: eight bedrooms, four baths, a large entertaining dining room, a well-equipped kitchen, a library, a study, an ample family room, and an exquisite living room. Two stories, balconies facing the sea. All for $1,056,700.

Marge was happy; George sighed with relief at not seeing another house; the realtor was ecstatic with a full commission. For a while, all went well. Then the bickering began.

"Oh, look, George! I can put a baby grand on that raised corner."

"We don't need a baby grand. We don't even play. What's the point?"

"All rich people have one. I want one," Marge pouted.

"You sound like a spoiled brat," George said, sneering. "'All rich people have one, so I want one.' That's not a reason to spend that kind of money."

"I'm not spoiled—you're unreasonable. You never want what I want. Why don't you settle into the rich man's life like you should?" she bellowed.

"Because it's not our money! I remember how we got it—don't you, Marge?" His voice rose. "We killed a good man for this stinking money. You act like nothing happened, like we were born rich. Doesn't it bother you?"

"Oh, shut up, you fool! Don't you ever bring that up again. People only need to know we sold holdings in an oil field back East. Nothing more! Sometimes you make me sick—your stupid small-town, poor-boy routine. I liked you better when you drank. Remember when I met you?" she snarled.

"Yeah—I remember. A loose-lipped idiot trying to impress people with how much insurance he carried. All I got was a gold digger. You want drunk, lady? I'll give you drunk," George growled, heading for the door.

Marge stomped after him. "And another thing, buster—I'm not your mother!"

"Thank God. I'd have left home a long time before I did," he shot back.

"Anyway, I'm hiring a maid. That's another thing rich people have. And a butler!"

"If you want a maid, fine—that's your business. But you're not hiring a butler. We don't need one, I don't want one, and I'll run every last one off until no one comes back. Got it?" he snarled, slamming the door.

He fired up his jeep. *I never thought money could change a person that much. She makes the Wicked Witch of the West look like a sweet puppy. I need a drink. No beer. From here forward—Jim Beam, get me out of here.*

He stopped a short distance away, guilt needling him, and returned. "Look—I'm sorry I blew up. I just can't play the rich nice guy."

"If you don't drop the good-ol'-boy routine, someone will suspect. And no one of importance will ever come to our house," she whined.

"I am dropping it. I've always wanted money, power, important friends—and I'll have them with you or without you. You choose!" Marge yelled.

George turned, climbed into the jeep, and headed for a bar. All he wanted was a bottle of Beam—enough to blur the murder of his best friend and, increasingly, the marriage to Marge. *If I'd known then what I know now, I'd have knocked her in the head and spared the world,* he thought darkly.

Marge's thoughts were no kinder. *How do I get rid of this leech without killing him? I will, if I must. I can't let him ruin what I've always wanted.* She grabbed the phone book and started with maid services. She wasn't going to lift another finger—she was rich. Why should she? She also needed to circulate. *Where to start?* Then: "Hairdressers know everything." In the mirror she decided, yes, it was time. *Who knows what I'll learn. George can go—well, whatever the high-society version of that is.*

George found the Salty Dog Tavern near the edge of town. He slid onto a barstool.

"J.B. and Coke," he said. "I'm here to push everything out of sight except a glass and a bottle."

"Sounds serious," an older man down the bar said.

"Nothing a little J.B. won't handle."

"You want the good stuff or the watered down?" the man asked.

"What do you mean, watered down?"

"Some places stretch a bottle—make it go twice as far as the peso."

"I didn't know that," George said.

"Señor, you spoil my business," the barkeep complained.

The old man chuckled. "Name's Wayne." He held out a big, bear-like paw.

George grinned and shook it. "I'm Terrance. From back East. Sold my holdings in oil."

"Sure, sure. On the run, are ya?" Wayne laughed.

"No—vac—ah—we came for vacation and decided to stay," George stumbled.

"On the run from the little lady?" Wayne clarified.

I wish she were, George thought. "Yeah—rich girl. Want, want; spend, spend. Then she's hunting the next fool."

"Blonde, blue eyes, spoiled, demanding?" Wayne said.

"Right on the money. How'd you know?"

"Lucky guess," Wayne said. "Been there—time or two. Found a good one, teamed up, and when the time was right—split down here."

"How'd you know the time was right?"

"That, friend, you'll have to take my word on. Maybe someday I'll tell you—when we're honest with each other."

George shot him a nervous glance and caught a twinkle in Wayne's eye. *Does he know? Cop?* He decided to be careful.

Wayne lifted his glass. "Here's to the webs we weave. Good or bad—they all get us here, eh?"

Yeah, George thought. *And what a web a black widow can weave.* "I've got a name for her, you know."

"Who?"

"My wife."

"Oh? What's that?"

"Black Widow."

"Does she know?"

"No."

"Be careful, lad. After mating, the female kills the mate."

George nearly choked. He'd almost forgotten. She had hinted at it. "You might be right. I'd better watch where the web is going."

"Bright boy. I've got to go. Maybe I'll see you around?"

"I'd like that. You live nearby?"

"I've got a yacht at Marina Puerto Rey. Stop by—Pier 24, slip 212."

"Okay—might do that."

The J.B. did its work. George drifted home in a soft haze.

Marge—Jody to everyone there—leaned harder into the rich and elite. She hired a maid, Abby Townsend. Marge didn't like that Abby was a Christian; George did. Abby was old enough to be his mother and kind besides. The "rich act," though? George wanted no part of it. Soon he became a nightly fixture at the Salty Dog, where he felt people were real—plain folks who knew what they were. Marge surrounded herself with the glittering set.

Their new life had started with a bang.

CHAPTER 25

THE LONG WAY HOME

Laura and Jeannie were up early Tuesday morning. Over breakfast, Laura said, "I want everything perfect for Jonny. It's been so long since he's been home."

"Valerie and I will do all we can, Mom. Did you know she called her mother the other day and asked her to move down here so we could all be together?"

"I wasn't aware of that at all. She's a sweet girl. I don't know what we would've done without her," Laura said.

"Nor I, Mama. Nor I."

After they ate, Jeannie slipped down the hall to Valerie's room. She eased the door open, thanking the good Lord for carpet as she padded to the bed. Gently, she lifted the unused pillow—then *whomped* Valerie across the rump. "Wake up, sleepyhead! You gonna sleep all day?"

Valerie sprang up, pillow raised. "Ah-ha! The wicked rascal from the swamp has invaded my castle. Take that—and that!" She swung wildly.

Laura rushed in, and within seconds all three were laughing too hard to land a hit. They finally collapsed to the floor, breathless and teary.

"You girls," Laura said, clutching her side, "I don't want either of you to leave. Having you here has done my poor old heart so much good."

Jeannie hugged her. "We won't leave unless we have to, Mom."

"That's right. We're family," Valerie said.

"Come on, lazybones," Jeannie added. "We've got a long day ahead."

"You're a hard taskmaster, Lucy Brown. Okay, I'm up. Let me shower and toast something, and I'll be ready for anything."

"How about housework?" Jeannie teased.

"Well—almost anything," Valerie shot back, grinning.

Jeannie and Laura returned to the kitchen while Valerie hopped in the shower.

"Mom, I know an excellent Chinese restaurant in Moscow. Think Pastor Kiely would want to try it after we pick up Jonathon?"

"I don't know. You could call and ask."

"I will." Jeannie went to the living room phone. "We're getting you a kitchen extension, Mom."

"That's what June said. Oh—she told me to tell you hi."

"When was she here?"

"While you were showering."

"I'll go see her later," Jeannie said.

"She'd like that."

"Mom, what was I doing?" Jeannie laughed at herself.

"You were calling Pastor Kiely, dear."

"Oh—right." She dialed. "Sometimes I get brain cramps and forget what I'm doing."

"We can't blame it on the blondeness; you've got brown hair," Laura teased.

Jeannie was still laughing when the pastor answered. "Oh—sorry, Pastor, my mother just made me laugh."

"I thought maybe I said hello wrong," he snickered.

"No. Do you and your wife like Chinese food?"

"Yes—love it."

"Great. There's a place in Moscow. We could stop there before or after we pick up Jonathon—your choice."

"On the way back might be good. It'll give us time to get acquainted," he said.

"Perfect. We'll plan on it."

"See you around noon. Bye."

"Jeannie," Laura said when she hung up, "I wonder what Jonny looks like now. It's been nearly fifteen years. We tried to reach him when your dad passed, but we didn't know where he was. Phillip only found him about six years ago."

"I don't know either. Surely he hasn't changed that much, has he?"

Valerie walked in, toweling her hair. "Mother Gunn, I think you'll know him. There's a bond between a mother and her children—no matter how long it's been."

"Maybe you're right," Laura said, smiling. "I believe I will."

They had two hours to straighten the apartment before Pastor Kiely and Gwen arrived.

The pastor pulled in, parked the van, and walked up the path. He glanced at the broken doorbell and thought of broken lives; before he could knock, the door flew open.

"Aaah!" Valerie yelped. "You scared the liver out of me!"

Pastor Kiely laughed. "I was about to knock—honestly."

"I was heading to June's to ask her to keep an eye on the place while we're gone."

"And I was coming to say we're ready whenever you are."

"I'll grab your coat and purse, Val!" Jeannie called. "Meet you in the van."

"On my way," Valerie said, jogging across the lot.

Gwen caught Jeannie's eye and slipped her an envelope unseen. Jeannie tucked it into her purse. Gwen mouthed, *Read it later—to her.* Laura didn't notice; she was talking with the pastor, and Valerie was hunting in her bag.

The drive to Spokane was quiet. They made small talk about children—the polite ones, the difficult ones, and everyone between. In Lewis Town, during a brief stop, Jeannie read the note: *Our church took up a collection for you and your mother. Times like these are hard. Please accept this check from Phil's church family.*

She blinked back tears, pulled Gwen aside for a hug, and whispered thanks. "Mom will appreciate this so much."

"We loved Phil," Gwen said. "And we love your family."

"I think I'd like to come to your church—and bring Mom and Valerie."

"We'd be glad to have you. Even Jonathon—ever since we learned about him, we've been praying."

"Good," Jeannie said, smiling.

They spotted deer and geese along the highway, even a distant line of elk. The pastor drove in thoughtful silence while the women chatted.

Jonathon's flight felt endless—Denver, Salt Lake, Portland, Seattle, and finally Spokane. He didn't mind. He needed time to brace himself. *Will they forgive me? Will I even recognize them?* He tried to push away fifteen years of running—and the war that broke him. *Am I ready for a new life? Ready to face Mom?*

The worst ache was Phil. There would be no chance to say *I'm sorry*—or *thank you*. Phil had kept sending money anyway. Jonathon stared out the window and fought the swell of grief.

He dozed and woke with a start, waving down a flight attendant. "Have we reached Spokane?"

"Not yet, sir—about thirty minutes."

"Whew. I thought I'd missed it."

"I would've woken you," she said kindly.

He nodded and sank back, the butterflies rising. *Now or never.*

When the wheels kissed the runway, he whispered, "Come what may," and gathered himself.

Laura and Jeannie stood at the end of the jet bridge, the others hanging back. Both were visibly nervous; Laura's hands trembled.

"Oh, Mama," Jeannie whispered, "will we even know him?"

"He's my son. I'll know him." Inside, Laura wasn't sure. Fifteen years is a long time.

Passengers streamed past—faces, coats, rolling bags—and then she saw him: a tall man in a suit that didn't fit his skin. Six-five, lean, brown hair, eyes the color of autumn. A scar tracked from his brow across his left cheek. She met his eyes, knew them instantly, and her arms opened as tears filled hers.

"Oh, Jonny—you've come home. You've come home!"

He folded into his mother and sister, and the dam broke. His tears fell like spring rain.

The fear evaporated in the embrace. After a long minute—then another—Jonathon drew a breath. "Momma, I've missed you all so much. Can you forgive me?"

"Oh, Jonny—yes. It's all forgiven and forgotten," Laura said. Jeannie nodded, eyes wet.

"Where's Dad? Didn't he come? Or doesn't he want to see me?"

"Jonathon... Dad's been gone six years," Laura said gently. "We tried to reach you, but we didn't know where you were. Phillip found you later."

The pain crested again and they held him. "I lost fifteen years," Jonathon said hoarsely. "I couldn't handle what I did in the war. When I got back, I couldn't handle *not* having the stuff. So I left. I made it more important than anything. I'm sorry."

Laura wiped his cheeks. "You're home now. That's what counts. I'm sorry it took Phillip's death to bring you, but he always said God would."

"Yeah—by killing him?" Jonathon muttered.

"Now, Jonny," Laura said softly, "I don't believe that."

"I miss him already," he said. "And Dad."

"I know. We do too. Come meet everyone." She led him to the group. "This is Pastor Kiely—Phil's pastor—his wife, Gwen, and Jeannie's friend, Valerie."

"Hello," Jonathon said, sheepish, feeling on parade. "So—you're a man of the cloth?"

"Yes," the pastor said easily. "I hear you were in the service."

"Yes. But I don't talk about it." His voice trailed off. "I forgot the war years ago."

The pastor felt the resistance and began to pray silently. He didn't know why Jonathon bristled at preachers, but he bore the burden gladly. *This man is lost,* he thought, *and needs a shepherd.* He prayed for peace in the car and for a door to open.

The ride back toward Moscow was quiet. Jonathon talked mostly with his mother and sister; Valerie slept; Gwen and the pastor prayed under their breath.

They ate at the Chinese place in Moscow. Jonathon shared a little about Oakland, apologizing for the fuzzy years. Laura and Jeannie filled in about Dad's passing and all Phil had done. Jonathon, in turn, admitted Phil had sent money when he barely remembered having a family.

In Lewis Town they stopped for gas. While the women went inside, Jonathon joined the pastor at the pump.

Words came easier than he expected. He told him about the war. "Sir, there was a boy—thirteen, maybe. His torso was ripped in half. He was still alive—looking at me. He said something and lifted his gun. I lost it. I killed him. After that I looked for any way to lose reality. That's when I turned to drugs and alcohol. I thought I had *them*—but they had me."

"Jonathon," the pastor said, "all men get addicted to something—alcohol, drugs, sex, TV—anything can take over. What matters is how we overcome it. And I believe you've done well already. If I can help, call me. I was there for Phil; I'll be there for you. Your brother was well loved by our church. Before it's over, I think you'll finish what he started—with your mother, and maybe with us."

Jonathon stared at him, unsure what to say, and only nodded. He climbed back in. The women returned with sodas and popcorn; soon they were on the road to Kamish.

As the van pulled up to Laura's place and the pastor and Gwen drove off, Jonathon watched them go. He didn't know how he knew, but he did: this was a man he could trust—maybe even confide in. *Maybe I'll visit his church,* he thought. *We'll see.*

Chapter 26

Something Rotten in Denmark

The following day, as Sheriff Gage and Officer Pipcorn walked into the office, the dispatcher said, "Sheriff Gage, you got a call from Sheriff Hasselblat from Lewis County. I left the message on your desk."

"Okay, thanks," he replied as he headed for his desk.

On top of a few folders was a piece of paper listing the lottery winners—Terrance and Jody Weinberger—and vehicle information:

The Wetzels' vehicles are a 1999 Dodge D-Blue 2500 series 4x4, VIN# HLM48830027, Plate# XLO995; and a 2000 Chevy Impala, white, VIN# JJH775S99732SR08, Plate# 064AMB.

"Pipcorn! Come in here!"

"You called, Sheriff?"

"We searched that road real good for any other bodies, didn't we?" asked Gage.

"Yes, I'll guarantee there were no more bodies up there," replied Pipcorn.

"Then there's something really rotten in Denmark," muttered Gage.

"What do you mean?" asked Pipcorn.

"I mean the Wetzels didn't win the lottery. A couple by the name of Terrance and Jody Weinberger did. So, if they're not the Wetzels—where *are* the Wetzels?"

"Boy! This is getting weirder by the moment," Pipcorn said, scratching his head.

"Yes, but we're going to figure it all out. And soon," replied Gage.

"How far do you think they might've gone by now?" asked Pipcorn.

"I don't know. But I do know we're putting out an APB on the Wetzels right now. And if we have to, the Weinbergers too. In fact, that might not be a bad idea. We can pick them up for questioning. I want to know how they got the ticket—and what they had to do with the Wetzels. Or if they did in the Wetzels for the ticket, after the Wetzels did in Gunn for the ticket."

"That sounds like a plan. Probably the best one we've got," replied Pipcorn.

"It could be, too, that the Wetzels and the Weinbergers are one and the same—though very doubtful. Oh, and Pipcorn, run the plate number on the car. Maybe we can come up with something."

"Got'cha, Sheriff." Pipcorn walked over to his desk and started typing.

Gage, meanwhile, not only put out the APBs on the Wetzels and the Weinbergers but also pulled the Wetzels' file. Then he tried running a background check on the Weinbergers—but nothing. It was as if they weren't even from this world. Let alone this continent.

"Hey! Did anyone see those lottery winners from last week?" called Gage.

"Yeah, I did," yelled the jailer from the next room.

"What do you need, Sheriff?" he asked, poking his head out.

"Tell me—do you remember where they said they were from?"

"All I heard was from up north."

"Yeah, that's what I thought. I'm finding nothing in Idaho or Canada. Hey, Sergeant Massey!"

"Yes, sir," came a reply from the back room.

"Get ahold of Alaska. See if they've heard of the Weinbergers. Somebody has to have heard of them. They can't just appear and disappear whenever they want."

Still, in the back of his mind, a nagging thought whispered that maybe they *could*. Maybe they were the same people—with new IDs. But no. That would be too easy.

"Here's something interesting," said Pipcorn. He picked up a sheet from the fax machine and handed it to Gage.

"What's this?" asked the sheriff.

"It's a fax from Boise. Seems they've got the car in question—a 2000 Chevrolet Impala, white, VIN# JJH775S99732SR08, Plate# 064AMB—in their impound lot."

"What in the world's it doing there?" asked Gage.

"Seems it was sitting in front of a motel for the last ten days. The manager finally had it towed yesterday."

"What's in it? Have they been through it yet?" Gage's voice was sharp now—impatient. He wanted that car up here, *fast*.

"Let me call and see what's up," said Pipcorn.

"Okay." Gage hit the intercom button. "Gerri, give me everything you can on the Wetzels—where they grew up, their parents, what they had for breakfast the last two days they were here, if that's possible. I want to be them. Maybe I can figure this mess out."

"I'm on it, Sheriff," replied Gerri.

"Oh—and Gerri, run their pictures on the news, both here and in Boise. In fact, run the pictures of those lottery winners too. Tell them if anyone has any information on these people to contact the nearest law enforcement agency immediately."

"Got it," Gerri said.

"Pipcorn! What have you found out?"

"I've got them on the phone right now. They say they just towed it in and parked it."

"All right. Tell them it's part of our investigation. We're sending a car hauler down to pick it up. Tell them not to touch it—I want prints. Everything in it stays in it. Oh—and if any of their officers touched it, I want their names so we can exclude their prints if we find them."

"Done," Pipcorn said, going back to the call.

He knew when Sheriff Gage was on a roll, you didn't interrupt. You just did what you were told and everything would be fine. He'd learned that lesson once—and almost lost his job over it.

Like a well-oiled machine, when Gage was working, the whole office followed his lead.

CHAPTER 27

BEYOND THE SUNSET

It was three weeks after the accident and finally time to bring Phil to his final resting place. With the investigation, finding Jonathon, and getting him home, time had flown without much thought of burial. But that was what weighed on Jonathon's mind—and on Laura's and Jeannie's. They didn't want to let go, but knew they had to, and today would be the day. The morning broke gloomy, as if a veil of sorrow had moved in over the land, turning down the sun until it was only a shadow. Even nature seemed saddened.

Jonathon and Valerie were the only ones up. They let Laura and Jeannie sleep in. Jonathon had been awake at least two hours; Valerie only part of that. Heavy with the day's weight, he felt alone. He had lost two parts of his family while he'd been gone, and it was finally hitting him. For the first time since coming home he knew exactly what he wanted—a fix. He wanted one badly, but knew he couldn't.

"God, if you're real and if you're here," he said, "help me get past this addiction to where I can live without that stuff. Let me be what Phil was. Please."

The service was scheduled for 10:30 a.m., and there was plenty to do. Jonathon took charge. "Val, if you make the toast, I'll get the eggs and bacon going."

"You're on, big guy," she said, teasing, and reached for the bread box. She pulled the bacon and eggs from the refrigerator for him.

"Thanks. Now I'll show you how to really cook an egg," Jonathon said.

Before long, breakfast was on the table.

The aroma of food and freshly brewed coffee drifted down the hallway. Even though neither Laura nor Jeannie felt hungry, the smell was tempting. Jonathon stepped into the hall between their doors. "Chow's on! Better hurry and get it or we'll throw it out."

"I'll be right there," Jeannie called.

"Me too," came Laura's muffled reply.

He knew she'd been crying—and for some time. If only he'd been here sooner, he thought, he might have eased her pain. He felt always a day late and a dollar short. What he didn't know was that his being home was the best medicine Laura had had in a long time.

Jeannie reached the table first, eating like she was famished—though they all knew it was nerves. Laura came slowly and picked at her food. Not much was said; each was lost in thought. By 8:30, breakfast was over, yet they sat staring at nothing. No one wanted the day to move forward, but they knew it would, and the sooner the better.

At 9:00 Jonathon broke the silence. "Mom, we should probably start getting ready."

She patted his hand, tears in her eyes. He leaned over and held her as she broke. After a few minutes, she looked up at him.

"Oh, Jonny, it's good to have you here. Jeannie and I need you now more than ever."

Jeannie joined the hug. "It's very good to have you home, Jonny. Please don't leave again," she sniffled.

They rose to get ready for the funeral. The breakfast dishes could wait. 10:30 was coming all too quickly. Jonathon, Laura, Jeannie, and Valerie arrived at the church where Phil had been a member for years. It was about 10:00, and Carl—one of Phil's dearest friends—met them at the door and led them to the front row. Three rows had been reserved for family: a few cousins, two aunts, three uncles, and one great-uncle. They'd all stopped by sometime in the past three weeks to console the family. But even among family, none were as close as those in the front row. Sadly, Phil had been the only Christian among them.

At about 10:15 the organist began "The Old Rugged Cross." Jeannie thought she had never heard it played so beautifully. Before long, the church was full—no standing room, even the foyer crowded. Though Phil was young, he had touched many lives. They came to pay their last respects to a friend taken so abruptly. Memories flooded the sanctuary, and would not be forgotten.

The organist began "Amazing Grace," and a choir member sang all the verses. Afterward, Pastor Kiely rose from the platform and moved to the pulpit. Sadness lay plain on his face. He looked at the casket and felt a lump so big he was not sure he could swallow. This was going to be harder than he thought. After a moment, he began—softly at first; then, as he felt the power of God, stronger.

"Brother Phillip—or Phil, as many knew him—spoke often about death: others' and his own. He said most funerals build up the one who's passed and leave nothing for the family to cling to. He told me—and his family—that he didn't want that (no matter when it came). He said, 'Don't feel sorry for me; I'm going home to be with Jesus. Rejoice with me.' What he wanted preached was God's saving grace—that through his death someone might find the Lord. His words were, 'I want someone to come into a relationship with God, to find the realm of God, as I go to meet my God.' Brother Phillip—Phil—this is for you."

For the next hour, Pastor Kiely walked them through God's plan of salvation—from Adam to Revelation. He preached as he had never preached before. When he finished, there wasn't a dry eye in the church. As the Holy Ghost moved among the people, many prayed for deliverance, salvation, and strength.

Everyone remembered how Phil had touched their lives: a fishing trip with Jim; changing Mrs. Taylor's flat; helping Mr. Carter in his garden; finishing the garage Burtrum had started before breaking his back; lending Mr. Townsend money for a car; giving Mrs. Baker the fare to get to her daughter in Florida when her son-in-law was killed during maneuvers. Tear by tear, memory by memory.

During the service a small group slipped in and sat in the back: a man, two women (one very small and much older), and three children. The children wore new clothes, bought with money Phil had pressed into their hands along with food that very morning of Phil's death. They'd come to thank the young man who cared so much—but it was too late to thank him. They could only pay their respects and thank God for sending him when they were in need.

Jill Bennett sat mid-pew, third in. Phil had only spoken a few words to her, but they were etched in her mind. She'd been in a foul mood that whole day until he walked in and spoke kindness. He was a breath of fresh air, kindling a place in her heart that had never been lit. Listening to the pastor, she learned what made him different from other men: salvation. That was what she had been looking for all her life. She would come here again. Often.

Mac and Betty were lost in their own thoughts—of another funeral six years before. A twenty-year-old boy stood there broken, weeping loudly because his dad had passed away. They had gone to console him. He had grabbed them and held on as if there were no tomorrow. A bond had been born that day. As the memories flooded back, tears filled their eyes. They would never see that boy—now this man—again. That is what broke the most hearts.

Mr. Torganson remembered a sixteen-year-old boy wanting his first car. There was an old 1958 Oldsmobile in the back of his barn, riddled with bullet holes and rust. The boy wanted it badly. When

Mr. Torganson started to give it to him, the boy said, "My dad said if anything is worth having, it is worth buying." They settled on $150. The boy worked it off on weekends, and before summer's end the car ran like new and looked it, inside and out. When the boy brought it back to show him, Mr. Torganson thought it was a different car.

Laura saw a newborn—then a small boy—then, in minutes, a young man. A young man leaving the café ... for the last time. The thought stabbed her heart like a sword. She nearly collapsed, crying out in grief. The floodgates opened; tears streamed down her cheeks onto her black satin dress. The veil hid her face, but the tears were plain. Jonathon put an arm around her, and she leaned into him. His other arm held Jeannie. Valerie held Jeannie too.

Valerie knew Laura's and Jeannie's world would never be the same. Her heart wept for them.

This church, this town, this valley—changed. It would be in the news for some time. Murder always makes the front page.

While the choir sang "What a Day That Will Be," Laura regained her composure. At the same time, Pastor Kiely began the closing of his sermon.

"So, my friends and brethren, Jesus died for every man, woman, boy, and girl—not only those in this building, but all in this world. The Bible says God would that none be lost. If we walk away today, then Jesus died for nothing. We were brought together by the death of this young Christian man. If we walk away and his last request goes unanswered, then his death, too, is for naught. His last request was that someone would find God as Lord and Savior as he met his God. If you feel the conviction, if God is working on your heart, if you want to know this Jesus—come. Today is the day of salvation. Come kneel before your Lord this morning and come home.

"We'll have the passing by in a few moments. Let's seek the Lord, the only true God. He is calling His children. Let's fulfill our departed brother's last request. Come."

Gwen and two other women joined the pianist and sang, "There's Room at the Cross for You." Many flooded the altar—silent prayers, spoken prayers, open weeping. Repentance was found; hurts were healed; souls and hearts mended. Most of all, many sought the Lord. The angels rejoiced. The bells of glory were ringing.

It took forty-five minutes for everyone to regain their seats. Pastor Kiely asked if anyone wanted to share about their friend and loved one. Stories poured out—many tender, some funny; all about friendship and the unconditional love Phil had shown in a short lifetime.

An old, bent man named Lyle spoke last. He summed it up. "This man showed us how to live a Christian life—how we should act, and how we should treat others." No one could say different. He was right.

Pastor Kiely prayed, and the organist began "The Old Rugged Cross" again as the people stood to pass by the casket. Row by row, one by one, they came. Because it was closed, a photograph rested on top. Most looked at the smiling face and left in tears, knowing it was the last smile they would see from him. The family's turn came: cousins, then aunts and uncles, then the great-uncle.

Jeannie stepped forward. Valerie beside her, she broke into sobs of pain and anguish. Valerie held and cried with her. Laura came and, somehow, found the strength to comfort them though she was breaking inside. Then Jonathon stepped up. He looked at his brother's picture—and fifteen years of hurt, pain, and anger broke loose in sobbing waves. He dropped to his knees. Pastor Kiely knelt beside him, held him, and prayed—and wept—with him. They stayed there many long minutes.

Then, just before they rose, Jonathon began speaking in a language he did not know—as the Spirit gave utterance. He had been born again, a child of God. As the Holy Ghost swept over him, he found the very thing he had sought for years. Now he knew what had been so real to Phil—and why Phil had been so persistent. He would never leave this newfound freedom, not as long as he had breath.

When the family finished, the pallbearers returned the casket to the hearse, and those who wished followed to the graveside. As they gathered, a man from the church sang "Lord, I'm Coming Home." Afterward, Pastor Kiely gave the eulogy and the final prayer. As they lowered the casket, the same man sang Phil's favorite, "Beyond the Sunset."

Just then the overcast sky parted and the sun shone on the small patch of ground where they stood. Some felt God's pleasure—as if He were saying, *Phillip's with Me now. Don't weep; rejoice.*

It was a bittersweet moment: the Lord's presence palpable, tears of awe mingling with tears of anguish.

When it was time to leave, Pastor Kiely announced that dinner was being served back at the church for those who wished to come.

CHAPTER 28

PAWN OF THE QUEEN

George felt that life as he and Marge had known it was slipping away. Ever since they bought the house in Puerto Vallarta, he'd been staying away as much as possible—and the more time he spent apart from her, the more he liked it. In his mind, she was clawing her way into *snobville*, and he wanted no part of it. He was plain old George, not some rich fool who looked down on others.

Marge, on the other hand, was thriving as queen of the hill. She was learning all the right moves—the breakfast parties, the luncheons, the makeovers. Yes, she was doing everything she could to be accepted into a world she had always wanted to belong to but never could. Did she miss George? Not a bit. He was just another pawn in her game. Now that she had what she wanted, he wasn't useful anymore.

Her guest lists grew longer each week, always including the most influential people. This Saturday morning was no different.

"Terrance"—she always called him that now, and he hated it—"are you going to be here for the luncheon today?" She joined him on the deck overlooking the ocean.

Looking out across the waves, he said dully, "Probably not. I've got some business to take care of downtown." He knew the kind of people who would be there, and he couldn't stand the stuffed shirts.

"Well, you're going to have to meet your neighbors someday," she said sharply.

"Someday," was all he said.

She pressed on, ignoring his tone. "Do you remember I told you about Senator Robinson from the States? Well, he and his family are coming over. Wouldn't you like to meet him? He might even have a business idea for you—something to boost our income. Doesn't that sound good?"

"Not really, Mar—ah, Jody. I don't get along with those rich guys. They're always talking down to each other, trying to outdo everyone else. They're not my kind of people, and I don't enjoy being around them. If you do, fine. Just leave me out of it, okay?"

Now she was fuming. "You're going to have to start acting like you're supposed to, mister!" she snapped, spitting the words at him. "You're rich! You're supposed to act like it! You're supposed to be talking about making more money, opening businesses, whatever it is rich men talk about. If you blow this for me, you'll pay big time, buster! Do you hear me?"

George's temper flared. "I'll tell you what—you have your little party, and if anyone asks where your husband is, tell them I'm at work or had an appointment or something. Just lie to them, Marge! You're good at it!"

He strode back through the living room to the wet bar in the corner, grabbed his car keys, and headed for the door. "I might be back in time to say goodbye," he called, "but I won't promise anything."

"Yeah, whatever!" Marge shot back, following him into the room. "At least try to come home sober this time. You're gone so much, I might as well join the spa. That's where all the girls go."

George opened the front door and paused, considering her words. "Good idea," he said. "That way you can be with your friends every day. You'll be happy—and so will I."

"You're right again, Terrance, old buddy!" Her voice broke, hot tears filling her eyes. "And you can join *your* friends at the Sundance, the Zoo, or Alcatraz—whichever of those you patronize. Or all of them!"

"Touché," George said, slamming the door behind him.

He walked down the long stone walkway lined with twin lion statues, each perched atop a twelve-foot column. His Jeep sat on the left side of the circle drive, a fountain bubbling in the center. He climbed in, realized he'd forgotten his jacket, then shrugged. "Who cares," he muttered. He started the engine and drove off.

"Well, Jasper," he said to his Jeep, "you should know the way by now. Take me to Alcatraz. I think we'll be spending a lot of time there."

But instead of heading to the bar, he turned toward Marina Puerto Rey to visit his friends Wayne and Muriel. They were an older couple—wealthy, yes, but down-to-earth. They never pretended to be more than they were. He could talk to them and feel understood.

They lived on a yacht. He had met them on a booze cruise a few weeks earlier. George had never been on one before, so he figured he'd try it. The yacht cruised back and forth along the coastline all night, lights glimmering across the bay. He'd often seen it from his balcony. That night, he'd drunk himself nearly unconscious, haunted by guilt over what he and Marge had done to Phil. Shame swallowed him whole. He wanted forgiveness but didn't know where to find it, so he buried himself in alcohol—until Wayne and Muriel came along.

A day and a half later, he woke not on the booze cruise but in a soft bed aboard another yacht—the *Jolly Anne*. His clothes hung neatly in the open closet. The gentle rocking told him he was still at sea. As he sat up, he tangled himself in the sheet and fell to the floor just as a booming voice called, "You all right in there?"

Wayne opened the door and burst into laughter. "Guess not!"

After introductions and some good-natured ribbing, they'd become fast friends. Later, he learned he had vomited on half the guests and nearly been thrown overboard before Wayne and Muriel intervened. The captain had agreed to let them take him off in their dinghy.

The *Jolly Anne* was a sixty-four-foot yacht with an eighteen-foot tender. Before George left that first time, Wayne had told him, "If you need anything—and I mean anything—you come to us. You'll get it, no matter what."

Now, as George turned onto Puerto Avenue and First, he murmured, "Well, Wayne, here I come again. I need some advice—and fast."

The marina was only a few blocks past Alcatraz, so it wasn't far out of the way. The sign arched over the road: Welcome to Marina Puerto Rey. Spotting Wayne and Muriel's 2001 silver-and-black Kia near the front, he parked four rows back. Locking the Jeep, he walked toward Slip 212 on Course 24. It was a long walk, but he didn't mind. The sun was warm, the salt air crisp, and Wayne always had a cold brew waiting.

As he passed rows of sleek sloops and fishing boats, he smiled to himself. *You know, this might not be such a bad life after all.*

When he reached the *Jolly Anne*, he called out, "Ahoy the ship!"

"Ahoy, mate! Come aboard!" Wayne answered, waving from a lounge chair. The older man, tanned and shirtless in gym shorts and white deck shoes, had been watching him approach. "You know where the fridge is—grab a brewski and pull up a cushion."

Muriel, seventy-one to Wayne's late sixties, soon appeared. Petite and spry, she wore bright pedal pushers and a floral blouse. Together, they looked as if they belonged to the sun itself—easygoing, weathered, and content.

"What's on your mind today? You look like you're ready to talk," Wayne said.

"Oh, I'm not sure," George replied. "I've got some things to work through, but I don't really know where to start."

"Sure you do," Wayne said with a grin. "Come on, Terrance—let it flow."

"It's Mar—ah, Jody," George began. "She wants me to become someone I'm not. I just can't do it. I'm me. I don't want to act like some rich snob who doesn't care about anyone else. I don't even fit in their world, and she's trying to force me to." He set his beer down and ran a hand through his hair.

Wayne studied him. "You thinking about leaving her?"

"I can't lie to you—it's crossed my mind, and it's getting stronger. Seems all she wants to do is throw parties and make me miserable. While she plays the rich lady on the hill, I feel like a hermit crab stuck in a shell I've outgrown."

Muriel came over and patted his shoulder. "Honey, we all have our trials, but you listen to old Wayne here. He's pretty sharp about this sort of thing."

"Well," Wayne said, "all I can tell you is this: things get mighty sticky when there's money involved—especially now."

"That's right," Muriel added. "We think a whole lot of you, and we don't want to see you hurt or taken advantage of. So, you listen to him. And if he doesn't give sound advice, come see me." She winked and carried off their empty cans.

Wayne chuckled. "You need a woman like her, boy—full of spit and fire."

Muriel returned with fresh beers, settled on Wayne's lap, and listened.

"Really, Terrance," Wayne said, "my advice is to hold out as long as you can. And by all means, get as much money as you can into a private account. If you'd like, we can hold it for you. Buy things and have the bills padded. I've got a friend who runs a garden shop on Lejon Drive—tell him I sent you. If you decide to stash the money with us, we'll keep it safe. Lord knows we don't need it."

"I wouldn't worry about that," George said. "I trust you both more than anyone. What you say sounds good. If you only knew Jody like I do, you'd understand. When should I start?"

"Tomorrow, today, next week—it's up to you," Wayne said. "Just make sure she doesn't find out. You'll have to be sneaky. Me and Muriel, we don't have secrets. We're like two peas in a pod. That's the key—you need someone you actually enjoy being around."

Muriel smiled. "And don't get one who tries to change you, dear. You're just fine as you are. Now, do you boys need another beer?"

Wayne chuckled and handed her his empty can. George grinned and did the same.

"So what's on your agenda today?" George asked. "I've got some time to kill. She's throwing her snobby party, and some senator's supposed to be there."

"If it's Robinson, you're better off away," Wayne said darkly. "He's into drugs—and worse. White slavery, corruption, you name it. How he ever became a senator, I'll never know."

George blinked. "Are you serious?"

"Dead serious," Wayne said. "Anyway—how about some fishing? Deep-sea style."

"You're talking my language now!" George said, smiling wide. His day had turned for the better. His problem with Marge was solved—or so he thought. He'd start putting his plan into motion soon. And somewhere in the back of his mind, a thought stirred: *Maybe I'll find a way to send something to Phil's mother.*

He didn't know how—but maybe, just maybe, he would.

CHAPTER 29

POWDER AND COMPANY

W hile George was off fishing, Marge got ready for her party. About 11:00 a.m., Shelly and Brenda showed up—friends she'd met on the tennis courts.

"Hello!" Marge greeted. "It's so good to see you. I could really use some help."

"That's what we're here for, remember?" Brenda said.

"Great, great. Shelly, be a darling and bring in the shrimp dip, will you?"

"Certainly."

"Brenda, would you get the sandwiches out and set them on the table? I have to make sure the punch is all right."

"I believe the guests will start showing up any time," Marge added.

"Did you remember to invite Danny, Jermaine, and Mel?" Shelly asked. "That was part of the deal."

"Oh no!" Marge put a hand to her mouth, then laughed. "Of course I did. A deal is a deal. Besides, Danny is cute. Who knows—maybe he could replace Terrance someday."

All three snickered and went back to work.

"Speak of the devil, Jody—look out there," Brenda said. Through the kitchen window, the three men were jogging down the beach.

"That's why Danny put all those clothes in the trunk of my car," Marge said. "They're not only cute; they're smart."

Next came the neighbors, and soon the other guests arrived in a steady stream. The party hit full swing. The last to arrive were the Robinsons. The senator—a tall, muscular Southerner in his late sixties with salt-and-pepper hair—was all polish. His wife, a petite bottle blonde of forty-five with at least two facelifts, hovered at his elbow. Their daughter was a voluptuous brunette with trouble in her eyes.

The trouble appeared immediately: the daughter, Ginger, laid out a line of cocaine and snorted it. Marge stared, unsure what to say.

"Want some?" Ginger asked.

"I don't know—I've never tried it," Marge said, reluctant but curious.

"Oh, go ahead. You'll love it," Danny said.

"Do you use it?" Marge asked.

"All the time," Danny replied.

"Well," Marge said, "I guess one time won't hurt."

As Ginger made another line, the senator walked up. "What on earth is going on here?"

"Just having fun, Daddy," Ginger said. "This is for our hostess."

"Oh? Do you indulge?" he asked Marge.

"This is the first time, but if you'd rather I didn't, I'll quit," she stammered, embarrassed.

"Not at all, not at all. I use a little myself," he said smoothly. "But I'd rather that not get out."

"Oh no, sir. I wouldn't tell anyone. My lips are sealed. How do I do this?"

"Here—take this straw. Put it in your nose, pinch the other nostril shut, and sniff," the senator said, helping her while shooting Ginger a warning look.

"O-o-o-oh, wow. I feel like I'm going to sneeze."

"Now do the other side," he said.

"Really?" Marge asked.

He nodded and guided her again.

"Your sinuses will go numb," he continued, "and you'll feel it run down the back of your throat. Next you'll notice a kind of tasteless sensation, and then—"

"Oh, wow." Her pulse quickened as euphoria bloomed. "This is great. I like this."

Danny laughed. "Yes, my little lady. We all do. That's why we call it nose candy."

"Can I have some more?" Marge asked.

"Later," the senator said. "Later."

By the end of the party, Marge, Danny, and the cocaine were fast friends. He even nudged her to make up her mind about the spa—he worked there, and that was all it took.

After the guests left, only Senator Robinson, his wife, and Ginger remained with Marge—now happily answering to "Jody"—and Danny.

"Well, Mrs. Weinberger," the senator began.

"Oh, please—call me Jody!" She was still buzzing.

"Well, Jody, I hope we can become good friends. I told Ginger not to be forward with our new friend until we knew you better, but she has a mind of her own. If there's anything you need, call. And here's a little present from me to you." He handed her two eight-balls. "I'm sure Danny will show you what to do."

"Thank you, Senator. I don't know how I can repay you!" She gazed at him, dazzled.

"Take it easy with that, dear," the senator's wife said. "The next won't be free. But it is nice, isn't it?"

"M-m-m—yes," Marge said. "I never knew it could be so good. I don't care what it costs—I want it."

"Danny, make sure she takes it easy," the senator said.

"You got it. I'll take good care of her," Danny said.

"And don't stay too late," Ginger teased. "We don't want our new friend getting in trouble."

Danny blushed as they laughed.

"Seriously," Ginger added, "if Mr. Weinberger comes home, you'd better have a good excuse for being the last one here."

"I'll say I'm telling her about the spa while waiting to offer him a membership," Danny said.

"Might work," Ginger said. "Well, Daddy, Mom, I'm tired. Shall we bid adieu?"

"Yes," the senator said. "Until we meet again, Jody." He took her hand and kissed it like the gentleman he played to be.

"Oh, Jody," Ginger said, "I'll come by tomorrow to pick you up. I have people you should meet. I like you, and they will too. Be ready around ten-ish, okay, love?"

"Okay," Jody said, smiling. "Good night, Ginger. Good night, Senator, Mrs. Robinson. Have a safe ride home."

"Thank you, dear," Mrs. Robinson said. "Good night."

"It was a lovely party," the senator added. "We'll meet again, I'm sure."

Marge walked them to the door, said good-bye again, and closed it. Leaning against the wood, she flashed Danny a flirty smile. "And now for dessert," she said.

Danny left around 9:00 p.m. George still wasn't home. Spent, Marge went upstairs, showered, slipped into a nightgown, and was asleep almost instantly.

All was quiet until George came in.

Pulling into the drive, he tried to stop in the right place, but the alcohol had the wheel. He rolled too far and clipped a lion statue by the walkway. Crash. The horn bleated as he jolted to a halt.

"Marge is going to kill me," he said aloud, then laughed. "It's only a lion."

After shutting off the Jeep, he eyed the rubble. "Huh. Six or seven pieces. They can glue it." He stumbled up the walk. "Back to the dungeon," he muttered.

At the door, he fumbled for his keys. The door swung open.

"Drunk again, Terrance?" Marge snarled. "You remind me of my brother. Do not expect anything from me tonight—or ever—if this is how it's going to be. Find your own room. Mine is off-limits. Do you hear me?"

"Yes, missy, I unnerstand," he mocked. "If you don't mind, Maaaarge, I think I shall retire. That's how rich folks talk, isn't it?"

She glared as he staggered across the living room to the base of the stairs.

CHAPTER 30

THE MORNING AFTER

It was 10:30 a.m. before Marge even stirred. *I wonder how Ginger knew I wouldn't wake up before now,* she thought. *Oh well—quick shower.* Ten minutes later she was dressed and headed downstairs. She brewed coffee, and the doorbell rang. She hurried to answer.

"Oh, Ginger! Come in. I was hoping you'd come early. I've got to get out of here before Terrance wakes up."

"So he finally made it home last night?" Ginger asked politely.

"Oh, he made it home, all right. That's his Jeep where the statue used to be. The drunken bum almost woke the whole neighborhood. Sometimes I wish I wasn't married to him. Since the money, he's changed. Before, he seemed grounded—had goals. Now it's... nothing. Just booze."

About that time George came down the stairs. "Oh—good morning, ladies!" He seemed cheerful. "I slept in a little late. Sorry I wasn't up to make your breakfast this morning, sweet Jody."

Marge rolled her eyes. "Oh please," she muttered. "Good morning, Terrance. I'm going downtown for a while. Oh—this is Ginger Robinson, the senator's daughter. Ginger, my husband, Terrance."

"A pleasure to meet you, Miss Robinson," he said.

"Thank you. Nice to meet you too," she replied.

"Jody," George said, "this may not be the right time, but I'd like to apologize for my behavior lately. I've been a real jerk. I let this instant success get to me. I couldn't handle it. Please forgive me. I'll honestly try to do better."

"Of... of course, Terrance." Marge blinked. *A true change of heart? And in front of Ginger?*

"To tell the truth," George added, "I never liked those lions out front anyway. I'm sorry I knocked one down. If it's all right with you, I was thinking of replacing them with something else."

Marge couldn't hold back a laugh—the boyish look she liked had crept onto his face. When she laughed, so did George and Ginger.

"You do what you think best, love. If you don't like them, change them. This is your house too." She wrinkled her nose. "I never liked them either."

They laughed again.

"You girls have a good day," George said. "Don't eat too much, Jody. I'm planning a nice dinner when you get back. Miss Robinson, you're invited if you'd like."

"Oh, I don't know—I..." Ginger stammered.

"Yes, Ginger! Please eat with us tonight," Marge said quickly, convinced now of George's change.

"All right. I'd be happy to," Ginger replied.

"I'm going to have a hot cup of coffee, then take care of the problem out front," George said. "Bye—and have a good time."

"We will. We'll be back in plenty of time for dinner. What are we having?" Marge asked.

"My secret recipe—*chops-ali-roi*." George kissed his fingertips, mock-Italian. "Mwwaa."

"Ginger, you're in for a treat," Marge said. "You'll throw rocks at regular pork chops after these."

She waltzed across the room, planted a kiss on George—his eyes widened; it had been a while—then rejoined Ginger. "Ready, dahling?" They left.

George watched them climb into Ginger's Mercedes convertible—one Marge had bought—and drive off.

"Wow," Marge said as they rolled away. "What's got into him? He wasn't like that last night. One night alone must be an eye-opener."

"You sure this is the same guy?" Ginger teased. "I was almost ready to go kiss him myself."

"It's the same guy... I think." She giggled. "Maybe my last words helped. I told him my room was off-limits." They laughed. "Oh well—let's have some fun. I hope you brought some of our friends?"

"You mean the candy?" Ginger said.

"Oh yeah—the candy. I could use some," Marge said earnestly.

"This is like my Master Charge card—I never leave home without it," Ginger laughed. "Ask and you shall receive."

She frowned slightly. "Hate to say it, but it's gotta cost you this time. I had to buy it."

"Name your price, girl. It's worth every penny," Marge said, dead serious.

"I've got enough for a line apiece, and I'll sell you this eight-ball for $250. All right?"

"Sold," Marge said, eyes on the white prize.

Back at the house, George whistled while he made breakfast. Moving from stove to toaster, he murmured, "Ahh, that worked like a charm. I'll go to Wayne's friend and pad the bill for the new statues, take the excess to Wayne to hold, and—hello, nest egg." He chuckled. "Knock down a lion, play drunk, win an Oscar."

He plated eggs over easy, toast, hash browns, and bacon—Phil Gunn's favorite. A chill ran through him as the thought landed. He went pale, then shook it off. Coincidence.

Dishes in the sink, he headed for the shower. Even on Sunday, most shops here were open. He'd driven past Wayne's friend's place and seen two massive cherubim—perfect replacements for the lions. He didn't know why he liked them, only that he did. Thirty minutes later he and Jasper were headed to town.

In under twenty minutes, he parked in front of Los Flores San Jacinto. The cherubim all but called to him. Plenty of other statues and fountains crowded the display, indoor and outdoor plants too—everything to turn a million-dollar house into a ten-million-dollar showpiece.

He climbed out. *If I can swing a $10,000 skim today, Wayne can start the stash,* he thought, ambling to the pedestals. The cherubim were gorgeous: six-foot-diameter, six-foot-high columns topped by six-foot figures, wings spread as if guarding whoever passed between.

"Good morning," a voice said behind him. "Beautiful day to be out and about, isn't it?" The salesman, Ted, wore a pin with his name on his shirt.

"Well, Ted, I haven't seen a bad day since I moved here," George said. "A little rain, sure, but mostly sun and ocean."

"So, do you like these cherubim?"

"Yeah. A lot. I'm going to buy them."

"Let's look around a bit more," Ted said, smiling. "Something else might catch your eye."

"Ted, may I call you Ted?" He nodded. "I'm not here to look around. If I wanted to look, I'd have kept walking. I want these. If I wanted something else, I'd be at something else. I'm here to do—" He caught himself. "Sorry. I've got a lot on my mind and not much time."

"That's okay. I know the feeling," Ted said.

"Do you know Wayne Abernathy?" George asked.

"Sure do. He sent you?"

"Yeah. He said you could help with a problem—and not just the statues. For starters: how much, and how much to deliver and set up?"

"The statues are $22,000. Delivery and setup are $250," Ted said. "We'll need to schedule it."

"I've still got one whole lion and the other in pieces. What about disposal?" George scratched his head.

"No problem. The $250 includes removal. I can reimburse you a little for the intact lion."

"Oh no—you can have it. Why should I get something out of that eyesore?" George grimaced. "Never liked them."

"Lions... lions... I remember those," Ted said. "You must be in the Douglas house."

"That's what the realtor said—their old place. She died; he moved back to Colorado to be near the kids."

"That's them," Ted said. "They came in after buying. She wanted the place to look kingly. She picked the lions. He hated them, tried to steer her elsewhere, but she won. We sold them, and there they've sat. To tell the truth, I hated them too. Ugly."

"Sounds like I should've met Mr. Douglas," George said. They laughed.

"So—these cherubim?"

"I have a set at my entrance," Ted said. "I wholeheartedly approve."

"Great. Second question: Wayne said you could help with a little financial problem."

"And that would be?"

"My wife and I aren't seeing eye to eye. She's the type to file for divorce and run with everything," George said. Ted nodded. "I need to pad this bill—make it look like I paid, say, ten to fifteen grand more—so I've got a nest egg."

Ted studied him. "It'll take more than a few thousand for a nest egg, won't it?"

"Of course. But I've got a lot of ideas to decorate the place—and you've got a lot to sell." George smiled. Ted did too.

"Come with me." He led George through the shop. "José! Watch the floor. I've got business in back."

"Sí," came a voice.

They wound through a storeroom to a small office.

"This is my space. Please—sit." Ted pulled a receipt book and pen from a drawer. "You'll need to keep the real receipt or destroy it—that's on you. For now, this is the fake one. We'll fill out the real one up front so José can witness it if anyone asks. Sound good?"

"Sure. How will anyone believe this wasn't a trick?" George asked.

"Watch." Ted wrote a perfect "2" with the tail nearly lost in the line below. Then, with a flick, he turned the two into a three. "There you have it: thirty-two thousand, two hundred fifty. Thoughts?"

George examined it. "Amazing. You're good."

"Thank you. Let's do the real receipt, then I'd dispose of this one if I were you."

"I will. How soon can we do this again?"

"I'd suggest every week or two. Gives us time to install the pieces—and keeps your wife from noticing."

"We'll do it your way," George said.

"When should we deliver?"

"You'll have to remove those hideous lions first. Can you start tomorrow? And... how many times do you think I can get away with this?"

"That's up to you. Me? I'd build a real cushion—three to four hundred thousand. That'll keep a guy for a while," Ted said.

"Boy, I guess it would," George said—then the thought of millions, and Phil, took some wind from him.

"Not as much as you have now, I suppose," Ted said lightly, "but it'll do in a pinch. We'll be there tomorrow at 10:00. All right?"

"I'll be waiting. And thanks for doing this." George shook his hand.

"No problem, Mr. Weinberger. Let's go write the receipt in front of José."

"Let's go," George said.

A few minutes later, he walked out with the purchase set and a counter check for $10,000 made out to cash. He headed straight for the marina and Wayne and Muriel's yacht—the proud soon-to-be owner of cherubim and completely satisfied with what he'd set in motion.

CHAPTER 31

THE CROCHET UNRAVELS

It was past 10:00 p.m., and with traffic finally calm, Hazel had settled on the end of the couch to crochet. It looked as though she were carefully watching every stitch, but in truth she was peering over her glasses at the news Harry had turned on, while her hands flew on autopilot.

"And now we are asking for the help of the community. If you have seen or know the whereabouts of the following couples, please notify your nearest police station. The couples are on your screen now..." the newscaster announced as two photos appeared.

"The first couple's names are George and Margaret (Marge) Wetzel. The second couple are Terrance and Jody Weinberger. As we said, if you know the whereabouts of either couple or have seen them, please notify your local authorities. Thank you."

Hazel's mouth dropped open; her eyes went wide. Her hands stopped mid-flurry. She was about to say something to Harry, then thought better of it. *No—he'll just make fun of me again.* She set her crocheting down, stood, and headed for the kitchen. She banged the coffee can to make it sound empty—Harry would never know; he never set foot in the kitchen except to eat.

"Harry!" she called. "I've got to run to the store. We're out of coffee, and I forgot to buy some earlier."

"Okay. I'll probably be in bed before you get back—especially if you run into anyone you know!" he bellowed. He knew that if she found a familiar face, she'd talk till the rooster crowed.

"Yeah, yeah. I'll be home later!" she hollered back. She grabbed her purse from the stand by the back door, unlocked it, stepped out, and locked it again. At the vintage '79 Lincoln Continental, she hit the dash button to raise the garage door—she'd once forgotten and Harry hadn't let her forget it for six years.

When the door was fully open, she started the car, reversed out, flipped on the lights, shifted to drive, and rolled away.

Fifteen minutes later she was at the store. She bought coffee. Her favorite checker tried to chat, but Hazel said, to the woman's surprise, "I'm so sorry, dear, I can't talk now. I've got something very important to do." She hurried out.

Another twenty minutes weaving through light traffic, and she sat in front of the Boise Police Department. She shut off the car, straightened her skirt, and headed inside.

"May I help you?" asked a friendly voice at the counter.

"Ye—yes," she stammered. "I'd like to talk to somebody about those people that were just on the news."

"And what people would that be, ma'am?" the officer asked.

"You know—the ones on just now... I think their names were... the Wetzels and the Bergers, or something like that."

"The Wetzels and the Weinbergers—those ones?" His face sharpened.

"Yes, that's them," she said.

"Please have a seat. Someone will be right with you." He vanished as quickly as he'd spoken.

In less than two minutes the door to the back opened and an older man entered with the officer who'd greeted her.

"Ma'am, this is Detective Alquist. He has a few questions for you. All right?" the officer said.

"By all means. That's why I'm here," she replied. She followed them to a back office, where a second detective joined them.

"Please sit," Alquist said, perching on the corner of the desk. "This is my partner, Detective Jackson," he added. Jackson sat opposite Hazel. "Tell us about these couples. That's why you came, correct?"

"Yes, I'll be glad to—maybe someone will believe me. My husband doesn't," she said.

Alquist glanced at Jackson. "We'll believe you—but first you've got to tell us what we're believing. Have you seen these couples?"

"Yes, sir. I have. They were at my neighbor's house. The first couple walked in, and a few days later the other couple walked out," Hazel said.

"What do you mean one couple walked in and the other walked out?" Jackson asked, confused.

"I mean they're the same people," Hazel said, beaming.

Alquist nearly slipped off the desk corner. He looked at Jackson; Jackson looked back—both in near disbelief. "You're saying they're the same people?"

"That's what I said. Do you believe me?"

"We want to," Alquist said, settling again. "But we'll need more. What makes you think they're the same?"

"Well, about a week ago the first couple—the Wetzels—came to my neighbor's house..."

"Do you and your neighbor get along well?" Jackson asked.

"Oh no. Not that little creep. He has people coming and going all hours. I've tried to tell my husband something's going on, but he just says to keep my nose in my own business and goes back to the television."

Jackson scribbled notes. "All hours?"

"Yes."

"And you say about a week ago you saw the Wetzels show up there?" Alquist asked.

"Oh, they didn't just show up. *He brought them*," she said.

"He—your neighbor. Mr...?" Jackson prompted.

"I'm not sure of his last name. His first name is Jerry. I think his last name is Kesselton—or something like that," Hazel said, rubbing her chin.

"Would you like something to drink—coffee? Soda?" Jackson asked. "We'd like to talk to our supervisor a minute."

"I'd like coffee, please. With cream," Hazel said.

Two minutes later a female officer brought it. "Here you are, ma'am."

"I wish everyone would stop calling me *ma'am*. I'm Hazel Blankers. Please call me Hazel," she said briskly.

"Okay, Hazel. I'll let them know," the officer said.

"Please do. *Ma'am* makes me sound old. I'm only sixty-seven," Hazel said—shaving five years off seventy-two.

Five minutes later the detectives returned with another man.

"Hazel, this is our captain, Robert Decker," Alquist said. "He'd like you to tell him why you believe the couples are the same people. All right?"

"Absolutely. They're the same because I saw the Wetzels when they arrived. He was around five-eight to five-ten, kind of chunky—early to mid-thirties. She was a beauty—like me a few years ago." The officers smiled despite themselves.

Hazel looked down her nose and continued. "She had to be in her twenties, five-four to five-seven, and a hundred pounds at most. Now, when the others came out, that's exactly what they were. They'd changed hair color and such. He must've worn a wig, because he had hair when he came out. And he had the same limp as before. She had the same voice—kind of whiny."

"Sounds like you looked closely," the captain said.

"I've seen some of the people who go there on the news when they get arrested," she said. "You know—for dope and all."

"So you think your neighbor is running drugs?" Alquist asked.

"Probably that and more," Hazel said.

"Do we have an address yet?" the captain asked Jackson.

"No, sir. We wanted you to hear this first," Alquist said.

"I live in the Eagle's Nest subdivision—south of town," Hazel said. "I'm at 2554, and this fellow is right across the street at 2555. The street is Talon Drive."

"Thank you, Hazel," the captain said, brightening. "I think you've been a big help. We'll probably be calling on you again soon."

"Then you do believe me?" Hazel asked, amazed.

"We believe you enough to stake the guy out and see what we can learn," the captain said. "If it checks out, we'll take him down and find out where to locate the others."

"How long will it take?" Hazel asked. "I want to tell my husband 'I told you so.'"

"It could be days or weeks—and if it doesn't go as planned, maybe months. But I don't think it will take too long," Jackson said.

"Good," Hazel said.

"Please leave your number with one of the detectives so we can reach you if needed," the captain said.

"Yes, I will," Hazel said, excited. Ten minutes later she was on her way home. When she pulled into the driveway, she could tell Harry was already in bed—the porch light on, house lights out.

"Oh, that man," Hazel muttered. "He knows I'm coming in through the garage; why can't he leave *that* light on? Sometimes I think he doesn't like me."

She parked, shut the garage door, and went inside to bed.

CHAPTER 32

THE ANGELS OF DECEIT

It seemed like everyone and his brother was at the marina that day, and finding a parking space was going to be tough. He finally found one about three blocks from where Wayne's car was supposed to be. At least he found a place. After he parked, he shut Jasper off, stepped out of the jeep, locked the door, and headed for the slip where Wayne's yacht was moored.

As he walked, he noticed Wayne and Muriel's car was gone, but he kept walking anyway. Wayne had told him how to get in if they weren't there. They trusted him, but not many others. When he reached the yacht, he stepped aboard and found the key Wayne kept hidden in the butt of the old fishing pole among fifteen others in the rack. The other poles were newer—used for guests who fished with him. Wayne always said that particular one was a keepsake and was never used, so no one suspected it held the yacht key. Once George had the key, he replaced the pole and unlocked the cabin door.

Just then, he heard Wayne and Muriel approaching.

"Wayne! You want a cool one?" George shouted over the rail.

"I would, but the only ones there are, are the ones I have with me!" Wayne shouted back, laughing like he'd pulled a fast one.

George went to the side and helped Muriel aboard first, then Wayne.

"How ya' doin', my boy?" asked Wayne.

"Well, I just made my first transaction for ten grand—and I don't feel guilty about it, I might add. Not to her anyway. You know, Jody—my wife."

"To who then?" Muriel grunted as she handed him her sack of groceries.

"Uh, no one, I guess. I just said that." George couldn't tell them how they'd gotten the money. *What in the world did I say that for?* he thought. *Now they're going to suspect something.*

"Oh, just put them on the table. I'll put them away. We have three more in the car if you'd like to help Wayne with them," Muriel said.

"I'm on my way," George replied, then turned to Wayne. "You ready?"

"No, but if you insist." Wayne puffed through a smile.

"You take it easy on Terrance—it's not every day we have guests who are willing to help," Muriel teased, giving George a wink.

"Yes, ma'am," Wayne drawled. "She'd make a good skipper, don't ya think?"

"I do believe you're right, Wayne."

Laughing, the two men turned back toward the deck and walked to Wayne's car for the rest of the groceries.

"We saw you come up—we were over here," Wayne said.

"No wonder I didn't see your car. You must've had a hard time finding a spot too! This is way out of the norm for you to park over here, isn't it?" George was amazed that Muriel and Wayne had walked nearly half a mile from where they'd parked.

"Yeah, it's not often we have to park this far away, but when we do, it's a chore. I'm glad you showed up—I don't think Muriel could've done another pack from here," Wayne panted. "In fact, I don't think I could've done a third one myself."

It took Wayne and George about twenty minutes to return to the yacht with the groceries.

As they boarded again, Wayne said, "I'm sure glad you took my advice, Terrance. You never know when that woman of yours will get a wild hair and decide it's over. I think you'll do all right if you make a few more of these little transactions."

"I think so too. Ted—the guy at the garden shop—told me he thought I could do it enough times to get around four hundred thousand before I should call it quits."

"He should know what he's talking about. Lord knows he's done it enough. I've sent quite a few people over to see him," Wayne said. "He won't steer you wrong. Just do what he says."

When they entered the cabin, Muriel was busy putting things away. "There are cool ones again, boys!" she announced.

"Ah-h-h, that's music to my ears," teased Wayne, chuckling as he reached into the fridge and grabbed two beers.

"Muriel, do you have that account ready for Terrance?" Wayne asked as he turned and handed George a beer. "He's brought his first investment over."

"All we have to do is take him to our bank, and they'll fix him up," Muriel said, stretching to put some cereal above the fridge.

"You want me to do that?" George asked.

"No, hon. I've been doing this for years. I'm used to it. Besides, if I let you do it, then I'll get used to it, then I'll be spoiled—and after you're gone somewhere else, I'll have to learn how to do it all over again," joked Muriel.

"I didn't understand a word of that," George said.

As soon as he did, Wayne burst out in a thunderous laugh.

"You tell her, boy—you tell her," Wayne chortled.

Muriel didn't miss a step. Smiling, she kept putting things away. "Well, how 'bout this then—thanks but no thanks?"

"Now that I can understand," chuckled George.

"So, what did you buy?" asked Wayne as he sat down at the table. He gestured for George to sit, and he did.

"I bought some cherubim. Remember I told you I hated those lions out front of my place? Well, I played like I was drunk and ran into one. I got the idea after talking with you yesterday—or whenever it was we talked about it. Oh, I wasn't feeling any pain, but I wasn't that far gone. I knew what I was doing, so I hit the one on the right. You'd have been proud of me, Wayne. That thing tumbled off that pedestal slicker than a whistle—broke in six parts, it did." George was pleased with his story.

"How'd the missus take it?" asked Muriel, who had finished half the groceries and decided to take a break.

"Oh, she fussed a little, so I fussed a little back. But this morning—Muriel, you could've given me an Oscar for my performance! She bought it hook, line, and sinker. She's taught me well. I talked her right out of the lions and into the cherubim. In fact, she was really sweet when she left. I can do anything I want to the house, she said, because it's mine too. Now wasn't that nice of her to tell me that?"

"Do I note a little sarcasm in there somewhere, dear?" Muriel asked, winking at Wayne.

"Well, maybe a little," joked George.

"So, you more or less have a free road ahead of you to buy anything you want, right?" asked Wayne.

"That's what it sounds like to me. Nothing extravagant, you know—just things like, oh, say, a jacuzzi, new patio furniture, a sweat house, a fountain or two, some more statues—you know, the important things," George said, smiling.

"I've always said, a man has to do what a man has to do—and it sounds like a good plan to me," Wayne said approvingly.

"Too bad you couldn't buy a yacht," Muriel mused.

"If that guy had one there, I would—even though I don't know the first thing about one."

And with this plan in mind, over the next few months George put more than four hundred eighty thousand dollars away in his secret hiding place. While he was busy doing that, Marge was busy with things of her own—mainly Danny, who was introduced to George as her tennis instructor. But soon he became her volleyball coach, then her weightlifting partner, and finally her masseur.

Even though George drank more than he should have, even he could read between the lines. He knew what was going on between them—and he didn't care.

The maid, on the other hand, was furious. Being a Christian woman, both Marge's and George's behaviors were far outside the lines of righteous living. She could tolerate the drinking for a while, but adultery was something she would never abide.

Abby and George got along quite well when he was off the booze. The only thing George knew he would regret about leaving Marge was losing this maid. She reminded him of his mother, whom he'd lost many years ago. If only he could take her with him. Maybe there would be a way. He'd just have to see. But he knew the time to leave was soon. In fact, the sooner the better.

Maybe Abby would pack up at the same time—he didn't know. All he knew was that this sixty-five-year-old woman was kind, quiet, and steady. Yes, he would miss her very much.

CHAPTER 33

CUTTING TIES

It was a stormy night. The wind whipped the waves against the rocks, and mist drifted like ghosts across the open stretches of sand. It caught on the nearby houses, bathing them in salty, whispering brine.

George decided to come home after drinking all day. Once again he had found the Salty Dog a place of refuge. He'd sat and tossed back tequila sours most of the day, thinking—and the more he drank, the more twisted his thoughts became.

Just before closing, the bartender came over and said, "Friend, it's time to go home. You can't stay here."

What George saw terrified him. As he looked into the man's eyes, all he could see was Phil. He actually believed it was Phil saying, "Friend, it's time to go home. You can't stay here."

George began to shake and almost screamed, but then his eyes focused and he realized he'd been confused.

"Looks like you saw a ghost, mister," the bartender said. "You all right?"

George looked at him for a minute, blinked, and left. But the picture of Phil was etched into his memory. He heard the words over and over—"Friend, it's time to go home. You can't stay here"—as he staggered to his new Jeep Cherokee. He could have had any car he wanted, but why he chose the Cherokee, he didn't know. Marge, on the other hand, bought a BMW. George didn't care anymore. What she did was her business. Tonight he didn't want anything more to do with Marge. They were going to have it out—tonight.

The road to their house seemed more crooked than usual. Though he drove extra slow, it still felt too fast for the curves, but at last he pulled into the driveway. He shut the Jeep off and stumbled as he shut the door. Regaining his composure, he climbed the front steps. Hearing the waves, he started thinking about how beautiful the view was from here. A person could stand on the deck and become mesmerized. The beauty and the constant pounding of the waves were hypnotizing. At any other time—before these last few months—George would have loved it. But not now. Not since that night on Speckled Bird.

"Jody!" he slurred. "Where are you?"

"Oh, Mr. Weinberger," said Abby. "Let me help you. Do you know that stuff is bad for you?" she scolded.

"I don't care about that now. I want to talk to Jody," he mumbled.

"Sir, I don't think... Well, she's getting a massage. I don't like it, but I don't think you ought—"

"Where is she, Abby? I don't care what she is getting or who she is with. I want to talk to her now!"

"Okay. If you want to, I'll take you," Abby said.

She had to struggle to help him up the stairs. Drunk, he leaned more on her than on his own strength. She, being only five-four and about a hundred pounds soaking wet, was no match for George's bigger, heavier frame. But somehow they made it.

Knocking lightly, then opening the door, neither George nor Abby was ready for the sight. As the door opened there was a flurry on the bed where two red-faced people looked back at them. The covers were draped over Marge and Danny—the masseur, tennis instructor, and ex-workout instructor from the gym.

"Ma'am, expect my resignation in the morning," was all Abby said as she turned and left, upset at what she'd seen.

"George—I mean, Terrance—it's not what you think. I'm, ah... a... a—" Marge stammered.

"Aw, shut up! I'm sick of you anyway! You can have your little boy toy and all of this! I've had it. I want my half and that's all. I'll be gone by morning. If you don't like it, that's just tough!" George shouted. Finally, he thought, I've found the guts to do what I should have done at the Speckled Bird!

"Well, fine, Terrance, if that's what you want. You've got it!" Marge snapped. "Just don't ever come crying to me again!"

"I'd never come back to such a sneak, play-acting, conniving witch as you," George snarled. "You've become the epitome of evil and I want no part of you. I'm going to Mexico City. You can have this place."

"That's funny—coming from an alcoholic," she laughed.

"Tomorrow I'm going to draw half the money out and I'm gone," George seethed. "You and your whatever there can do anything you want. I don't want you anymore. I just want my Jeep."

"Fine—and good riddance!" Marge shouted. Tearing a water glass from the nightstand, she threw it. George's reflexes were off just enough that he couldn't get out of the way, and it caught him above the left eyebrow. The glass shattered and opened a wide cut on his forehead.

Furious, George started toward her. Danny jumped up and kicked him in the stomach, doubling him over.

"You'd better just leave, George, before I turn Danny loose on you," Marge sneered. "If you want, we'll meet you at the bank at nine. Goodbye."

Beaten and bewildered, George somehow managed to get downstairs before falling to the floor.

Abby came to help him up. "Oh my," she exclaimed. "Sit down here and let me take care of that cut."

"I'll be all right. I just need to get out of here tonight."

"Well, if you'll let me get my bag, I'll drive you to town. This is going to need stitches. Hold this towel tightly and give me your keys. I'll drive," she ordered.

George foggily thought, *All the orders she's been given have finally caught up with her.* But he did as he was told. He didn't feel like fighting anymore. He just wanted his money and to be gone.

As Abby gingerly helped him to the Jeep, Marge and Danny were getting dressed.

"It's time I was rid of him," Marge said. "I should have done it right after—I mean, a while back."

"Do you want me to take care of him?" Danny asked.

"No. Let him have his leave. He'll get his money tomorrow and he'll be gone. Then we can start our lives together," she said sweetly.

"That's what I like to hear," Danny said, putting an arm around her. "You know, Jody, I think we're a perfect match."

"We'll see," she said as they walked out the door. "Abby! I want something to eat! Abby! ABBY! Where are you now? She's never here when I need her."

Looking out the window to see if George had left yet, she saw Abby getting into the driver's side of the Jeep, starting it up, and taking off. "Just what George needs—a mother. Yeah, why not. He's dead anyway," she laughed loudly. "What a couple they'll make."

"Mr. Weinberger," Abby said as they drove, "I apologize for giving my notice. I really like you. You seem sincere, and after watching your wife when you are gone, I suppose I understand your drinking. But I won't put up with what she is doing now. I'll drop you at the hospital. Then, if it's all right, I'll use your Jeep and go rent a couple of hotel rooms, then come back and get you."

"That will be fine, Abby," George said, trying to figure out what was going on. Ever since that night on the Speckled Bird, he'd never seemed to have a hold on reality. And it was getting worse. Dear sweet Marge had turned into a demon out of west hell—a creature now no one would want. Well, Danny could have her. From what George had found out, they deserved each other.

"You know, Abby, I just want my half of the money. Then I don't care if I ever lay eyes on her again. In fact, she can have Puerto Vallarta. I'm going to Mexico City. Do you want to come? You can be my maid there."

"Well, I don't know, Mr. Weinberger... I suppose it would be all right," she said hesitantly. "No alcohol, though."

"You got a deal," George said. "Tomorrow morning, after I get the money, we'll sell this Jeep and take a taxi to the airport. Then, adiós, Puerto Vallarta—hello, Mexico City. Olé!"

"What we've got to do first is get you stitched up," Abby said.

"You sound like my mother. She always fussed over little cuts, too," George chuckled.

"Well, I'm old enough to be your mother, and that's no little cut. It'll take ten stitches if it takes one," she said.

The rest of the trip to the hospital they were silent—George thinking of Mexico City, Abby thinking whether she'd made a good choice.

At the hospital, Abby escorted George into the emergency room.

"I help you?" a nurse asked in broken English.

"Stitches," Abby said. She'd dealt with this nurse before she met George and Marge.

"Sí," the nurse said, taking George by the hand.

"What about the paperwork?" George asked.

The nurse looked at him as if she didn't understand, then looked at Abby.

"Cash—mucho—peso," Abby said.

The nurse smiled and led George to a small room. Before long a doctor came in. Thank God, George thought—he was an American.

"What happened to you? Looks like someone said, 'Shut up,' and you thought they said, 'Stand up'!" the doctor said.

"You could say that," George muttered. A comedian, too.

The doctor spoke in Spanish, and the nurse began setting out sterile soap, gauze, needles, antiseptic—the works. Man, George thought, I wish I knew those words. They seem to really work.

In another half hour, George was escorted to the front desk where a bill was already prepared.

"You pay?" the nurse asked.

"Yes," George said. "How much?"

"One hundred fifty dollars," she said with a smile.

George pulled out his wallet, showed her five different credit cards, and she picked the gold Visa. "Gracias."

"You bet," he replied.

Abby was back to pick him up. "How many stitches?" she asked.

"Twelve," George answered.

"See? I told you. Maybe next time you'll believe me when I say you need stitches," Abby said.

"Abby, the only thing I want to hear right now is that our rooms are waiting," George said, half sarcastic.

"They are. And cheer up—you have the ocean view," she said.

This hardly helped. What he wanted was out of this city—and away from Marge—forever. One more meeting with her tomorrow and he'd be through. With that thought, he was ready to call it a night.

"What time do you want breakfast?" Abby asked.

"I'll let you know when I wake up, okay?" George replied. Then he felt bad for being gruff. "I'm sorry, Abby. I've got a headache. How about we eat around 8:00 or 8:30 a.m.? Would that be okay?"

"That will be fine. Apology accepted," she said.

Abby turned left mid-block and drove into the parking garage of the La Hacienda Hotel. "We're on the fourth floor. Four-twelve is your room, and I'm in four-thirteen," she said.

After parking the Jeep, they walked silently to the elevator. The only words between them were at the fourth floor.

"Here's your key. Good night," Abby said.

"Thanks—and good night to you, too." George retired to his room.

At 6:00 a.m. he heard a tap-tap-tap on his door. He threw back the covers and drowsily grabbed his bathrobe from the floor beside the bed. "Just a minute!" he shouted. "What's the matter—the world coming to an end? It's only six a.m. Give me a break." As he straightened up, his head felt like it would explode. "Augh," he cried out.

He opened the door with one hand while holding his head with the other.

"Good morning, Mr. Weinberger. I thought you might need these." Abby opened her hand: four Tylenol 500-mg tablets.

"I thank God for you, Abby!" He reached for them. "How'd you know I'd need these this morning?"

"Well, I know hangovers are bad enough, but to have your head cut wide open on top of it—well, you needed them," she said.

"You're a lifesaver."

"No, I'm a maid. I know these things," she said with a smile, turning toward her room. Over her shoulder: "Breakfast at 7:30 a.m."

"Okay, I'll be there."

He found his way to the bathroom for a glass of water to take the pills. Since he was already there, he decided to shower. He should have turned on the water first to let it warm, but he didn't and—"Ho—ho—wow, that's cold!" He jumped back out. If his head ached before, it was bursting now.

It took five full minutes for the water to warm. By then he was eager to get in and out. He didn't want to wear the same clothes, but he'd forgotten to grab any from the house. So on went the same old outfit. He was about to step onto the veranda when he heard the tap-tap-tap again.

He opened the door. Abby again.

"I thought you might need these. I took the liberty of charging them to your room: shirt, underwear, pants, and socks. Thirty-eight waist, I believe."

"Yes, that's perfect. Thank you, Abby!" George said, genuinely relieved.

"Well, I wouldn't want you going around in a blood-soaked outfit. Especially if I'm your maid. That wouldn't speak well for me, now, would it?" she said.

"You've got that right. Thank you, Abby," he said earnestly.

"You're welcome," she said. He ducked back inside. When he came out ten minutes later, she was still by the door.

"I could have let you come in. I wasn't thinking," he said.

"That's all right. It didn't bother me," she sighed. "I just want to get out of here. I really don't care for this town."

"Well, after ten o'clock today we'll most likely be on a plane out of here," George said.

"Good," was all she added.

As they headed to the hotel restaurant, George asked, "Do you have any specifications on what kind of house we should get?"

"Well, I don't mind a big house if I have help with the chores, but if I have no help, then I'd rather not have too big of a house," she replied. "We'll see what's available when we get there, then decide."

"Sounds good to me."

"Besides, you should really choose anyway. I'm just the maid, remember?"

George didn't reply. He was thinking about getting away from Marge and starting over. He had become part of a scheme he should never have been in. I wish I'd never met her, he thought. I realize now that was the darkest day of my life. Then another thought entered his mind—three words he agreed with though he didn't know where they came from: evil draws evil. Maybe that's what this meant. He told himself, *It's going to change. I'm going to become like Phil was, just as soon as I can. I'm going to be a Christian, too—if God will have me.* Then he set the thought aside.

In the restaurant a waitress hurried between tables.

"May I help you?" she asked.

"Yes, a table for two," George said.

"Smoking or non?"

"Non-smoking," Abby said quickly.

"This way, please." She seated them by a window. Outside were hotel shrubs; to the right, a swimming pool; to the left, the office. Out front was Main Street.

"Menus?"

"Please," George said.

After bringing menus and coffee, the waitress disappeared.

"I think we should discuss my salary," Abby said.

"Do you want more?"

"No. In fact, I want less because I'm only taking care of one person now."

"Well, I think you're worth more than what—Jody—was giving you, so I'm upping it two hundred a month," George said.

"Really, Mr. Weinberger, I don't think I'm—"

"Abby, I appreciate your loyalty. Please let me do this."

"Well... okay. But you don't have to, you know."

"Yes, I know. I've never been to Mexico City, so let's play it by ear."

"No, we won't!" Abby exclaimed. "You've never been there?"

"No."

"Mr. Weinberger, you'd better listen to me. I've been there, okay?"

"Go ahead. I'm listening."

"First, the landings in Mexico City are atrocious. The runway—or the pilot, I don't know which—is very rough. When they set the plane down it's bumpy. The airport is really big. There'll be a lot of people pushing their cabs, but don't you dare go with any of them."

"Why?"

"You've never heard the horror stories?" she asked.

"What horror stories—are you trying to scare me?" George teased.

"I am very serious, Mr. Weinberger. Most of them are after your money. They'll take you out, rob you, and in some cases even murder you. You'll be left without money or baggage—or you'll end up dead."

George whistled. "Maybe we shouldn't go there."

"It's all right if you do as I say."

"Okay. We'll do it your way."

"The best thing is to go to the Fiesta Americana. It's a hotel across the freeway from the airport. We don't have to drive or get a taxi. We'll use the glass breezeway above the freeway—it's air-conditioned."

"Okay. I follow."

"It's a beautiful hotel: a plaza in the center with a restaurant and a fountain. Out front, shrubs and a glass elevator so you can look over the city. What a view!"

"Okay, but what about traveling?"

"Leave the driving to taxi drivers. They're very skilled, but everyone is doing their own thing down there. No one follows traffic laws. If you're slow, they'll cut you off and think nothing of it. They do it all the time."

"Does anyone get mad? Road rage or anything?"

"No. They figure you'd do it to them, so everyone stays happy. Let the cab drivers do their job and they'll make New York cabbies look like newborns."

"You're kidding."

"Not a bit. Always let the bellboy get you a cab. You'll get a good one. You can negotiate for an hour, a half day, or a full day. Give them a hundred dollars for the day—you'll have a friend for life."

"So I won't have to buy a car?"

"Exactly."

"I'm sorry it took so long," the waitress said, returning with coffee. "We had an emergency in the kitchen."

"Did anyone get hurt?" Abby asked.

"No—not seriously. Would you like time with the menu?"

"This number four sounds good to me," George said.

"Yes, I'll have one too," Abby said.

"Great. I'll have it out in a few minutes."

"So how's the food at that hotel—what's it called?" George asked.

"The Fiesta Americana—and the food is excellent. You'll love it."

"Maybe we'll live there for a while. Do they have two- or three-bedroom suites?"

"It's high-scale. I don't see why they wouldn't."

They fell into thought. When the food came, they said in unison, "Thank you," and began eating, their new adventure riding high in both minds.

"There are beautiful parks in Mexico City," Abby said at last. "Parque América, Parque San Martín, Parque España. Then the National Museum of Art, the Palace of Fine Arts, and the Museum of Modern Art. Oh, and Chapultepec Castle and the National Museum of History. There's also the National Cathedral and the National Palace, not far from City Hall. If you like fine dining and discos, go to La Zona Rosa—very exquisite."

"Well, at least we'll have some things to do," George said.

"What do you mean we? I'm the maid, nothing else," she replied.

"So the maid never has any fun?" George asked.

"I suppose I can go once in a while. But you need your privacy, too. You'll need to do your things and I mine."

"Yes, I know—but not all the time."

"Agreed," Abby said.

After they ate, George asked for the check and they walked to the cashier.

"We hope you enjoyed your meal," she said with a smile.

"Oh yes, very much. Say, is there someplace I can sell my Jeep? We're leaving and don't need it. We're flying out today," George said.

"There's a car lot about three blocks down on your right, sir. They might take it off your hands—you might take a loss, though."

"Not to worry. They can have the fun of making money on it," George said, smiling as he and Abby headed to the parking garage. "By the time we get to the bank, it should be opening."

"Yes, sir. The quicker we get out of here, the better," Abby said.

It was 9:00 a.m. on the nose when they pulled into the bank's lot. Marge and Danny were already waiting.

"Isn't this cozy?" Marge asked as George and Abby got out.

"Whatever you're thinking, Mrs. Weinberger, you can stop," Abby said. "I'm old enough to be his mother, for one, and for two, I'm his maid."

"Yeah," George said. "I'm not jumping in bed with anyone. You've got that base covered." He nodded toward Danny.

Danny made a move, but Marge caught his arm. "He's not worth it. Let's give him what he wants and get him out of here."

"Good," George said. "You can have this place. I'm out."

"You and your maid?" Marge sneered.

"That's none of your business. If you want to reach me to send the papers, I'll be at the Fiesta Americana. Send them there," George said.

"What papers?" Marge asked.

"Divorce papers, of course."

"Danny, did you hear me mention a divorce? I'm sure I never did," Marge said smugly. Danny shrugged.

"If they aren't there in two months, Mar—er—Jody, I'll send them your way," George snapped.

"My, my, aren't we testy," Marge mocked.

They walked inside. About a half hour later they emerged—George with his half and Marge with hers, not in hand but in separate accounts. George was ready to move his funds to Mexico City as soon as he arrived.

Danny and Marge strutted to the BMW. The last thing she did was make a ridiculous face at George as they left.

George and Abby, on the other hand, took the Jeep back toward the restaurant to find the car lot. George made the best deal he could: nineteen thousand five hundred for it.

"I guess we call a taxi," George said.

Not long after, they were in the air, taking their last look at Puerto Vallarta. In another three hours they were standing in the large suite they'd rented at the Fiesta Americana—hoping, praying all the trouble was behind them.

CHAPTER 34

THE HIDDEN ROOM AT 2555

It had been six months since anything was done on the murder case of Phillip Gunn. The trail had gone cold—until Jerry's house sold.

"Boise Police, Sergeant Brokerman here. How may I help you? A secret compartment? Oh—door... that leads to the basement... uh-huh... it's got what? What's your address? 2555 Talon Drive? Okay, I'll have someone come out and check it. Yes, they'll be right over. Yes, ma'am—thank you." *Boy, that address sounds familiar,* he said to himself.

The sergeant finished his notes, then called out to the room: "Hey, listen up. Why does 2555 Talon Drive sound so familiar to me?"

"Sounds familiar to me too," said Pointer. She went to her records and looked under Unsolved Cases. If the address was ringing a bell, it had to be there. "Here," she said. "That address used to belong to a Jerry Kettleman. Jonesy and I were on stakeout across the street, and it seemed like the feds took our boy away from us. Why—what'd you get?"

"Well, a Mrs. Zanders just called in and said she was polishing a bookshelf when—this sounds crazy, but I'm quoting—'a knot gave way a little and the wall opened up.' She says she went down a narrow stairwell to an automatically lit room and found not only drugs but files on people, plus materials and machines to make false IDs, among other papers."

"You interested? Or should I give it to someone else?" asked Sergeant Brokerman.

"You do, and neither Sarge nor Jonesy nor I will report back from lunch," Pointer threatened.

"Okay. Let's roll then," they said in unison.

"Want some help?" asked Sergeant Brokerman.

"Yeah, but not just yet. Let us see what we find first, then we'll bring it in and we can all go through it. But us first. We're looking for a special couple. They might be involved in the murder of a Kamish man," said Pointer.

"Where's Jonesy? He'd better be starting the car if he knows what's good for him," she muttered, grabbing her coat. It was a cold winter, but for once she felt warm as the adrenaline kicked in. She was on the trail again.

"Hey, where you going, Pointer?" shouted Jonesy.

"Grab your coat. We might have a break on our murder case!"

"Which murder case? I didn't know we were on one!"

"Remember the family members of Phil Gunn over in Kamish?"

"Oh, that one. All right!" He snatched his coat and ran after her. "We going to see them again?"

"Nope. We're going to the house we had on stakeout."

"What about the feds?"

"They're not involved. The house was sold."

"Fantastic. What we got?"

"A secret panel, a narrow stairwell, a basement. Drugs, machines, files—plus the papers they processed. We are going to get our people. I can feel it."

"Boy, I've wanted a break on this for some time. Thank God they sold the house."

As they all but ran to the car, thoughts spun. Are we going to find our perps? How far have they gone? Can we get them? Wonder how they're spending the money. Yes, it always went back to the money.

Well, if it were me, Jonesy thought, I'd find a spot with no extradition. Even if I got caught, they couldn't do anything. Then I'd have fun. A house—not huge—lots of rooms, cooks, maids, butlers, the works. Of course, I'd have to get rid of Rita. She's too old. I'd have to marry younger. Hey, I might even get in shape for that!

"So how d'you want to play this?" asked Pointer.

"Huh? What'cha mean?" Jonesy snapped back to reality.

"We can call for help to sift through everything, or we can go through it first—fast—then call for help to haul it back to the shop."

"Let's go through it first, looking for our people. You remember the names?"

"Of course. I've had them on my mind 24/7 since we lost our pigeon."

"Yeah, me too." Silence fell again.

Now Pointer thought about the money. "Jonesy, what would you do with all that money if you got your hands on it?"

"Oh, I never really thought about it," Jonesy said, blushing at the lie.

"I think, for that much, I might even be tempted," Pointer mused.

"Not you, Pointer! You really mean that?"

"Well, we'll never know, will we?"

Shocked, Jonesy mumbled, "No," and gave her a sideways glance. I would too, he thought. But I won't tell her that. Shoot, I might even ask her to come with me. She ain't too bad. Besides, she's divorced—and I know what they say about divorced women. It'd be fun for awhile. Then I'd get tired of her and look for something else. Come to think of it, that's a lot of work. Maybe I'm not so bad off right here.

"Yeah, I'd pay off my bills, sell out, then go where no one could find me."

"Let's just hope our pigeons weren't that smart. I want to catch them. Right now we've got a stone-cold trail. I'm hoping we can pick up the scent again."

"Amen to that, Pointer. Amen."

"I didn't know you were religious."

"I'm not. Figure of speech."

"Oh. Okay."

As soon as they pulled up, they heard banging on a window. Across the street, Hazel waved at them. Pointer smiled and waved back.

Jonesy followed Pointer to the front door. After two rings, a young blonde woman—about twenty-two—answered.

"Are you the police?" she asked.

"Yes. I'm Detective Pointer, and this is Detective Jones. Are you the one who called?"

"Yes—but my husband said maybe I shouldn't have."

"Why would he say that?"

"Well, if somebody finds out we told you about the room, they might get back at us. Try to hurt us."

"Ma'am," Jonesy said, "if there were going to be trouble, don't you think it would've happened in the last six months? Fire. Explosion. 'Burglary.' Something?"

"Well, I guess that's true. Okay—come in."

Pointer gave Jonesy a thumbs-up for quick thinking. "Nice house," he said.

"Thank you, Detective Jones. We bought it because we like the area. But now we're wondering. We might sell and move. Neither of us likes trouble."

"Is this your husband?" Pointer asked, lifting a picture.

"Yes. He's a great librarian. He's written a couple of books on criminal theology, and we're going to use the money for this house as soon as the royalties come in."

No wonder he didn't want trouble, Pointer thought. He couldn't fight his way out of a wet paper bag with a shotgun and a dagger. She nearly laughed but kept her composure. "Looks like a fine man," she said.

She glanced at Jonesy, who rolled his eyes at the puny ninety-seven-pound wonder in the photo.

"Here's where I was cleaning—and here's the button." She pressed it. "It only stays open about forty-five seconds, then closes. There's another button on the other side. I found it when I came back up."

"Did you touch or move anything?"

"Just the papers on the table. Then I realized what they were."

"Okay, we'll need your fingerprints so we can exclude you from the scene."

"Sure! I've always wanted to give my fingerprints—but I never wanted to go to jail to do it," she squealed.

Jonesy rolled his eyes again. Pointer kicked him lightly. "Jonesy, see if that machine still works. Maybe we can print her here so she won't have to go to the station."

"Oh, goody," she said.

"Right this way, Miss. We'll see what we can do," said Jonesy.

Pointer started through the files. She found the names of George and Marge—and their aliases. As she kept thumbing, her eyes lit like a kid in a candy store. "Oh, Jonesy—"

"Don't bother me, can't you see I'm busy?" he grunted. Taking her fingerprints was worse than he thought. She kept bumping into him and giggling, like she was flirting. "Well, Miss, maybe we'd better let the experts do this," he said abruptly and walked over to Pointer.

"Remember those people who came up missing three years ago? No trace?" Pointer asked.

"Yeah. What about them?"

"They're in Colorado. Scott and Connie Julias. Their kids: Scott Jr., Sadie Ann, Jacob."

"Well, what d'you know."

"Remember—the house ten miles out of town? Isolated. A little blood, bullet holes, the place torn up. Remember?"

"Oh yeah. That case was never closed, was it?"

"No. But now we can. And the IRS will be interested in these people too."

"Right—their business was about to be audited."

"Bingo."

"You want me to call the station?"

"The captain will want this. Yeah—go. Tell him we need a big truck and a crew to move this stuff. We may have to work with the feds. But this time we make a deal: we get our people; they can have the rest."

"Best thing I've heard you say in a while, partner."

It seemed to Pointer that the captain and the truck arrived faster than it took her to think it—but that was the adrenaline, and the hope of a fresh trail.

"My God." The captain put his hands to his head, eyes wide. He whistled softly. "You weren't faking."

"No. Here's the dope—looks like about a million in street value. And the files—you're gonna like them. Might explain a lot of missing people," said Pointer.

"Tell him about the drug deals too," she added to Jonesy. "It's all here, Captain."

"Okay. Before we touch anything, get the feds over here. They're going to want to see this."

"Captain, before you do—can we talk you into making a deal with them for us?"

"What's that?"

"For all the material and information they're going to get—ATF, FBI, who knows how many—we want all rights to George and Marge Wetzel. Can you do that?"

"I'll try. Seems they ought to give us something out of this haul."

"Captain—take a look at this!" Another officer had been tapping on the walls. He'd found a hollow section. On top of a cabinet he found a sheet with a computer name and access code. He entered it. The wall opened on another room—full of weapons. From M16s to surface-to-air missiles, and everything in between.

"I wonder..." the captain said, flipping through logs until he found, under the phrase hold me in your arms, another code. He entered it and pulled up a list of sales—to militant groups and terrorist organizations.

"Don't touch another thing. Get the feds. Now!" the captain bellowed.

After the feds saw the scope, they gladly made the deal: the Boise PD would get everything on George and Marge Wetzel.

It took fourteen hours to remove the files, machinery, weapons, and drugs. The new owners were sent to a luxury hotel while the house was swept top to bottom. Good thing, too: three more hidden rooms under the basement floor. More drugs. Information on murders. More files—many more files.

Back at Boise Police Headquarters, Pointer and Jonesy read, looked, searched for clues.

"I think one of the first things we ought to do is go to all the airlines, bus lines, and trains to see if anyone fits these descriptions," said Jonesy.

"Why, Jonesy? We've got their aliases. Let's ask whether anyone under those names bought a ticket—and to where," Pointer said.

"Okay—that's what I meant. But which name?"

"They're not going to use their own, so we've got four to run. We'll push all four until something hits."

"You buying lunch?"

"On two conditions. One, you drive. Two, no Mexican. I can't stand the car with you after Mexican—and it's too cold for windows down."

"How about Wendy's?"

"Now you're talking."

They walked into the Boise airport. Jonesy was still munching fries. "Man, I haven't been here in a while. It's bigger."

"When was that, Jonesy?"

"'Bout five years ago."

"What! You haven't been here for five years?"

"I said about," he corrected.

"Why? No one come see you?"

"Yeah, but Rita drives. Why should I take time from my busy schedule?"

"What busy schedule?"

"Well, when I'm not working, I like a snack and to relax. TV. Paper. That kind of thing."

"Okay," she said, and let it go.

They flashed badges at the ticket counter. "Do you have records of passenger lists for previous months?" Pointer asked.

"Yes, Officer."

"How hard would it be to trace someone, say six months ago?"

"To where?"

"That's what we need to find out."

"I'll have to get my supervisor. He can help you better."

"That'll be fine."

Two minutes later an older man appeared. "Good afternoon, Officers. How can I help?"

"We'd like to see your records for the past six to seven months to check some names and destinations."

"Sure. This way."

Not long after, they left the airport confused.

"I was sure they'd want to get out as fast as they could," Jonesy said, scratching his head.

"Well, we've got the train station and the buses," Pointer said.

"Yeah, but I'm getting a weird feeling."

"Me too."

"What if we don't find anything?"

"Something will break somewhere."

But after checking the train depot and the bus station, they were back at square one. Many leads, same wall: nowhere.

A week in, they were still racking their brains. Jonesy sat with elbows on his desk, head in hands. Pointer stared off into space. A young officer walked by, chatting with another: "Yeah, my mother-in-law had to hire a private jet to make the wedding because she forgot what day it was. A week behind. I can already see what she'll be like." They laughed and disappeared into the locker room.

Five minutes later, Pointer's chin dropped. Jonesy wore the look of brilliance. "You thinking what I'm thinking, Jonesy?"

"Sure am!" They began calling private jet rentals. That too was a dead end.

"Some idea that was. I'm going home," Jonesy said.

"Yeah, me too. See you tomorrow." Dejected, they grabbed coats and left.

It bugged Jonesy all night. Something kept trying to punch through. They'd used all four names for George and Marge, but no one had heard of them. No registrations under those names, anywhere.

He went to bed about 10:00 that night with it still grinding. After four hours of fitful sleep, he sat straight up at 4:00 a.m., eyes wide. He grabbed the phone and dialed. Five rings. A muddled "'H'lo."

"Pointer, that you?"

"Who do you think—the Wicked Witch of the West?" she grumbled.

"I've got an idea!"

"It'd better be good, or I might be the Wicked Witch, Jonesy. I don't like being woken at night. Remember?"

"Yeah, yeah—but listen."

"I'm listening."

"Okay—say they never rented the jet under any of their names—"

"Duh. Isn't that what we found out?" she snapped.

"Yeah, but hear me out. What if Jerry rented the jet in his name? That's why we never found anything under the other names."

"Wait—let me wake up." A beat. "You're saying if Jerry rented the flight—public or private—or even bus or train, he could've handed over the tickets or, on a private charter, just given them the flight info?"

"Bingo."

"That's not bad, Jonesy. Not bad at all!" She jumped out of bed. "I'm hungry. Let's get breakfast."

"Sounds good. I'm famished."

"Good to see your appetite back."

"Well, when I stop eating, I think better."

"Evidently. See you at Cheeno's."

After a long breakfast they hit the airport, the bus station, and the train depot before 8:00 a.m. At the station, Pointer said, "You want to call the private jet companies again?"

"Yeah."

"Okay—let's go."

About the fifteenth call, Pointer said, "You do have a contract with him? When was the last time he used it? About six months ago. Great. Can you tell me who he contracted it for? A man and his wife? Could you identify them if I showed you a picture? Yes—yes, that's right, they were the lottery winners. Oh, you took a picture? Fantastic. Is it okay if my partner and I come see you? Great. Thank you so much. We'll be there in thirty minutes." She covered the receiver. "JONESY! I could almost kiss you. We've got 'em."

CHAPTER 35

POWDERED PROMISES

During the month after George left, Marge and Danny became an item—Marge, Danny, and candy. By now they
had quite a habit. They would easily spend ten thousand dollars
a weekend and not bat an eye. There were parties upon parties,
day after day, and nighttime would find them crashed in a heap of
wasted flesh, waiting for morning just to do it all over again.

Both had lost weight. Eating was no longer a necessity—just a
pastime at parties. The Robinsons were always the main guests.
The senator had to be gone a lot, taking part in United States
government affairs, you know. But Ginger and Mrs. Robinson
were always there—with the candy.

On Saturday morning, Ginger stopped by to make sure they
were ready for the party she and her mother were hosting with Jody
the next evening.

"Hi, love! How are you two doing these days?" she asked.

"We're doing fine. Poor Danny's still asleep. He was quite spent
last night," Marge reported.

"I hope he'll be ready for the party tomorrow," Ginger said. "It
won't be the same without him." Mainly because she knew his
habit and that the sell would be bigger. Marge's habit was coming

along nicely too—almost as much as hers—but Ginger's didn't cost anything.

"Is your dad going to be there this time?" Marge asked.

"No, he had to go play senator," Ginger replied.

"That's too bad. I really like him."

"He likes you too, Jody," Ginger lied. "In fact, he was asking about you the other day. I'm glad we've become friends."

"Me too. Say, I do have a question. Is there any way I can get more candy? It seems I could really use some in the mornings. I hope I'm not running you folks out, though—I mean, I'm taking a lot of yours lately."

"Oh, pshaw, don't even worry about it. We do a transport to the U.S. every month worth ten million dollars, plus we have more than enough for everyone here," Ginger replied.

"Wow, really?" Marge was all ears now. This was good information to file away. "Man, how do you do that and not get caught?"

"My dad owns a coffee plantation. After it's ground and roasted, it's packed in fifty-pound bags, and by chance there's always some candy inside. You've heard of Flavors Blend Coffee, haven't you?" Ginger said proudly.

"Wow, I would have never guessed," Marge said.

"But of course, I never told you. Daddy would skin me alive if he knew."

"Oh, my lips are sealed. This is our little secret." This time, Marge lied.

"Well, darling, I've got to run. I must pick up a few things for Mom for the party tomorrow. Oh, be sure to bring Shelly and Brenda. I've got two adorable guys for them to meet."

"Okay, hon. Danny and I will be there at noon," said Marge.

"Oh! Jody, here—why don't you and Danny have one on me?" Ginger said, holding out an eight ball.

"Oh, thank you! Thank you so much! I could sure use it this morning. I'm sure he could too," Marge said, almost grabbing it from Ginger's hand.

"See you later," Ginger said.

"Bye." And with that, Ginger walked back to her BMW and was gone in a flash.

By the time Marge watched her go down the driveway and turn toward town, Danny lumbered into the living room.

"Good morning, sleepyhead!" she greeted him brightly. "Look what I got."

"Mmmph," was all he could muster.

"Just what I need," he said. "Let's hurry and get it ready."

The very next Monday, two days later, Marge went into the bank to get some money.

"I'm sorry, ma'am, but your account has been frozen."

"What? Are you out of your mind? You have no right!" Marge screamed in exasperation.

"Ma'am, a freeze has come down from the United States. It says here something about an investigation or something," explained the teller.

"We'll see about this!" Marge said in a huff. "Where's the manager? I demand to see him now."

About this time, an older, well-dressed, prudish-looking man stepped up. "May I help you, madam? I'm the branch president," he said, looking down his nose at her.

"Yes, yes, you can! This imbecile said I can't get any more money out of my account, and I haven't even got enough to last me a week, let alone a month!"

"I'm sorry, madam. There's nothing we can do. This order came from higher up, and we can't override it. Now I must ask you to leave," he stated.

"You must ask me to do what? I've got people in high places, you know! You're going to be sorry you ever messed with me, mister!" she sputtered, then turned and stomped out of the bank.

"How much did you get, baby?" Danny asked, leaning against her BMW as she stormed out.

"Oh, shut up and get in the car!"

Stunned, Danny did as he was told. Marge slammed the door so hard the window shattered into a million pieces. All she could do was scream. And scream she did. When she finally calmed enough to start the car, Danny took the first truly frightening ride of his life.

Back at the house, they said little. Two hours later, after cooling off, Marge muttered, "Seems we didn't cover our tracks too well."

"What do you mean?" Danny asked.

"Nothing," she said, disgusted, walking to the front door. She stood there ten minutes, arms crossed, staring. Then her eyes stopped on the statues. "Yes!" she shouted.

"What?" Danny asked again.

"Well, my assets are frozen for now," she said.

"Why?"

"Oh, it's nothing. But until I get it worked out, we can sell everything Terr—uh, George—spent so much money on. The lawn furniture, the fountain, the statues, the exotic figurines—everything."

"Yeah, that's something. We could do that," Danny agreed, still not following.

For the next hour, Marge went through paperwork until she had thirteen receipts in her hand. When she added it all up, she came to four hundred fifty thousand dollars.

"This is a start," she said.

"What on earth is going on? I'm not going to sit here in the dark like a mushroom while everything goes to blazes! If we're going to be together, you tell me right now what's happening—or I'm gone!" Danny shouted.

Marge turned slowly and glared. "If I wanted you to know, I'd tell you! Don't push me right now!"

"Fine! I'm outta here. I thought we were a couple who talked things over—but—" He started for the door.

"Danny, wait! I'm sorry. You're right. If we're a couple, we should talk," Marge said, running to him and hugging him. "I'll start from the beginning. I inherited this money when my mother died. But when we got married, I was coerced into signing a prenuptial agreement with Terrance to split everything if we ever divorced. Now my account's frozen, and I think Terrance is behind it."

"What about the tracks not being covered?" Danny asked.

"Well, we left the States to start a new life together. Then his parents—they're the ones causing all our problems—are trying to get the money I inherited. I think they're behind this too. I told Terrance his brother Phil made a pass at me just to get me to leave. Now they're all working together to get the money and run." Fake tears streaked her face. Boy, she thought, if he doesn't buy this, he's a real fool.

"Why didn't you tell me before, Jody? No one's getting a thing while I'm here," Danny said bravely. "What's our next move?"

"We're going to the store to tell them to take back everything Terrance bought. That'll give us money to find him and figure this out." She smiled slightly. She had bigger plans.

It took Marge and Danny about thirty minutes to get ready and drive to town.

Finding the Complete Garden & Patio Shop open, she pulled in.

"Want me to wait here?" asked Danny.

"No, come in," she said, shutting off the car.

They entered. Marge walked straight to the counter.

"Good afternoon, madam. Can I help you?" asked the clerk.

"Yes, is there a Ted here?"

"Yes, madam. Would you like to speak with him?"

"Please."

"No trouble. Just a moment." He paged, "Ted Newsome to the counter, please."

Soon Ted appeared. His nametag confirmed it. The clerk pointed to Marge and Danny.

"May I help you?" Ted asked.

"Yes. I'm Mrs. Weinberger. My husband, Terrance, has left, and I'd like to return some things he bought. I don't like them and want the cash to purchase new items," Marge lied.

"Of course, Mrs. Weinberger. Which things?"

"I have a list here that totals four hundred fifty thousand dollars, and I—"

"Oh, I assure you, Mrs. Weinberger, he never spent that much here," Ted said, pretending ignorance.

"Of course he did! Look!" She shoved the receipts at him.

"Let's compare, Mrs. Weinberger. We have your husband's file."

Ted stepped behind the counter, briefed another clerk, and took the file. "Thank you," he said, flipping it open. "Now, here are his receipts: statues, patio furniture, Jacuzzi, fountain, and sweat house. My figures add up to fifty-one thousand, nine hundred seventy-five dollars and eighty-nine cents."

"I don't believe it! Look at these prices! How do you account for this?" Marge shouted.

"For one, that number in front isn't my handwriting—see how it trails? I don't write my numbers like that. These are my figures," Ted said evenly.

"I believe he must have gotten to you," she snapped.

"Well," Marge said, trying to compose herself, "how much will you give me to take this stuff back?"

"Let me ask the boss."

Ted went into the back room for ten minutes. He knew he could resell the items for full price but didn't want to refund the entire amount. When he returned, he said, "Yes, ma'am, I'll explain. The best I can do is forty thousand. The boss says we'll have to pick everything up, restock it, and sell it as used."

"Are you sure that's the best?"

"Yes, ma'am."

"Fine. We'll take it. But I want it gone by three o'clock tomorrow!"

She was furious, but there was nothing to do but take the money and go. Go where? She was going to find George—and he was going to pay.

"If you'll wait, I'll get your check," Ted said.

"Thank you," Marge replied with a fake smile. As soon as the check hit her hand, she said, "Come, Danny. We have things to do."

After they got in the car, she said, "We're going to the bank to open a new account under your name. That way they can't freeze it again. Then we'll go home. But tomorrow—we're going to find Terrance and make him pay."

"I'm all for that. Never liked him. Does that mean I can do anything I want to him?" Danny asked.

"I said make him pay, didn't I?" she smirked.

"All right."

The plan was set. They went to the bank, then home. Once there, they called Ginger and bought some candy for the road.

CHAPTER 36

THE WAGES OF SIN

I t was late Tuesday morning when Danny rolled over and shook Marge awake. "Jody! It's 11:30 a.m.! If we're going to find George, we've got to get going."

"Wha... oh yeah. What time is it?" She was awake now.

"It's 11:30 a.m.," Danny repeated.

"Quick—call the airport and see if anything's going to Mexico City today," she ordered, jumping out of bed and grabbing her bathrobe. "I need a shower."

As she headed into the master bath, Danny picked up the phone. He knew the number by heart—he used to have a girlfriend who worked out there.

"Hello? Yes, do you have anything to Mexico City today? ... 2:40 p.m.? ... May I book two round-trip flights, please? Danny and Jody Stenopolus—S-t-e-n-o-p-o-l-u-s. Stenopolus. All right, thanks."

Danny smiled. Terrance was going to be sorry—very sorry. "I'm going to make some coffee!" he yelled toward the bathroom.

"Okay, I'll be down in a minute. See if we have any candy left. If we do, we'll share it. I know I need some," Marge called back.

"You can have it all, baby," Danny said out loud. "I'm doing fine." And he was—on an adrenaline high. He could already feel Terrance's face mash under his knuckles. What a rush, he thought, heading downstairs to the kitchen.

He had just finished the coffee and was setting out a pan when Marge came in.

"What do you want to eat?" he asked.

"Nothing," she said.

"Yeah, me either," he admitted.

Both had dropped weight over the last month. Since she'd met the candy—and been with Danny—food wasn't much of a thing. Money, on the other hand, went fast: one hundred fifty thousand dollars, maybe more.

"What did the airport say?" she asked.

"We've got round-trip tickets waiting at the Island Airways counter. We're on the 2:40 p.m. flight. How's that?"

"That's great," she said. "Now—did you find any candy?"

"At your service, my dear."

"Did you already have yours?" she asked.

"Yes, matter of fact I did," he lied.

He cooked up the fix for her while she wrapped surgical tubing around her upper arm and hunted a vein—harder and harder to find. The needle had become her friend. Rocks did nothing now; lines weren't enough. When the barrel filled with the nectar she craved, she shook like a spooked pup, and Danny had to steady her arm. Then came the feeling she yearned for—that false swing toward the gates of hell that greeted her every time she shot up.

At 2:44 p.m. they were aboard the small Island Airways jet headed for Mexico City—and the money they so desperately needed. Minutes later they were rolling down the runway and gone. What felt like no time after, they were landing again.

Marge stared out the window. "What a big city. It goes for miles."

"It's one of the largest in the world," Danny said.

"How are we going to find George?"

"First, we get a room at the hotel by the airport," Danny said. "Then we go from there."

"Okay."

They left the airport with small suitcases and stepped into the glass breezeway to the Fiesta Americana. "After walking all this way, I hope they have a room," Marge whined.

"I'm sure they will. It's big."

"Maybe we should've taken a cab," she muttered.

"Not unless you get inside the hotel first. The wrong drivers'll beat you up and rob you—maybe kill you," Danny said.

"Oh. I didn't know that."

"It's the truth. I swear to God."

"Don't say that," she snapped.

"Say what?"

"Anything about God. I don't believe in Him. He was never there, and the way He let me grow up—I want nothing to do with Him."

"Are you sure, Jody? He might do something for you. Not me, though. I sold my soul—just to make sure," Danny said.

"Yeah? Well, so did I." She said nothing more, but her mind jumped to a Chevy heading to Moscow, hearing herself make a pact for money. "And as soon as I find George, I'm going to get more," she said aloud.

"Who's George?" Danny asked. "I've heard you say that name a few times—at least try to say it."

"It's just that 'Terrance' reminds me of my brother before he died. I hated him, too," she said.

They reached the front desk.

"May I help you?" the clerk asked.

"Yes, we'd like a room," Danny said.

"Smoking or non?"

"Smoking," Marge said.

"Sign here, please."

As Marge dug for her pen—she always used her own—she spilled her purse across the counter.

"Oh, I'm so sorry," she said, red-faced.

"That's perfectly all right, madam," the clerk said, helping her gather things. He picked up a photo of George and Marge after their makeovers. "Oh—you're acquainted with Mr. Weinberger?"

"Say what? Mr. who?" Marge asked, stunned.

"Mr. Weinberger," the clerk said, pointing to George in the picture.

"Oh. Yes, yes." She recovered. "How do you know him?"

"He has a suite here on the twenty-third floor, with his maid. Very fine man."

"He is here? In this hotel? In room...?"

"Room 2312, ma'am. What is he to you?"

"He's my ex-husband! I'll never spend a night in a place where he stays!" She spun and stormed out, Danny on her heels.

"Did you get the room, Danny?" she asked outside.

"Twenty-three twelve. Why?"

"We're going to pay a visit. When no one's looking, we dive into the elevator."

"Okay."

They slipped back in, waited for the clerk to turn away, then ducked into the elevator and pushed button 23. Marge hummed like a little girl about to do what she wasn't supposed to do. Danny's adrenaline had his palms slick and his breath short. When the doors opened, neither intended to leave without damage.

He counted door numbers. "Here's 2364, 2366... Guess we turn around." They backtracked past the elevators until, finally, 2312—George's suite.

Danny rang. Marge tilted her head and shook out her hair.

The door opened to a smiling Abby. "Hello. Well, hello, Mrs. Weinberger. How are you?"

"I'll be doing much better as soon as I talk to that no-good husband of mine," Marge said, brushing past her with Danny right behind.

"Mrs. Weinberger, I assure you he's not here—he's out of town. I'm going to have to ask you to leave before I call the manager."

"Abby," Danny said, yanking the phone from the wall jack, "I don't believe you're calling anyone."

"Danny, make sure she stays put. I'm going to see if he's here," Marge ordered.

"I've told you he's not! I demand you both leave right now!" Abby said.

"Abby, shut up. One more word and I'll have Danny shut you up."

"Go ahead. God will take care of you. He doesn't like adultery, either—and me being a Christian, I don't like it any more than He does," Abby said. "I love you both, but not what you're doing. You should be ashamed."

Marge laughed. "I knew there was something different about you. You're a little goody two-shoes, Miss Priss." Phil flashed through her mind. "You're just like him—and I hated him enough to kill him because he was a Christian. So you'd better tell me what I want to hear, or guess what?"

"I know nothing except Mr. Weinberger is out of town and won't be back for some time. I can't tell you a thing more. Wouldn't if I could. At least he's quit drinking and is doing nicely."

Marge stepped close and shouted, "Shut up, old woman!"

"As you wish."

Marge slapped her hard. Abby flew back onto the couch, eyes wide but unafraid. "May God forgive you," she said.

"Where did he go?"

"Danny, she's all yours. I'm looking around," Marge said, disappearing down the hall.

"Lady, you should've answered her," Danny growled.

"She never asked anything I could answer."

His front kick folded her over the back of the couch. She hit the floor, gasping. "What's the matter, old lady—cat got your tongue?" he said, then backhanded her when she tried to rise. Blood poured from her mouth and nose. He spun and kicked again. She crumpled against the kitchen doorway, a deep split opening down her face. Her jaw broke. He kept kicking—ribs, back, legs—until he could do nothing but wheeze.

"Did you kill her?" Marge asked, returning.

"I don't know. She made me mad. I couldn't stop."

"Don't feel bad. She deserved it. Huh—a Christian," Marge sneered. "Let's get out of here before someone calls the cops."

"Yeah, we don't want the federales. They're mean," Danny said.

He yanked the tablecloth, dumping flowers and unlit candles, and wiped at the blood on his hands and shirt. Then they slipped out the way they came.

Two hours later, George returned to find the door ajar. "Abby, you left the door— What the... Abby!"

She lay in a heap on the kitchen floor. He ran to her. "Abby!" She was unconscious. He felt for a pulse. Very faint.

A bellhop passing in the hall heard him and stepped in. "Mr. Weinberger. Is anything wrong?"

"Call an ambulance—or the police. Call somebody, quick!"

"I'll go next door, sir—your phone's been pulled from the wall," the bellhop said.

"Okay—hurry!"

It felt like hours before the police and ambulance arrived—really only minutes.

"Meester Weinberger?" a policeman asked.

"Yes, that's me."

"Deed you do dees?"

"No! I wasn't even home."

"I'm sorry, Meester Weinberger, but I must ask you dese questions. You deed not see it happen?"

"No."

"Do you have any idea who might have done dis?"

"No."

"Have you checked de rest of de apartment for anyting missing?"

"No."

"I theenk we betta do dat now," the officer said.

"What about Abby?" George asked.

"That's okay, sir. We'll take care of her. We won't leave until you're ready," an EMT said.

"Okay—I'll be right with you."

George and the officer walked the three-bedroom, two-bath suite. Drawers dumped, clothes strewn, lamps broken, closets torn apart, mirrors shattered, dressers cleared to the floor. The only room not ransacked was the kitchen—just a crumpled, bleeding Abby.

"I theenk it might be a robber," the policeman said.

"Could be," George said.

"Ees anyting missing?"

"I can't tell. Let's get her to the hospital—then we'll come back and check."

"Eef you weesh. I will leave a man outside to protect everyting that ees still here."

"No—just lock the door. We'll both come back and go through this later."

"Sí, Meester Weinberger."

The desk clerk, the hotel superintendent, and a security officer rushed in. "Oh my word! We're so sorry, Mr. Weinberger—we didn't know!"

"I'll talk to you later. Right now I've got to get Abby to the hospital."

"If you'll allow it, we'll post our house detective at your door until you return."

"Fine." George followed the gurney to the elevator.

Fifteen minutes later they were at Hospital de Nuestra Señora de Guadalupe, an elegant place with portraits of presidents on one wall and former chief physicians on the other. Rooms were plush—sixteen thousand pesos a day.

Abby was rushed into emergency. George, lost in the Spanish, fixed the room's location in his head by landmarks. About forty-five minutes later a doctor appeared. He spoke Spanish; George caught only señora.

"No comprende," George said.

The doctor held up a finger, pointed to a chair, and left. Soon he returned with a nurse.

"Do you know who did this?" she asked.

"No."

"She's very badly beaten. Broken jaw, broken sternum and nose, fractured skull, broken arm, broken pelvis, six broken ribs—besides many bruises and lacerations. She's in a coma. We don't know when, or if, she'll come out. Is there anyone we should call?"

"I don't know. She's my maid. That's all I know right now. I'll be here. I'm not leaving."

"Meester Weinberger," the officer said, reappearing as if from nowhere, "I hate to mention dis, but what about your apartment? What eef someting ees missing? Shouldn we check?"

"Can... we do that later?" George asked.

"I theenk we do it now, señor."

"Okay. If she wakes up, please tell her I'll be right back."

"Certainly," the nurse said.

Back at the suite, it took two hours to search. Nothing obvious was missing.

"I am glad we find no theft, Meester Weinberger. I hate paperwork," the officer said. "I go now."

"Aren't you going to file a report—or take me back to the hospital?" George asked, confused.

"If no one is here, I cannot arrest anyone. If I don't arrest anyone, I have no paperwork. And I cannot use my car as a taxi." He shrugged and left.

The bellhop stepped in a moment later. "May I help you, Mr. Weinberger?"

"It'd be nice—but you're working, and I've got to get back to the hospital somehow."

"You're in luck. I just got off. If you'll let me help you clean up, I'll drop you there."

"Great," George said.

They worked for an hour and a half setting things right. Then the bellhop drove him back and walked in with him.

"Miss," George asked at the desk, "where's the woman who was in emergency?"

"She's been moved to intensive care."

"Where—?"

"Room 712, I believe."

"Thank you. How is she? Is she awake?"

"I can't tell you, sir. Ask them upstairs."

"Okay. Thanks."

In the elevator, the bellhop—Philippe—said, "I hope Miss Abby will be okay."

"Me too, Philippe. Me too. I don't even know why this happened—let alone who did it."

On seven, they followed the numbers to 712. A nurse stepped out. "Mr. Weinberger?"

"Yes."

"Could you help me with some papers, please? Insurance and such."

"Sure. How is she?"

"She's still unconscious, so no promises. The brain swelling seems to have stopped—that's good. But she was severely beaten. Looks like whoever did it knew some martial arts. What she needs now is complete rest. Maybe she'll be all right."

"Whatever it takes," George said. He signed quickly and returned to find Philippe praying. George waited quietly.

"I'd do that, but I don't know how to pray—for one thing or another," George said at last. "And after what I've done, God could never forgive me anyway."

"Don't be fooled. God will forgive anyone," Philippe said.

George hung his head. In his mind, he could never be forgiven—he'd killed a man for money. Doomed, he thought. He sat silently beside his maid and friend—the only friend he figured he had, besides Wayne and Muriel, who felt far away. Except for Philippe's brief visits, George kept his vigil. He even had meals brought to the chair. Four days and nights passed.

Midway through the fifth day, George whispered, "Lord, if you're there, I'm not asking anything for myself because I'm not worthy. I don't even know if you can forgive me. If you can, I'd appreciate it—but I'm really asking for my friend Abby. Please, sir, touch her. If you are real, heal her and make her well again. Thank you for your time."

He'd never done that before, but he felt... lighter. Relieved, somehow.

An hour later Abby's swollen eyes fluttered. She tried to rise, then fell back with a groan.

"Abby, Abby—easy. Everything's going to be all right now," George said, calling for the nurse, who brought the doctor.

They removed tubes and wires, took vitals—and were surprised at their strength. Then they brought George in.

Abby looked at him through wired teeth. She whispered, "Are they gone?"

"Who?"

"Jody and Danny."

"They did this?" George felt the heat rise.

"It's all right," she whispered. "It's over now. Will you stay for a while?"

"Yes," George said. "I'll stay."

CHAPTER 37

RECKONING FIRE

Abby had awoken only a couple of times through the night. Even in her sleep, moans and soft cries escaped her now and then. During those hours, George did some deep, aching soul-searching. By early morning, he had decided: he would tell her everything—everything he and Marge had done to reach this point. But first, there were a few things he needed to take care of.

At daybreak, he went down to the hospital office as the staff began arriving. He spoke with the doctor about Abby's care and the cost, then paid the bill in full—with enough extra to cover any unforeseen expenses. From there, he went to the airport and bought a one-way ticket to Bend, Oregon, in Abby's name. She had mentioned once that her son and two daughters lived there. Then he returned to her bedside.

Just after 11:00 a.m., Abby stirred awake. George leaned forward. "Abby, we've got to talk."

He began from the beginning and told her everything—his friendship with Phil, the murder at Marge's urging, the makeovers, the false names, and finally, his guilt and shame for living a lie. Tears streamed down his face.

"So, you see," he said at last, "I'm not the man you think I am. I'm a liar, a cheat, and a murderer."

Abby looked at him with eyes full of compassion—spiritual love, not pity. "You know, George—or Terrance, whoever you are—Jesus died for you as well as for me. If you ask Him to, He will forgive you and dwell in your heart."

"I don't know, Abby," George said, his voice heavy. "I don't know if He ever could. I've been a mess all my life. Always scoffing. Maybe someday I'll try, but I've got a few more things to take care of first."

"George, you shouldn't wait. How do you know you've got time?" she asked.

"It's a chance I'll have to take, I guess." He reached for her hand. "Abby, I've paid the bill, and there's a plane ticket waiting for you at the airport—to Bend, Oregon, where your kids are."

"But I can't accept that—not from money that..." she trailed off.

"It's not," he lied softly. "It's money from my friends in Puerto Vallarta." In truth, Wayne had given it to him, but it was money George had once given Wayne himself. "Besides, everything's been paid for. You might as well use it."

"Well, all right then," she said. "In that case, I'll do it. But where are you going, and what will you do? I think you should turn your life over to God, turn yourself in, and face whatever's ahead—let Jesus give you strength. If you're thinking of going after Jody, or whatever her name is, the Lord says vengeance is His. Let Him handle that."

"I'm not there yet, Abby. I've got to do some things my way," George said.

"Please, listen, George—"

"Shhh." He coaxed gently. "Don't worry, my friend. I'll be all right. I hope to see you again."

He bent down and kissed her forehead, then turned and walked out. It hurt him to leave her that way, but he knew she'd be all right now. All he wanted was to find Danny and Marge.

At the airport, he checked the monitor for flights. There was one at 3:00 p.m. He asked the attendant if it was the earliest.

"Yes, sir. Mexican Air only has three flights a day to Puerto Vallarta—9:00 a.m., 3:00 p.m., and 9:00 p.m. If you're in a hurry, you might try Gulf Express."

"Well, it's 1:00 p.m. now. I'll just wait."

He bought his ticket and sat in the concourse, lost in thought about what he would say—and do.

"Sir... sir, I believe this is your flight," said the stewardess, shaking his arm gently to wake him.

It took him a moment to get his bearings. "Oh, yeah. I must've fallen asleep. I'm sorry."

"That's all right, sir. I just didn't want you to miss your flight."

"Thanks—a lot," George said as he hurried down the ramp.

He took his seat by the window, still unsure what he would say. Then Abby's words echoed: *Jesus will forgive you and dwell in your heart. Give your heart to Him and let Him lead you.*

As he pondered those words, he decided—he would ask Marge to turn to God with him, and they would both face the consequences. It was the only way.

When the plane landed in Puerto Vallarta, George moved quickly through the terminal and flagged a taxi. There weren't many passengers today—about eight cabs sat idle.

"Where to, sir?" asked the cabby in broken English.

"LaJon Drive."

"Sí," the cabby said, turning on the meter and pulling away.

George felt his adrenaline spike. Fifteen minutes later they pulled up in front of the house he and Marge had bought. "Stay put. I'll be back," he said.

"Sí."

George's palms were damp. He walked up the path, noticing the cherubim were gone. Without knocking, he opened the door.

"Is anyone home?" he called into the living room.

Marge appeared from the kitchen, wide-eyed. "Danny!" she shouted. "Guess who's coming to dinner!"

Danny stepped out behind her, smirking. "This has got to be a dream come true."

"Marge, we've got to talk," George said.

"You got that right. Where's my money?" she snapped.

"Listen. I've been thinking. Abby's right. We need to look to God for help—for guidance."

"What?"

"You know—turn ourselves in. Let God lead us from here."

"Are you crazy? You stupid idiot! You're gonna listen to an old windbag? You'll let someone like Phil run your life again? I want no part of it! Now where's my money?"

"What money? Go to the bank—you got your half," he shot back.

"Evidently, you haven't been to the bank lately, have you?" she yelled.

"No."

"Well, Mr. Smarty, if you had, you'd know all our assets have been frozen."

"If that's the case, then what money are you talking about?"

"The four hundred fifty thousand dollars you swindled me out of before you left here! The extra money you got padding the bills for your toys! Oh, I found out, George. And now I want it all—or Danny will talk to you like he did Abby."

George's anger flared. "And that's another thing—why did you even touch her? She had nothing to do with this! You almost killed her!"

"It's a pity we didn't," Marge snarled.

George couldn't hold back. He lunged, slapping Marge so hard she hit the wall by the glass doors. As he started toward her again, a boot struck his stomach, hurling him backward to the front door. He rolled just as another kick missed his head. Jumping to his feet, he took a fist to the cheek—blood spattered the floor.

He swung wildly, landing a blow. His eyes watered from the hit, but as he wiped them, he saw Danny staggering up, nose bleeding.

Danny lunged. George ducked, but a left kick caught him in the back and sent him sprawling. He rolled right, stomped, missed—grabbed Danny's ankle, twisted, and dropped him. George scrambled up and kicked Danny square in the face, sending him over backward. But Danny rose again, circling like a tiger ready to strike.

Hands raised in a karate stance, he struck. The kick to George's head landed fast and solid. Everything slowed. George saw the coffee table tilt beneath him, the dish of scented oil sail over the couch, ignited the fabric, the next kick crash into his mouth—and then the wall. He slid down, dazed.

"Danny! Stop! Don't finish him yet. I've got something to say," Marge shouted.

What's this? George thought. *Why is she stopping him?*

"George, do you hear me?" she asked.

He tried to speak but could only groan. His mouth was too swollen.

"George, if you think I'm going to kill you and collect your insurance—you're right. I'm going to tell them it was your idea, that you forced me to go along, and Danny rescued me because you were going to kill me. Oh, and George—about Phil? I lied. He never made a pass at me. I just said that to get you to go along."

She laughed—a shrill, manic sound.

Then, from somewhere deep within George came a low growl. It rose until Marge stopped laughing. His leg lashed out, catching her squarely and knocking her to the floor.

He started toward her, but Danny's kick sent him crashing against the kitchen doorframe. George rebounded, swung, and caught Danny under the chin, sending him sprawling in front of the burning couch.

For the first time, Danny froze. Fire was his weakness. He stared at the flames, paralyzed.

George seized the chance, pummeling him—fists to the face, stomach, ribs, anywhere he could reach. All the rage he'd buried surged through his blows.

Then—a blast. Pain ripped through his left arm; it went limp. Marge stood, pistol raised.

Without thinking, George dove through the window. Glass exploded around him. He hit the ground running, sprinting for the taxi.

The cabby's eyes went wide, white as dinner plates. George dove through the open window. "Get out of here!" he shouted.

The driver slammed the pedal down. Tires screamed for half a block before catching.

"Where to now, señor?" he asked, voice shaking.

"To Marina Puerto Rey—and hurry!"

"Sí. I know a shortcut."

"Fine. Just don't make it too bumpy," George said through gritted teeth.

At the marina, he slipped a hundred-dollar bill into the cabby's hand. "Help me get to Pier 24, Slip 212," he said, light-headed.

"Sí, señor."

The cabby stopped, came around, and helped him out. "You lose a lot of blood, meester."

"Yeah, I know. If I can just make it to Pier 24, Slip 212, I'll be all right."

"Okay. Let's get you there."

The driver looped George's good arm over his shoulder and steadied him by the waist. Slowly, they moved forward.

It seemed like forever before George heard Muriel's voice. "Wayne! Wayne! Come quick—it's Terrance, and he's hurt!"

He could barely see, the world a brown haze. Then he felt Wayne's strong hands catch him as everything went dark.

CHAPTER 38

THE DOVE ON THE STERN

George awoke to the slow, steady hum of an engine piercing the darkness in his head. Shards of light kept busting through the blackness as his eyes fluttered, trying to open. When he did get one open, it was only a slit; the other was nearly swollen shut. The fight with Danny had taken more of a toll than he thought. His nose was broken, one eye blackened, his split lips bandaged. His ribs—every breath hurt. If this wasn't hell, it felt close. His shoulder throbbed, and every time he tried to move his arm a searing pain shot through him—bad enough to make him want to scream, if he hadn't been so weak.

Then a cool rag wiped his forehead. Oh, that felt good.

"So, you decided to rejoin the living?" Muriel said.

George blinked a couple more times until things began to form. "Yeah. That you, Muriel?"

"It's me, sweetie. How do you feel?"

"Like the last rites are past due. Where are we?"

"We're about five miles out and sixty miles south of where we were. Once we got you aboard, we figured it was time to leave. We were ready anyway—we get tired of a place if we stay too long."

"What's our destination?"

"Not sure right now. Wherever Wayne decides to set down, probably. He likes land fine, but he sure loves the sea. Sometimes I think he loves it more than me. I don't mind—she's a beautiful woman." She paused. "By the way, who shot you?"

"Shot me? What do you mean, who shot me?"

"Someone put a hole in your shoulder. Didn't hit bone, so you'll be all right in a few days."

"I don't know... I think... well, Danny and I were fighting and the couch caught fire. Danny... was afraid—yes, he was afraid of the fire—and I heard a loud bang, a blast, something." George grabbed at his shoulder and went on. "That's when my arm went limp and burned like fire. I turned, and there was Marge pointing a gun at me. I dove out the front window, ran to the taxi that was waiting, and told him to hurry and take me to your yacht."

"So who's Marge?" Muriel asked as she worked an afghan.

"She's my wife. Or was."

"But I thought you said her name was Jody. Come on, sweetie—spill the beans."

About then the engine slowed and shut off.

"Muriel, we're going to drop anchor here tonight. Is our guest awake yet?" Wayne called down the comm tube.

"Okay, dear! Yes—he's awake! Hurry down; he's going to tell us something!"

"Be right there!"

They heard the chain rattle and the splash as the anchor hit the water. Then Wayne's heavy steps crossed the deck and thumped down the companionway. Muriel helped George up from the bunk and carefully eased him into the galley.

"Hey, my boy! How do you feel?" Wayne asked.

"Let's put it this way—now I know what a rabbit feels like after it gets hit by an eighteen-wheeler," George wheezed.

"Hahaha—yeah, I guess you would." Wayne grinned. "Muriel says you're going to tell us a story. What about?"

"It's about me. I'm not Terrance Weinberger. I'm George Wetzel. My wife—Marge, not Jody; Jody's fake, too—and I killed a man for his money. He won the lottery, so we took his ticket, changed our names, had makeovers, and ran for parts unknown. We ended up here in Puerto Vallarta. She started acting like some rich snob and I couldn't. She hooked up with a guy from the gym, I started drinking, and I split—took half the money and tried to start over in Mexico City."

Wayne wrinkled his nose. "Why on earth would you try there? That's the last place I'd go. Lucky you had sense enough to look us up this time."

"I couldn't go back there. They knew my hotel room. They were there first. They beat my maid unconscious—she was in a coma for six days. When she woke up and I knew she'd be all right, I paid the hospital bill, bought her a ticket home, then came back to find Marge. I tried to talk to her. My maid said God would forgive us and we should turn ourselves in after we turned our lives over to God. What do you think? Should I try to pray?"

"Whoa, wait up. Number one, that's just a myth. Don't get caught up in that foolishness," Wayne said. "People been saying that for years. 'Repent, repent, repent! Jesus is coming back. God's going to punish this world.' Ever since I can remember. Don't believe it—it's just something else to spend your money on. Muriel, could you get Terrance"—he winked—"and me a beer?"

"Okay, sweetie, but I want to hear the rest," Muriel said.

"That's about it," George said. "You've got it all. Only thing I left out were the dumb details."

"Phooey! That wasn't very exciting. Tell him our story, Wayne," Muriel said.

Wayne's eyes twinkled. "Boy, you ever hear of Marc Williams and Penny Martin?"

A light clicked on behind George's bruised eyes. "Not since I was about fourteen. Biggest criminals in fifty years. Supposedly killed."

"They were," Wayne said, "and I'll tell you why. They killed six cops, robbed eighteen banks, and hit one Brink's truck—and walked off with, I might add, a tidy sum. Twenty-three million plus. How d'you think we got this boat?"

"You're M-m-m-arc Williams? She's P-p-p-enny Martin?" George sat with his mouth agape.

"In the flesh. Ain't been caught yet. Now we're so old, even if God were real, He couldn't catch us," Wayne snickered.

"Who'd have guessed. You're not spoofing me?"

"On my word." Wayne raised a Scout salute.

"Wow. I'm amazed," George said.

Muriel grinned. "Now that's a story!" They all laughed. She patted Wayne's knee and stood. "You boys want anything besides beer? Something to eat?"

George couldn't remember his last meal, and the word *food* hit like a drum. "Well, now that you mention it, you got a small snack—like a whole side of beef?"

She winked. "You're gonna be just fine, sweetie," Muriel said. Wayne chuckled.

"You stick with us, son. We won't guide you wrong," Wayne said.

"I figure we'll stay offshore about six days—get you past any relapse or pneumonia. Then we'll head for Tahiti. Ever been?"

George shook his head. He was so flabbergasted he almost set his beer on the floor instead of the table.

"'Tis a beautiful place. You'll like it. Maybe even find yourself another gal. Pick one like my Muriel—she's the greatest," Wayne mused.

"It sounds nice, but I can't afford it. I'd like to help with expenses, but..." George trailed off.

"Hey, you're the only kin we got," Wayne said. "We'll head around the Horn and plot our course from there."

"Why not go back up to Panama and take the locks?" Muriel asked.

"Ever been there?" Wayne said to George.

"No," George admitted.

"Wayne's taken us through a time or two. It's a nice way to reach the other side of this landmass," Muriel said, looking up from her crocheting.

"Yeah, might be better. The Horn gets rough this time of year. Besides, Panama's got good beer. You'll like it, Terrance," Wayne boasted.

George smiled. "You, my friend, are truly a wise man. Tell me—how'd you get away without being caught?"

"From where and by whom?" Muriel teased.

"I mean everybody was looking for you two—and found nothing... right?"

"Oh, but they did, my boy," Wayne said. "They found our plane at the bottom of the mountains in Colorado—took 'em four years. Found a man and a woman—well, skeletons—in our clothes with our IDs. Found a little money. Just enough to close the case. That's how we got away. They figured the rest either blew off or burned up. We made 'em think that—parachuted before the crash, hiked back in, scattered luggage, broke open a case with some money and threw it around. The plane wasn't burning yet, so we lit it and tossed in some cash. No trees around—no forest fire. We walked out under new names. First thing we did was head to Mexico. Been gone ever since. Never went back."

"Amazing they didn't check for DNA," George said.

"Weren't none back then. That was fifty years ago. They found bones thrown from a plane—no way to walk out. Last cops on our trail never put two and two together," Wayne said.

"Well, Captain Wayne, if you want, we can have a bite to eat," Muriel said.

"Muriel, you're a doll. Don't you just love her, kid?" Wayne said.

George smiled at the two of them and wondered how two ruthless killers had become lifelong mates—and whether they'd be together to the end.

It took quite a while to reach the Panama Canal, and more time to work through the canals and locks to the Atlantic. A canal pilot guided them. They saw the Thatcher Ferry Bridge, towns like La Boca, Balboa Heights, Balboa itself, Cristóbal, Colón. Then the locks—Mica Flores and Jatin Locks. By the time they reached Limón Bay at Cristóbal, George had almost given up on ever seeing the East Coast. The pilot left there; after they picked up a few things at the harbor market, they headed for the Atlantic and then north to new adventures.

It was pretty dark when they reached the shipping lanes, set their course, and settled in for the night. Around 2:00 a.m., the engine quit and all power died. No lights—nothing. Wayne tried everything to bring power back. The batteries were dead, and so was the boat—dead in the water. Worst of all, they were in the shipping lane at night in a blacked-out yacht.

Wayne was getting frantic when his worst fear came true: a giant container ship was bearing down. Muriel screamed. Wayne stood wide-eyed, mouth open. And the only thing George could think of were Wayne's words: *We're so old now God can't even catch us.* George knew it was over—for them, and for him.

He shouted, "Oh, Lord, not this way! Please—I'll do anything. Forgive me—tell me what to do! Please don't let me go out this way!" He burst into tears as the ship closed in.

The container ship caught the yacht midship. It came apart like pickup sticks. What felt like twenty minutes of destruction was over in seconds. Water rolled over George's head as he went under. He thought he'd never surface, then burst up and gasped for air. Nothing of the yacht remained. The only thing in sight was the small rowboat Wayne had always said was just for looks. Now it was George's only hope.

He scrambled in and scanned the water for Wayne and Muriel. He called and called. No answer. Nowhere. God had caught up with them—the hard way.

As George drifted, his mind spun. Had God heard him? Was he still going to die? He remembered Phil and began to weep again. *Why did I let greed in? I was doing fine before the ticket. Why did I let Marge talk me into killing Phil?* He wrestled with that and with every lie and cheat. After two days of such thoughts, he looked up—and there on the stern sat a dove, staring at him.

Now this is strange, he thought. *Middle of the ocean—nowhere to go, nothing to eat—and you're still here. Why are you still here?* The dove just looked back. His thoughts returned to Phil, to Marge, to Wayne and Muriel—and again the words echoed, *We're so old now God can't even catch us.*

George looked up and said, "Okay, Lord—forgive me for the wrong I've done. I give myself to You right now, and if You get me out of this, I will serve You—no matter when or where. As of now, I'm Yours." He wept hard.

At that, the dove lifted off and flew away.

The very next day, George saw a ship on the horizon—the only one he'd seen. Why? He couldn't say. But he knew it was of God.

CHAPTER 39

MERCY IN CHAINS

It took a good half hour after being seen by the ship before George was on the deck. Then, after a meal, a bath, and a set of clean clothes furnished by the captain, George sat in the captain's office. He learned the ship was headed home to Brazil.

George told the captain his story and how he wanted to face what he had done and turn himself in. The captain tried to talk him out of it. "But you're free now! Live in Brazil. It is a beautiful country and no one can find you there."

George was adamant about going back.

After docking, George figured that if he turned himself in to the authorities in Brazil, they would send him to America to face charges. So he did. The authorities, in turn, thought he was crazy. They said, "Why tell us about it? We've got our own problems. If you're dead set on doing that, find a ship going back to America and turn yourself in. We don't want you."

George asked the captain to help him find a ship going to America, and he did. It took another couple of days, but after meeting the new captain, the first captain from Brazil left. George decided to tell the new captain his story as well.

They walked and talked along the dock. George said he had to get to Florida to turn himself in and then be sent back to Idaho to face charges for what he had done.

"Are you sure you want this?" asked the captain in broken English. He sounded German to George—another hint was the ship's name, the *Heikendorf*.

"Yes, sir. I'm sure of it. That's the only thing I want to do," said George.

"Ah, but you got your freedom. You can go anywhere you like," the captain said.

"No. I've got to go back. I can't live with what I've done."

"I'm going to have to lock you up in the hold, you know."

"Well, if you must, you must," George agreed.

"Done. But I must say, I like a man who is honest. I'll take good care of you until we turn you over to the authorities in America."

"Thank you, sir."

George found himself in a 10-by-12-foot room in the belly of the ship. It was a cargo ship, well loaded, heading for America. The room wasn't bad. The captain made sure he had reading material, a toilet, and a radio. His meals matched what the crew and captain ate—good on the captain's word.

It took a while to get to Miami, Florida. On the last day of the trip, the captain came down to visit George.

"This is your last chance, my friend. I can let you go if you'd like. Anywhere you go you'll be—"

"No, sir. My mind is made up. I've got to go back. I will never be free until I do," George said.

"I understand," said the captain.

"I'm not so sure I do, but I've got to do it," George answered solemnly.

"Well then, I'll call the authorities just before we dock and have them waiting for you. Take care, and I wish you the best. May God have mercy on you."

"Thank you, sir. You've been most kind."

George's demeanor had changed. He didn't want booze any-more. He didn't know what he wanted other than to be polite and kind. He felt like a new man, and deep inside was an urgent desire to go back and pay for what he had done. He knew he would never be completely free until then. About five hours later, whistles and horns began to blow. They were entering the harbor.

The captain went to his office and called the Miami Police De-partment.

"Hello, this is Sergeant Hansen. Can I help you?"

"This is the captain of the *Heikendorf* out of Germany. I have a prisoner in my custody who would like to turn himself in."

"Do you have a name for me?" asked Sergeant Hansen.

"Yes. His name is George Wetzel. He says he is wanted in the state of Idaho. Can you help me?"

"Okay—Wetzel, George. Does he have a middle initial?"

"Yes. It is W."

"Got it. I'll contact Idaho and see what I can find out. Will it be possible to have you hold him for a few hours until we confirm?"

"Of course. We'll be in dock for three more days."

"Great."

George heard several footsteps coming his way. One set was the captain's—he knew that stride. The others had to be at least two officers. He heard the key enter the door and couldn't swallow the lump in his throat. *Why didn't you take the boat? Why didn't you run? It's all over now. What have you done?*

The door opened. The captain stepped in with another ship's officer and two plainclothes detectives. They showed badges and placed George under arrest. Before the cuffs went on, the captain shook his hand once more and said, "I wish you would have taken my advice."

George smiled. "Me too."

He spent four days in county jail before a lawyer came to see him. "My name is Lonny—Lonny Stuckland. I'm here to represent you in your extradition hearing."

"Just waive it," said George.

"What? You can't. I'm going to defend you!"

"Do you not work for me?" George asked.

"Well—yeah," said Lonny, dumbfounded.

"Then waive it."

"Nobody ever does that. I mean, how can I get paid—I mean—"

"Yeah, that's what I thought. Just waive it, or I'll find someone who will," said George.

"But they can't prove—"

"Waive it! Guard! Guard!"

"Okay! You win. I'll waive it."

Looking out his cell window at the warm Miami sun, George wished he had taken the captain up on his offer—yet he knew he had made the right decision.

Time dragged while paperwork and transport slips were processed, connections made with the Boise office, and word sent that they had the man they'd been looking for. Boise notified Sheriff Gage in Main Ville and asked if he wanted to help escort George Wetzel back.

Since Boise had been working the case, two detectives were cleared to retrieve George and bring him back. Not quite believing it was happening, Detective Pointer and Detective Jones boarded a plane for Miami.

"Too bad we don't have time for the beach. That would be nice," said Pointer.

"Sure would," said Jonesy, already looking for a menu. "Ah, stewardess—do you know what we're having for lunch?"

"We'll be serving trays soon, sir—in approximately twenty minutes. I think it's Salisbury steak," she said.

"Is it fresh?"

"No, sir. It's precooked and prepacked. We warm it up and serve it."

"Is it any good?"

"Well, the captain ate it—but he had to go home as soon as we landed."

"Was he sick—diarrhea or something?"

"No, he lives here."

"Oh. You had me scared," Jonesy said, wide-eyed.

"Jonesy, you're such a putz. Why do you always have to eat? Can't you get a hobby?" asked Pointer.

"Eating is my hobby. When I get nervous, I eat. When I get scared, I eat. When I get bored, I eat. When I get—"

"I know, I know—you eat," Pointer finished.

"No. When I'm happy, I read a book. So there."

Pointer had to smile. This was going to be an interesting trip. She shook her head and looked out the window.

"Hey, Pointer, you got any peanuts?"

"What is it now?"

"What?"

"Are you scared, nervous, bored, or what?"

"Oh, I'm scared. Never been on a plane before."

"Relax. Safe as driving a car," said Pointer.

"Yeah? Did you know two planes went down yesterday in the world—and across this country alone probably 400 people were killed in car wrecks?"

"You're impossible. Just go to sleep. That way it won't bother you."

The plane started to taxi away but stopped, then taxied back to the concourse.

"What's happening now? See? I told you something would go wrong," stammered Jonesy.

Pointer gave him the oh-please-shut-up look.

"Ladies and gentlemen, this is your captain speaking. There will be a slight delay. We have returned to pick up a couple of late arrivals. We apologize for any inconvenience. Rest assured—there are no problems. Thank you, and have a nice flight."

"Sure, they say that now. Just watch—they'll have the mechanics out here shortly," puffed Jonesy.

"Jonesy! Read a book or something, will you? You're getting on my nerves," said Pointer.

"I can't help it. I—"

"Do you want me to gag you?"

"All right! I'll be quiet."

As the two passengers boarded, they spoke to the stewardess, who pointed toward Pointer and Jonesy. They walked down the aisle.

"I'm Sheriff Gage, and this is Deputy Pipcorn. We're from the Idaho County Sheriff's Department in Main Ville. We've been working with you on this case and thought it best to go down with you to get the prisoner. We'll want custody—no problem with that, I hope."

"Yeah, but he's our prisoner!" Jonesy blurted.

"We appreciate your work with our department, Jonesy," Gage said evenly, "but we're trying him in my county. The murder happened there, and he's going back there."

"Jonesy," Pointer said, "the sheriff is right. We've been aiding him—this isn't our case. Sheriff, please join us."

"How long have you been on the force?" Pointer asked.

"Here in Idaho, ten years. Law enforcement in Dallas for six before that," Gage replied.

"What brought you to Idaho?"

"My parents were up north in Main Ville. I loved the country. I applied, got accepted right off, and here I am."

"I thought you were from the South," added Jonesy. "Heard your accent."

Gage smiled. "You folks have an accent to me."

"You'll have to forgive my partner," Pointer said. "He's peculiar—but he grows on you."

"What do you mean peculiar? I'm just hungry, that's all," Jonesy muttered.

Somewhere over Tulsa the jet hit bad turbulence. Jonesy jumped halfway into the aisle. "Hostess—I mean maid—I mean attendant! Are we going down? What do we do? What happens when we hit?" Sweat beaded on his forehead; his eyes looked too big for their sockets.

"Please, sir—back in your seat and buckle up. We are not crashing. This is just turbulence. No need to panic. We're fine," she assured him.

"I'm sorry, miss," Pointer said. "He's never flown before."

"I figured—but didn't want to say it. Sir, I'm sorry for being forceful, but you know what happens if panic breaks out? Please—let me get you something."

"Peanuts. Lots of peanuts," Jonesy mumbled.

Sheriff Gage woke at the commotion. "Jonesy, let me tell you a story. Two kids—a boy and a girl—visited their grandma in Dallas. She sent them to the store for bread and eggs. A drunk driver came along and just missed them. He swerved into a picket fence fifty feet away. One picket flew back and killed the little girl."

"So what's the meaning?" asked Jonesy.

"No matter where you are or what you're doing, when your number is called, you're gone. Not before, not after," said Gage.

Jonesy blinked, mouth open, then sat back to ponder. He was quiet the rest of the trip.

With the exceptions of stops in Salt Lake City and Dallas—where Jonesy, of course, had to eat—the Dallas-to-Miami leg was uneventful. Jonesy slept, to everyone's relief.

Officer Pointer leaned toward Sheriff Gage. "This is the last trip I make with him," she said, nodding at Jonesy. "All our expense money has gone into his stomach." They chuckled. Since it was late afternoon when they arrived in Miami, Sheriff Gage and Detective Pointer decided to stay the night and start paperwork and pickup in the morning.

Upon hearing they were staying the night, Jonesy immediately wondered about room service and the menu. "Boy, Jonesy," said Pointer, "just how much of your paycheck goes for food?"

"I can't help it," Jonesy said. "I get hungry when I get—"

"Yeah, we know," said Sheriff Gage. "Whenever something comes along." They all laughed—except Jonesy.

After dinner, the four retired. Thankfully, Sheriff Gage and Deputy Pipcorn shared a room, Detective Pointer and Jonesy had separate rooms. Jonesy, snored like thunder. Even in another room, he was so loud that Gage and Pipcorn both woke twice. Jonesy sounded like a locomotive plowing through a nitro factory.

Morning came. Jonesy, after a restful night, headed straight for the breakfast buffet. The others followed, reluctantly.

At 9:00 a.m. they walked into the Miami Police Station to pick up the prisoner.

"May I help you?" asked a clerk behind the desk.

"Yes. I'm Sheriff Gage; this is Detective Pointer, Deputy Pipcorn, and Detective Jones. We're here for the prisoner, George Wetzel."

"Oh, great," said the clerk. "I'll need to see some IDs and your transport papers."

"Of course," said Sheriff Gage, as Detective Pointer produced the paperwork and they all showed IDs.

"Everything looks in order," the clerk said after a few minutes. "I'll notify my supervisor and we'll bring out Mr. Wetzel."

George had just finished biscuits and gravy with bacon when the jailer walked up. "Hey, Wetzel. Looks like your wish came true. The officers from Idaho are here. They'll be ready for you in about an hour, so be ready to go."

"Thank you, sir. I appreciate the heads-up," George said.

"Just doing my job," said the jailer.

About a half hour later the jailer cuffed George and led him to the foyer. Sheriff Gage exchanged cuffs. "I'm not going to make these too tight—we have a lot of traveling to do. Might as well be a little comfortable."

"Thanks," said George.

In the next 30 minutes the officers came in, introduced themselves, transferred custody, and told him they would leave for Idaho within two hours. In a way, George felt relieved; in another, dread. He didn't know what would become of him in Idaho. For now, they took the cuffs off and placed him in a holding cell. The air-system compressor kicked on, sounding to George like it might blow apart. He thought what a blessing that would be if it did—and blew the room he was in to smithereens. It would be over then. Or a plane wreck on the way back to Idaho. Anything, just to be done with it all. He even prayed for something to take his life. Nothing happened. He had to go back.

Two hours became two and a half. George began to sweat. Did they forget him? Did something come up? Were they ever going back? His first time in trouble—he didn't know what to expect. He even wished he'd gone down in the shipwreck. But here they came.

After the jailer opened the cell, Sheriff Gage and Deputy Pipcorn stepped in and cuffed George. "It's time to go, Mr. Wetzel. Are you ready?" asked Sheriff Gage.

"Would it matter?" George half smiled.

"No—no, I guess it wouldn't," the sheriff said, smiling back.

"I guess I am," George said with a nervous smile.

The Miami Police Department took them to the airport. Gage and Pipcorn rode with George; Pointer and Jonesy rode in a second car.

"Mr. Wetzel," asked Sheriff Gage, "since we'll be on a long trip back, do you mind if I call you George? Or would you prefer Terrance?"

"Please call me George. I never liked that rich garbage anyway."

The sheriff nodded. "Thank your lucky stars we came down here, too. Ol' Jonesy would probably have driven you crazy on the way home. Almost drove us crazy coming down."

George smiled. "Reminds me of some of the guys I met while waiting for you."

"Yeah, I bet," said Sheriff Gage.

They fell quiet until they reached the airport; the radio dispatcher was the only voice.

After boarding the first flight back, George fell into a sort of trance. His mind re-ran the events that put him on this ride—so many regrets. Letting Marge talk him into the ticket. Killing his friend. Why would I do that? Why let money become my lust for life? Why believe Marge about Phil's supposed pass? How many times had she lied before? So why believe her then?

"Are you buckled in?" the stewardess asked Sheriff Gage.

"Yes. Buckled up and ready."

"You ready, Wetzel?" Jonesy smirked.

"Huh? Oh—yeah. I'm okay," George said.

As the plane took off, his mind shifted. Lord, I deserve what's coming. I can't blame anyone but me. I went along with it all; let me face it. But please—walk beside me. I can't make it alone. And please, Lord, let Marge see the error of her ways. Maybe she'll come around too.

Peace came. He and the officers spoke now and then, except for Jonesy, who peered down his nose with a loser's smirk. George let it go and closed his eyes. Maybe he could sleep—maybe.

After a long flight and two connections, they arrived at the Boise Airport. A police van met them; George was secured in back. They piled in for the station.

"Mr. Wetzel—" Sheriff Gage began.

"What are you being so nice for, Sheriff?" Jonesy cut in. "This guy is wanted on murder and everything else!"

"Jonesy! That's enough," Detective Pointer snapped. "One more outburst and you'll go on report." She meant it.

"Mr. Wetzel," Sheriff Gage continued, "we'll spend the night here and in the morning take a commuter to Main Ville. Anything you'd like?"

"No, sir. Well—maybe a bottle of water or two," George said.

"Sure. No problem," the jailer said.

"See you in the morning," said Sheriff Gage, and off they went.

"If you need something to eat," the jailer added, "we have leftovers from tonight's dinner."

"That would be fine," said George, settling on his bunk. Thin mattress, cement bed—the night would be long.

After breakfast, Sheriff Gage and Deputy Pipcorn returned and took custody. "Are the cuffs too tight?" Pipcorn asked.

"No, they're fine," said George. "One thing, though—this 'Mr.' stuff is mainly for the rich and snobbish. Could you just call me George?"

Pipcorn smiled. "Okay. George it is."

"As you wish," said Sheriff Gage.

As they walked out the front door, Jonesy met them coming in. "Have a nice trip, Officers. Hope he won't give you any trouble."

"Jonesy! Shut up and get in here," the duty captain barked. Detective Pointer stood beside him; Jonesy looked scared. He knew he was in trouble. Sheriff Gage and Deputy Pipcorn smiled at each other—then at George. Gage winked. "Justice at last." All three chuckled as they headed to the airport.

The plane was a small Learjet; the flight to Main Ville was short. A Main Ville Sheriff's Office van met them. Minutes later, George lay on a bunk in a cell with three other men—his home until the preliminary hearing scheduled in three weeks.

For three weeks George ate, had one hour of recreation a day, and talked with the guys in the cell. Not much happened—except on Sundays, when he went to a church service held in a larger jail cell at the courthouse. Only a few men came, but George liked it.

On the day of the hearing, they brought him in. Three others waited for prelims. George went first. The judge asked, "Do you have a lawyer?"

"No," George said. "Sir, I'd just like to get this over with so I can get on with my life."

"Mr. Wetzel, you should have counsel to help with what's ahead," said the judge.

"Well, sir—I'm guilty, and I'd like to tell everyone exactly what happened so all the questions are answered," George said.

"Well—okay," said the judge. "But I'll make sure you have a lawyer the next time we meet. Let's say—will three months give you enough time to prepare, Mr. Wetzel?"

"Yes, sir. I believe it will," said George. And with that, he was led back to his cell.

CHAPTER 40

BLUEPRINT FOR EVIL

M arge stood with the fire extinguisher in her hand, shaking so badly it trembled. It wasn't fear. It was the frenzied madness that had come over her from her hatred of George—worse now because he'd gotten away. She took a moment to regain her composure after putting out the fire and thinking of Danny. Then she ran to him.

"Danny! Are you all right?" He had finally tried to sit up. He had been beaten ruthlessly. "What happened? How come you couldn't beat him?"

"The fire. The fire—I'm afraid of fire," he sputtered.

"What do you mean you're afraid of fire?"

"When I was young..." He tried to explain, but the beating made him hard to understand. "My sister and I were playing in my father's garage. I'd seen those guys on TV protesting things. They pour gas all over themselves and set themselves on fire." At this point he became really nervous, shaking and breathing harder. "I've never told no one how it happened. I told them I wasn't there. But I lied!" He started to cry and looked around as if terrified. "I poured a can of gas on my sister. I lit a match... and... and..." He covered his head, rocking as if someone were about to hurt him.

"No, no... I didn't know what would happen. Leave me alone!"
He started to scream.

"Danny! Danny! It's all right. Calm down. It's me—Jody! Remember? "

He peeked out over his arms, eyes darting as if searching for an attacker. Slowly he let his arms down. Marge saw he was visibly shaken.

"It's all over now. Take it easy," she said.

"Terrance is gone? What are we going to do now?"

"We'll think of something. We still have one bird in our nest. Remember Ginger?"

"Yeah?"

"Well," Marge said, helping him up and steering him to the kitchen to clean him up, "I believe her daddy would pay a pretty penny to get her back."

"You mean kidnap her?"

"In a way. It's more like extortion. Her for some money. Say... about $20 million."

"Do you think he'll pay it?"

"What do you think? She's the apple of his eye. All we've got to do is get her over here somehow. After that, it'll be a piece of cake."

"Ow! Take it easy!" Danny flinched.

"My poor baby. Did we hurt him?"

"Don't talk to me like that!" snapped Danny.

"Then man up a little. You're beginning to act like George—or Terrance, I mean."

"I heard you call him that once before. What is his name—George or Terrance?"

"Terrance, of course. I've told you he reminds me of my brother George. Now let's drop it. We have to come up with a plan. Let me see your ribs."

Danny lifted his shirt, wincing. Nothing felt broken, but his ribs were already turning black and blue; so were his legs, back, and arms. His face was a mess. Both eyes were swollen almost shut and blackened. His nose was broken and a few teeth loosened; only two were missing. A gash along his forehead bled until Marge cleaned it and set a butterfly bandage, which held for now.

"You're gonna be sore for a while," she said.

"What are we gonna do about the money?"

"Well, Danny, I'm thinking we'll probably never see Terrance again. We'll have to find ourselves another pigeon..." She was smiling now, a plan forming. "Danny, you know any abandoned, remote places no one goes anymore?"

"Well, there's one I used to prospect a few years ago. It's haunted, though."

"What do you mean it's haunted?"

"I mean it's haunted." Danny's heart began to race as he thought of the mine shaft. "I only went there three times, and I swore I'd never go back."

"What happened?"

"To start with, I felt watched. Every move I made—someone was watching. Then the moans and the screams... it was horrifying."

"Are you serious? Moans and screams? Probably just the wind," Marge smirked.

"No. There was no wind." Danny paled. "I'd set down my pick, look at a piece of ore, go to pick it up again—and it'd be ten feet away. After that, I tied my tools to me. But then I heard whispers."

"Yeah, people talking—only there was no one!" he said shakily.

"Well, sounds like the place we need. Can you find it again?"

"Sure."

"Then we're in business. Where is it?"

"About fifteen miles into the Sierra Madre from Mexico City. There are old Inca temple ruins there. Go three miles east of that, back in the canyon. The mouth of the shaft is hidden by a big rock and mesquite trees. You edge around the rock on a narrow path and through the trees, and then it opens into a small clearing—about thirty feet wide. To the left, maybe thirty feet, you'll see an opening in the mountain barely big enough to walk in if you bend over. It goes back quite a ways, I guess."

"You guess? Didn't you ever go to the end?"

"No. I was too scared. Let me tell you what happened. I dug through a wall and found myself in a room—about twenty square feet. There was a doorway at the far right. I went through it, down a little corridor, into a big room—maybe fifty square feet. In that room were many, many bodies. Looked like they'd been chained there and left—chained alive and left to die." Danny trembled. "That's when I swore I'd never go back. That place is cursed."

"Cursed?" she scoffed.

"Haven't you heard of Montezuma's curse? It's on this whole range—especially where the Spaniards made the Inca dig gold. It's supposed to get anyone who digs and takes any."

"Well, we're not going for gold, are we? At least not in that form. Will anyone find us there?"

"Like I said, it was my third time there and I went farther than before. I had my headlamp on. It seemed I'd left the opening miles behind—really it was only a couple hundred yards. I rounded a bend and saw a cave-in. I saw rocks that could've held gold, so I started digging. All of a sudden, I heard whispers—*Drop the rocks and leave.* Then louder: *Leave now!* So I dropped everything and got out. I haven't been back."

"No one would find you unless you told them and maybe drew a map. That's the only way."

"Well then, that's what you do—draw a map. I've got a plan. I want to see this place. Feel up to traveling?"

"Can we wait a couple of days?"

"I'd rather start now," Marge said. "We'll go up there, get a motel till you heal a little, then go see it. I don't want to wait—cash is tight. And we need to get our pigeon before she goes somewhere we can't reach her."

"Okay. Let's go, I guess."

"I want you to draw a map first. Make it readable, okay? Make it so they can find it easily. I want them to find her alive—so we get our money."

"I'll do the best I can. What are you going to do?"

"Pack some clothes."

While Danny drew the map—hard as it was with swollen eyes—Marge packed two suitcases. *Shouldn't take more than a couple of days,* she thought.

An hour later they were on the road. At first they didn't speak. After a while Marge said, "Let me see your map. I'm going to try to follow it right to the place."

"Okay."

"Are you sure this is right? You've got a lot of crossroads and forks here."

"I'm positive. I'll never forget that place—or how to get there."

"Okay. I'm going to study this map till I know it by heart." For the next few hours, she ran the route in her head—every crossroad, fork, and landmark. Six miles of road before the first crossroads; three forks and two small streams. On the first two forks, take a left. The two streams were before and after the forks, but before the crossroads—go straight there. Two and a half miles later, another fork—left again. Another mile to the second crossroad. Two more forks—left both times—then another stream, larger than the first two. The last five miles were switchbacks, with two forks and one more crossroad where they were to go right. That led to the ancient Inca ruins.

From there, turn left and go east about three miles. There would be the mouth of the ravine that led to the mine shaft—about one hundred fifty yards to the mouth, behind the boulder and through the trees.

"At last," she said. "I could take you there in the dark, I believe."

"We'll see. I'm no artist, you know."

"Oh, you'll do. Before we get lost in Mexico City, we'd better find a motel."

"I know one on the far side of town. Close to the road we want."

"Great."

Night fell before Danny pulled up in front of a very dilapidated building. As bad as it looked, a light glowed in a small window.

"Where are we?" asked Marge.

"This is the place. Doesn't look like much, but it's comfortable and the food's good."

"How did you ever find a disgusting place like this? I don't know if I want to stay here. *Yuck.*"

"It's better than it looks."

"It had better be."

Inside, a short, heavyset woman watched from behind the desk. She flashed a toothy grin—two teeth missing. "You like room? You hungry? Maybe you want both, no?"

"Yes, we'd like both," Danny replied.

She beamed. "You eat now. Get room later!" She ushered them to a corner table in the next room. Two other tables sat with dirty dishes.

Marge had to admit: the food wasn't bad. Whether it was truly good or she was simply starving she wasn't sure. Later, in the twin bed she had to sleep in, she found it surprisingly comfortable. *Maybe I'll get one for myself.* In no time she and Danny were asleep.

Morning sun breached the small window. As it hit Marge's eyes, she blinked a few times. She was about to yell when she remembered where they were and why. She rolled over, picked up her watch from the little stand between the twin beds, and read 8:35 a.m. Danny was still out, so she let him sleep until after her shower.

She slipped from bed, dropped her nightclothes on the floor, and crossed to an old dresser that had seen better days. On it: clean towels, washcloths, soap, and a cheap shampoo. She sniffed the soap. Pleasantly fragrant. Her brows rose; a small smile curled. Then she sniffed the shampoo. She nearly choked.

"Yuck!" Her brows furrowed; her nose wrinkled. She shook her head. "Revolting. No way I'm putting that on my hair!"

"What?" Danny mumbled.

"This shampoo is truly gross. I don't know what it's made of, but it stinks."

"Oh, that's aloe and lanolin. Down here they figure—why make it smell good? It's some of the best stuff for your hair, but yes, it stinks."

"You could've warned me! I'm not getting that smell out of my nose for weeks!"

"What do you mean? I just woke up. How am I supposed to warn you while I'm sleeping?" He was a little irate.

"Oh, never mind. Go back to sleep. Maybe you'll wake up in a better mood."

"Yeah, sure. You're in the bad mood, not me," he growled, rolling over and punching his pillow.

Marge made a face at him and stuck out her tongue—felt better already. She stepped into the bathroom, and locked the door. She wanted a nice, long, hot shower. First things first. She relieved herself, then, elbows on knees and chin in hands, started running the map in her head—every creek, crossroad, and fork. She pictured the entrance to the mine shaft—and jerked upright. *How are we going to see anything in the shaft? What were we thinking?*

"Danny!"

"What now?" He was more awake—and irritated.

"How are we going to see anything in the old mine shaft? We forgot about that!"

"No, we didn't. We'll stop at a friend's—Julio Martinez—and pick up a light there. Might need a few other things—a pick, a shovel. He's got it all."

"We're not digging for gold, you know," she retorted.

"That's true, but we'll need them anyway. Also, we'll need a gun. There might be snakes."

"Snakes? *Yuck.* Maybe I don't want to go."

"You're going. I'll protect you," he snickered.

"Yeah, I'll bet," she muttered. *Soon I'll be rid of you, too. I hope the next man I use is more eloquent than these last two.*

She stepped into the shower and, without looking, turned on the water—used to instant hot and clean. She got neither. With a scream she jumped back out. A brownish solution—*water*—flowed from the showerhead and down the drain.

"Danny!"

"Shee-e-e... I might as well get up! I guess the word *sleep* isn't used around here." Now he was fully awake. "What do you want this time?"

"Don't tell me this is the only stuff to shower in. Surely this isn't water!"

"It's the only water there is in these parts. Take it or leave it."

"Yeah? Maybe I should take or leave *you!* What do you think of that?"

"You know something? I don't think I need to spend any more time here. We're not going to work out. Your plan isn't going to work out. You're out of money and out of dope. I think I'll blow this place—without you!" Danny was furious.

Marge stormed out of the bathroom. "Oh, you do? And how long do you think it'll take me to sic the police on you? Look at my house. George is gone. My couch was set on fire, a window broken. I could smack myself around a bit, blame you. I could tell them about Ginger and say it was all your idea—that you forced me. *You* drew the map. I could give them that. I could also tell them about the secret compartment in your car—with money and some dope. You want to run, big boy? Go ahead. I dare you!" Her eyes were wide, tiger-bright. She watched his every move. She had him.

"What do you mean? You think I won't?" he stammered.

"Go ahead. I should let you. I can find someone else to help me while you spend the rest of your life in prison. Oh, and the pistol I shot George with? I bought it in *your* name. I wiped my prints before I gave it to you, so yours are the only ones on it. If he dies, you've got a murder beef. Yes, the gun's illegal. So if you want to run—" she smiled—"a few more charges won't hurt. Huh?"

He glared. "You can't get away with this. Anyway, what's in this for me?"

"Oh, I promise—if you stick around, you'll get whatever you've got coming," she gloated. "Then I'll gladly let you go. I only needed you to get rid of George anyway. Oh—did I say George again? We know I meant Terrance. And let's not forget the candy connection. Now the only thing I need you for is this last endeavor. I need money, not men. If I have money, I can get one anytime. I hate men, but every once in a while I can use one—like I used you. So it's up to you. Stick around and get rich, or go to prison. Your choice."

"Okay, you win. But I want half of everything we get. Then I'm gone. You hear?" Danny stormed back. "And how do I know you won't turn me in and keep everything?"

"You don't. That's the beauty of it. I've got all the bases covered and you've got nowhere to run." She wrinkled her nose and smiled. "Do we have a deal?"

"I guess so," Danny conceded. "I have no choice."

"Now you're getting the picture."

For the next hour they didn't speak—each lost in their own thoughts: hers on how to pull this off, his on why he'd ever gotten tangled with her. By 10:00 a.m. they'd thawed toward each other again.

"Jody," Danny said, earnest because he had nothing else, "I'm sorry for yelling. I'm tired and sore all over. I feel like I was hit by a steamroller that backed up to see what it hit and rolled over me again."

She laughed. "Danny, you have such a way with words. Yeah, me too. We both said some things that weren't nice." *(But they were all true.)* "Feel up to driving up there today? I'd like to get this done so we can have some money again."

"Yeah. I suppose I'm well enough. Sitting around won't help."

"Good. Let's get breakfast. We can leave after that."

By the time they'd eaten and Danny had called Julio to arrange a key for the shed—under the flowerpot by the door—it was 11:00 a.m. They hit the road to the mine shaft a little after 11:30 a.m. Another half hour and their tempers had cooled. He was in charge again; she was all loving. He thought she was faking every move.

Five miles down the old dirt road to the ruins, Danny pulled over. "Jody, honey, I'm sorry about earlier. I was being self-centered. Do you forgive me?"

"Well, let me see," she teased. "Maybe—if you forgive me. I said some things, too."

"Okay, then let's start the day over." He leaned over and kissed her. "Good morning, sweetheart."

"Mmm—good morning, love," Marge replied, pleased. He was eating out of her hand again.

She scooted beside him. He smiled, dropped the car in drive, and they started out. Another hour and a half put them at the temple ruins—the road rough, the pace slow.

"Let me drive from here," Marge said. "I want to see if I read your map right."

"Okay, the wheel's yours." Danny stopped, put it in park, circled the hood, and opened her door. She giggled like a schoolgirl, hopped out, and practically ran him over on her way to the driver side—like there was a prize for speed.

She smiled at him, wrinkling her nose, slid the shifter into drive, and they were off. A few minutes later they sat before a big boulder. Marge killed the engine.

"This must be the place."

"This is it," he agreed. "Hasn't changed much."

They got out. Danny stretched, then opened the trunk and pulled the lights and tools—shovels, axes, hammers.

"You really ready for this? I mean this spooky adventure?"

"I don't believe in spook tales," she giggled.

"Let's see what you say after we get out. I'm already scared—from what happened last time."

"We'll see," Marge said. "We'll see." They belted on the tools, set the hard hats, and flicked on the lamps. It took a few minutes to work around the boulder—the brush thicker than Danny remembered—but soon they stood in the clearing.

"I think the entrance is over there," Danny said, pointing left. "Behind the brush. Man, I've never seen anything grow so fast. This is outrageous. None of this was here before."

"Don't knock it. This makes it better. Nobody looks for what they can't see. If they don't know about the mine shaft, they won't find her—until Daddy dear does." Marge seemed six steps ahead of everyone.

"Yeah, I guess that makes sense," Danny said. "I hope he finds her—or she might die."

"Wouldn't that be a pity," Marge mocked.

Danny only stared. He was starting to see her cold side, and it scared him.

They finally found the entrance, nearly filled in. After a few minutes of hard work, it was open again. Then they went in.

CHAPTER 41

WHEN GOD CAUGHT UP

Slowly, they made their way back into the shaft—so slowly. Danny's heart was in his throat, his mouth dry. "Y-y-you all all right?" he stuttered.

"Boy, you are spoo—" Marge stopped because, at that moment, she heard a moan coming from somewhere in the darkness. She grabbed Danny's hand. "Maybe I misjudged your adventure. Let's keep going."

Even though the moaning kept up—and at times grew louder—they kept going and soon came to the place where the wall had caved in. The moans turned into whispers as they entered the big room. They could see where animals had been coming and going. They went down the corridor at the end of the room. Only this time Danny had brought along another marker to keep him from losing his way back to the opening in the wall. He had been so afraid the first time he almost missed it.

The corridor opened into another room, and there were the bones. The whispers stopped, but now a small rustle seemed to be coming from the bones that lay in front of them. Marge pushed closer to Danny when she heard the noise. Suddenly there was a piercing scream—Marge—because two rats ran in front of her. As the moans and whispers started up again, she said, "Let's get out of here. It's too creepy for me. It will, however, be perfect for Miss Ginger."

They couldn't get out of the shaft fast enough, and soon they were driving past the temple ruins on their way down. They never spoke until they reached Mexico City again.

"Danny, can we just go home? It will take a while, I know, but I just want to go home. I know I promised you a few days' rest, but that scared the devil out of me."

"Yeah, I suppose we could. I don't feel like doing anything but driving right now," Danny said. "Besides, the quicker we get there, the quicker we can get this whole ordeal done."

"True," was all Marge said.

It wasn't until they were sitting in front of Marge's house in Puerto Vallarta that Danny found his present consciousness. It seemed that when he got on the road, he left everything real and went somewhere else in his mind. What he realized was this: he wanted to run from this woman. He had found out how ruthless she was, but he couldn't, for the lust of money had him and was reeling him in like a fish on a line. Yes, he would stay—stay and hope all things worked out.

Marge, on the other hand, had succumbed to the realm of deep sleep. She wasn't even moved by the deed she was planning. Money was her god, and she didn't care what she had to do to get it. She had it figured out long ago: if you had money, you could do anything. You were the queen of the ball, and everyone would be at your beck and call. Nothing bothered her except the thought of no money.

"Jody... we're home." Danny coaxed her awake. The last thing he wanted now was a vicious wildcat in his hands. This was the second day since the beating, and he was aching in every part of his body.

"M-m-m—what?" asked Marge sleepily.

"We're home, dear." He winced at the word but figured it would soothe the beast lying under the surface of that beautiful face.

"Why didn't you wake me? I would have helped you drive." She was suddenly apologetic and sincere. "You must be completely worn out. Come on, I'll help you in the house. After a nice hot bath you'll feel much better." She rubbed her hand on his face, then pulled him close and kissed him. "Does that feel better now?"

"It's getting there," Danny smiled. Even though she was an evil beast, he still felt love for her. He now knew the feeling George—Terrance—had: wanting to get away but being chained to her. What a web he had woven this time.

It wasn't long before they were in the house. Danny had worked most of the soreness out by going into the mineshaft, but he was still a little stiff from being in one position for so long.

As they walked in the door, Danny asked, "So when do we make our move?"

"Well, we need a plan first—what we're going to say to get her here, even though that will be the easy part. But we also need to figure out what we're going to tell her father and where to meet him. You know, all the main things. The little things we can fill in as we go," Marge said.

"You've been thinking! That's good. You have a cell phone, so that will help," Danny said.

"What are you thinking?" asked Marge.

"Well, there's a small turnoff about two hours out of Mexico City. If we go there and go two miles, there's a small white building. We can meet him—or whoever he sends—there. We can let him know where to find her then," Danny suggested as Marge led him across the living room to the recliner. It was tipped over from the fight, so Marge righted it and Danny sat down.

"Yeah, that's great. You just sit there and I'll clean up a bit. You think of some more things and so will I, and we'll bring our ideas together. I'd like to get this done as soon as possible," Marge said.

"Me too," Danny agreed.

"Wait—I told you I would help you to the bathroom so you could have a nice bath, didn't I?" Marge, a little beside herself, helped him out of the chair and headed him up the stairwell to their room. "Okay, let's go up the stairs. Sometimes I let myself get distracted. I'm sorry, Danny."

"That's okay," he said. "That chair didn't seem too bad."

It seemed like Marge had cleaned for hours. But she was used to being a maid and forgot how hard it was to keep a house. It had really only been an hour and a half when she finally thought the job was finished. She would call a contractor to fix the window George jumped out of, and she and Danny would remove the couch. Hopefully before Ginger was brought over.

Danny, in the meantime, had finished his bath, dried off, slipped into George's bathrobe, and stretched out across the bed. He fell asleep.

Marge let him sleep until six in the evening. She had prepared a nice dinner, one of Danny's favorites: pork chops and shrimp scampi. She liked it, too, but she wanted to do something good for Danny. For some reason she felt sorry for him. She thought it might have been because he was so helpless when the couch was on fire. She thought he was much like a child then. Though she didn't want any children, she did let her heart be open to them.

At six-thirty that evening, Danny and Marge sat on the patio looking out over the ocean while eating their meal.

"Do you think we should let him know real soon?" asked Danny.

"Who—the senator?" Marge returned.

"Yeah. I thought maybe get him on the phone in Mexico City. Then, as he sends his man around with the money—I mean, I don't believe he'll bring it himself—we can call him and tell him to wait at the ruins of the temple. From there, when his man meets us, we can direct him to Ginger. Then we take the money and we're gone," Danny said slowly.

"Sounds good. But I want to leave her there for three days," Marge said sternly.

"Why?"

"She's been ripping me off for cocaine," Marge snapped. "Friends don't treat friends like that. They give them breaks. She didn't. The truth is, she has kept raising the price. Nope—she has to be taught a lesson. Just like her old man."

"Hey, I've got an idea," Danny said.

"What's that?"

"Why don't we have him bring us a new car? That way, if anybody wants to say they saw our car anywhere around there, they won't find us. We'll be long gone in a brand-new car."

"That just might work," Marge said. "We could take a taxi to that place, then take off from there. When they find our car, we'll be long gone."

"We could sell your car," Danny suggested.

"To who?"

"To Julio. He could even take us there and drop us off at that place."

"Perfect! That's perfect. That will work," Marge gloated. "Tomorrow morning... I think I'll give Ginger a call. We got enough candy for tonight?"

"Yeah, I think so. You might want her to bring some extra tomorrow, though," Danny added.

"Way ahead of you, dear."

The phone rang four times before Marge heard fumbling on the other end and a sleepy, "Hello?"

"Ginger, darling! I thought you'd be up by now. It's almost eleven-thirty in the morning!" Marge feigned a joyous mood while, in the back of her mind, a plot brewed—sinister and black as coal.

"Is it really that late, Jody?" Ginger asked. "I must get up, then. Is it a nice day?"

"Beautiful! The sun is up, the birds are calling, life is wonderful! Hurry and come over and we'll have some brunch," said Marge.

"I could use that! Okay, I'll be there shortly."

"Love, could you bring about four or five of our little friends?" Marge asked, meaning eight-balls of cocaine. "I've got a little get-together planned for later."

"Oh really? Maybe I'll bring more than that. You never know who could use some."

"What's for brunch anyway?"

"What would you like?"

"How about some BLTs? Does that sound good?"

"BLTs it is!"

"Oh—and plenty of coffee, okay?"

"That's perking right now, girl," Marge said.

"All right. See you in a bit. Ta-ta." The line went dead.

"Well, what's up?" asked Danny.

"She'll be here in a little bit. What we have to do is crush up some sleeping pills so we can put them in her coffee. Then after we have our BLTs, she'll be out like a light and we can be on our way," Marge said, pleased with herself.

"Is she going to bring five or so of our little candy friends?"

"More, I figure. Much more." Marge smiled and licked the spoon she had just stirred her coffee with.

Danny smiled. "Are you sure Julio will buy this car?"

"Sure. Might not be as much as you want, but we're after twenty mil, aren't we? So I figure a little less here will be better in the long run," Danny said.

"Yeah, I guess you're right. How much do you think? It's worth about thirty-eight grand."

"Well, I'm sure I could talk him into twenty-five thousand, but not much more."

Marge thought for a minute, then said, "I guess twenty-five is better than nothing. I sure wish we could have gotten money out of Geor— I mean Terrance. It would have saved us a bunch of trouble now."

"I can't believe he left like he did," Danny said. "There's not a trace of him anywhere. He just vanished into thin air."

"Yeah, that was strange. I wonder if he got any of his stuff from Mexico City?" Marge mused.

Abby, George's maid, had gone back for their things when she left the hospital. She figured she'd hold on to George's things until he came for them. She figured he'd look her up in Bend someday.

Before they knew it, Ginger had arrived.

"Danny, you keep her busy on the deck and I'll bring out the brunch. Okay?" Marge instructed.

"Okay, doll. I got everything under control."

As Danny stepped out on the deck, he waved at Ginger. "Hello, Ginger! Come up and grab a chair. Jody said she'd be right out."

"Hi, Danny! Can I walk across the grass here?" Ginger asked, noting the sidewalks were eight feet apart.

"Sure—no problem. We're not like a lot of people. We figure our grass can be looked at as well as walked on."

Ginger laughed. "When is this get-together going to start?"

Not knowing about the get-together, Danny played along. "Oh, I think Jody said the guests will start arriving around three-thirty or four."

"Great, maybe Jody and I will run in and do some shopping before it starts. Oh—you don't mind, do you, dear?" Ginger cooed.

"Not a bit," Danny assured her.

"I noticed your front window was busted out. What happened?" Ginger asked.

Marge appeared through the sliding glass door with a tray of coffee, mugs, and saucers.

"Danny and I were away for a couple of days."

"That's why I couldn't raise you on the phone," Ginger cut in.

"Yeah, probably. Anyway, while we were gone somebody broke in. Didn't take anything more than a few dollars and some food," Marge lied.

"Really?" Ginger asked, incredulous.

"Yeah. We think it was Terrance. He even set our couch on fire, whoever it was. Kind of looks as though it went out by itself, though—probably trying to cover his tracks," Marge said.

"If it was Terrance, he probably wanted the house and figured if he couldn't have it, neither could you," Ginger said.

"I never thought of that. But you're probably right," Marge said, lowering the tray. She deliberately gave Ginger her cup first, then Danny, then herself, taking a sip before she set it down.

Marge quickly went back in the house to get the sandwiches. Upon her return she heard Ginger say, "My, this coffee has a bite to it, or is that just me?"

"Oh," Marge said, "I forgot to tell you—these are some new beans I'm trying out. I don't think I'm going to use them again."

"Tastes like the beans were too green when they roasted them," Danny added.

"Exactly," Ginger said. "So, Jody, my dear, are you all ready to go shopping this morning?"

Knowing the crushed sleeping pills would take over long before shopping time, Marge said, "Of course, love. I'm always ready to go shopping." She should have put Irish cream or something in the coffee to disguise the taste, but all was well; Ginger suspected nothing.

"What are you going to do, Danny?" Ginger asked.

"I think I'm just going to stay home and do something I haven't done in years—surf fishing," he said, the best he could conjure on short notice.

"Sounds fun. Maybe we can join you when we get back," she said.

"You can join him, dear, but I don't touch fish unless it's on my plate," Marge said with a wince, and they laughed.

Ginger was yawning before the brunch was over. "Man, I don't know why I'm so tired. I slept a good ten hours."

"Maybe you're catching something," Marge suggested.

"I don't know, but I feel drained. Do you mind if I lie down before we go shopping—just for a little while?" Ginger asked.

"Tell you what—let Danny and me help you to the car, and then I'll talk Danny into going with us and we can go to Manzanillo and shop there. That way you can rest before we get there, and it's not too far, so we can get back for the party later this afternoon. Remember the fun we had last time? Well, you can sleep until we get there, then we'll wake you up in time to go shopping. Sound okay?" Marge's trap was sprung.

"You don't mind missing fishing, Danny?" Ginger asked sleepily.

"Not at all. Anything for Jody," Danny said.

Danny took one side and Marge the other as they gently lifted Ginger from her chair and walked her to Marge's BMW. They laid her in the back seat. Marge even fetched a pillow for her head and a blanket to cover her with. By then, Ginger was out.

Now came the time to search Ginger's car and purse. They found fourteen eight-balls of cocaine, which they eagerly divided; fourteen thousand in cash; credit cards; and a checkbook. While looking under the seat one last time, Danny found a small compartment with a snub-nosed Smith & Wesson .38 Special and another six eight-balls. He hurriedly hid the gun and cocaine without Marge's knowledge. He didn't want her finding out about either.

"Okay, she has enough of that stuff in her to keep her asleep for at least a good day and a half. We can find a good turnout and tape her arms and legs so she can't move. Oh—and her mouth too," Marge said.

"What do you want to tape her mouth for?" Danny asked.

"I know how softhearted you can be toward her. I saw you both giving each other the eye more than once. That never bothered me, and when this is over you can have her—but we need the money first, and I don't want her talking you out of it."

Danny didn't look up; he just shook his head. "I don't recall us looking at each other that way. But if you insist, I guess it's all right with me."

"Can you rig a small generator to last three or four days, constantly running?" Marge asked.

"I'm sure Julio can help me. Why?"

"Well, I want her to wake up and see where she is. Maybe she'll enjoy her surroundings," Marge said, sarcastic. "I'll gladly pay for it. I'd like to see her face when she wakes up, though."

"Isn't she even afraid of scary movies?" Danny mused.

Marge gave a little giggle as she brushed back her hair. "That's right. She almost wet her pants watching Scooby-Doo cartoons."

Danny laughed. His thoughts of pity for Ginger now in the past, he too wondered what she would do. "Besides, the twenty million will please us well, won't it? Won't it appease the hunger to see what she'll do?"

Greed reared its ugly head again.

"Yeah, it will... I guess. It will have to, because we won't be there to watch her wake up." Marge paused, then nodded. "Yeah, it will."

"I'd kind of like to see her daddy's face, too—when he finds her. Boy, I'll bet he'll be madder than a hornet," Danny said, smiling at Marge. "What do you think?"

"I think he will be quite devastated." Marge giggled again. "He'll be very disgusted about even going into a mineshaft, let alone finding his little girl there."

"Yeah, that ought to really blow his stack," Danny said.

After that there wasn't much talking. Danny got in on the driver's side and started the car. Marge got in on the passenger side, and Ginger was fast asleep. Then the journey began. There was a little small talk along the way, but mostly silence. Mile by mile caught them in deep thought—both miles away.

Danny was caught up with the scenery. First, there were the palm trees and the salt air of the ocean. Sometime after that came the pine scent of the mountains, first mixed with salt air, then just the sweet smell of pine. As the scenery changed, his thoughts changed too—from the plans at hand to what they would do after. Would they be together? Only time would tell. He thought the best would be to divide the cash and go their separate ways.

The trip to Mexico City seemed to fly by. They stayed at the same motel as before. Only this time, they did their business beforehand. They took Ginger into the room first, then called Julio. Between grunts, uh-huhs, and a couple of yeses and nos, Danny finally sold the BMW for twenty-seven thousand cash, no questions asked. He also told Julio he had to deliver Marge and Danny to the place where the senator would leave the money and the car.

After that, Marge called the senator. "Senator Robinson, hello! How are you? I'm fine. Yes, this is Jody. Oh, I just needed to talk with you. Yes, it's real important. Yes, it's about your daughter... Yes, Ginger. Oh, she's all right—for now. Well, let me finish, please. The rest is up to you. We want you to follow our instructions perfectly or she might not be."

Danny looked at Marge. "Jody, I'll go rent a four-wheel drive to take us up there, okay?" Marge nodded and waved him off, then covered the phone. "Is she still asleep?"

Danny checked. "Yeah—like a baby."

"Calm down!" Marge yelled into the phone. "Now listen to me. You will come to Mexico City and stay at the airport hotel. Number two, you call me on Ginger's cell phone. After three days, we will let you know where she is—after we get the money."

"You will get the money when I get my daughter!" the senator boomed.

"We can work that out, but you will send us a car with the money. Do you understand? I'm sure you won't do anything silly, now, would you?"

"No... no, of course not. Not with Ginger's life at stake," the senator said.

"I thought not," Marge said. "After you call us on the third day, we will tell you where to bring the money and the car. Fair enough?"

"Yeah, I guess it will have to be, now, won't it? Will you tell me then where I can find Ginger?"

"No, we're going to take the money and run," Marge mocked. "Of course we'll tell you where to find her!"

"I want Ginger in my sight before you get it. You can at least let me have that. Can't you?"

"I suppose... but that's it. No tricks. Deal?"

"Deal," Senator Robinson said. "Is it all right if I send one of my people to you? It's only natural I'd like to be with my daughter."

"I thought that's what you'd do. Yeah—but he has to be completely unarmed. Got it?"

"Yes, I've got it. One car, one driver, and twenty million."

"Exactly."

"How is he supposed to get back?" the senator asked.

"You'll have to come and get him after you pick up Ginger, now, won't you? What do you expect us to do—drive him back? One car, one driver, and twenty million. That's all that better come up that road. Or else."

"Okay, okay—you win. It'll be as you say. I'll leave tonight."

"Don't call me before the three days are up or the deal is off." Marge hung up. As she waited for Danny, she started to smile. She would get hers at last.

Meanwhile, the senator was on the phone. "Harry, pick up Becker, Junior, and Jensen, then get over here as fast as you can. We're leaving for Mexico City tonight. We've got some things to do. Oh—and tell Becker to bring some papers. We're going to need them. And hurry!"

"Be right there, boss," Harry said.

Danny held the gun he had found in Ginger's car on the man sent by Senator Robinson. "The car looks kind of expensive. We would have rather had a smaller one, but this will do. Where's the money?"

"The money is here in the case," the man said, holding up a suitcase.

"Open it," Danny snarled. Marge stood just behind Danny on his left. She watched intently as the man laid the suitcase on the trunk of the Cadillac DeVille and opened it. The money danced in her eyes. The lush green was superb, she thought.

"Give it to Jody," Danny ordered.

"Not until I hear from the senator. That was the order," the man said.

"What's keeping him? He should have found her by now," Marge said. "They said they left the temple ruins thirty minutes ago."

"We'll wait," Danny said. "We've waited this long; a few more minutes won't hurt. Just remember—the money."

"Okay, but I've never liked to wait," Marge said.

After another ten minutes, there was the chirp-chirp-chirp of the man's cell phone.

"Sir," the man said.

"Becker?" the senator asked.

"Yes, sir."

"Do it. Just like we planned. Wait until they are on the steep part of the mountain before you do it."

"Got it, sir," Becker said.

He put the phone away and turned to Danny. "Here's your money, and here are the keys to the car."

"Give her the keys," Danny said.

Becker tossed the keys to Marge.

"You sure the whole twenty million is in there?" Danny asked, pointing to the suitcase.

"Would you like to count it?" Becker asked, indignant.

"No, I guess I'll have to trust the senator," Danny said, sarcastic. "We haven't got the time."

"After all," Marge said as she brushed past Danny and sauntered to the car, "he wouldn't play around with his precious little girl's life, now, would he?" Ice rolled off every word.

"Just put it in the back seat," Danny said.

Becker opened the door, gently placed the suitcase on the back seat, and shut the door.

"Now back away. And—oh—give my regards to the senator," Danny said with a sly chuckle.

He held the gun on Becker as he made his way around the other side of the car. Just as he reached the passenger door, Marge hit the locks and smiled at Danny through the glass.

Marge already had the key in the ignition. "You know something, Danny? It was real and it was fun. But it wasn't real fun. Goodbye. Oh—don't think about shooting me. I saw you take the gun, so when you were asleep, I unloaded it."

As Marge started the car, Danny stood in disbelief.

"What are you saying? What do you think you're doing? We were a team! You can't—" But Marge threw it in reverse, eased back, turned down the road, dropped it in drive, and was gone. Danny pointed the gun and pulled the trigger, thinking she was bluffing. Click. Click. Click.

Danny looked up to see Becker's gun jump and smoke. Something hit him in the left shoulder, spun him around, and threw him six feet, flat on his face. He blacked out. When he woke, he was alone.

Becker didn't wait to see if he had killed Danny. All he wanted was to finish the job.

Marge had headed toward Mazatlán, on her way back to Puerto Vallarta. She glanced in the mirror and saw Danny on the ground and Becker. She reached into the back for the suitcase, feverishly opened it, and dug below the top layer. Blank paper. As she looked up for the last time, she saw Becker point something at her car. A sudden blast—her car swerved hard left. A piece of tire flew past her window. Just as fast as she saw the flapping rubber, she felt the car go over the cliff. Another explosion—this time the fuel tank—triggered by Becker's device.

The car plunged. End over end it tumbled down the mountain. Every time it struck, Marge saw another face of a person she had harmed or used or hurt. To her it seemed to take forever to hit bottom, but when the car finally did, it burst into flames. As she watched the demons dance in the fire, the last thing she heard in this world—and the first thing she heard in the next—were her own screams as she passed from the car fire to the lake of fire below.

CHAPTER 42

MERCY IN OPEN COURT

"Mr. Wetzel, I'm Leroy Jennings. I'm your public defender. Judge Wilson appointed me to your case. How are you today?" asked Jennings.

"Hello. I'm okay, I guess, under the circumstances," George said.

"I see that you want to plead guilty and that's it," said Jennings.

"Well, kinda. I want to tell the court what happened. I want to tell them the whole story, and that's why I'm pleading guilty," replied George.

"Why do you feel you are guilty? I mean, we can plead not guilty for a lesser sentence. You do know they have you up for second-degree murder, right?" Jennings spoke up.

"I want to plead guilty and get it over with. I don't want a long, drawn-out trial that benefits no one—especially the family of Phil," explained George.

"Did you know him?" asked Jennings.

"Yes," stated George, as tears filled his eyes. "He was my friend—yeah, he was my best friend. And I believed a lying, money-grubbing woman instead of talking to him about what she said happened."

"Do you want to tell me about it?" asked Jennings.

"Do you have the time?" George asked back.

"I'm here for as long as it takes," responded Jennings.

For the next four and a half hours, George told Jennings the whole story—up to the point where he came back to Idaho. "I don't know where Marge is. The last I knew, she and Danny were in our house in Puerto Vallarta," George said.

"Wow. What a trip," exclaimed Jennings, trying to take in everything he had heard.

"So, you haven't seen her since she shot you," Jennings said, kindly to himself; but George heard it.

"No, I've not seen her since. As far as I know, she and Senator Robinson's daughter, Ginger, and Danny are having the time of their lives," said George. "Oh, and the money that I got is in a bank in Mexico City—if it hasn't been taken by the feds like the rest of it that Marge had. I think it should go to Phil's family. It belonged to him anyway."

"I'll check into it, and I will see if there is anything on Marge as well. Do you have the numbers or anything for the accounts? You know the password and all?" asked Jennings.

"I'm sorry to ask you this, but can I trust you with the money?" asked George.

"Mr. Wetzel, there are some around here I'd watch myself around, but you can trust me. In fact, I'll get a call set up to the bank and will let you find out how much is there and if it is still there. Then we will see if the judge wants to seize it for evidence or if we can give it to the family of Phillip Gunn," Jennings answered.

After Jennings left George, he went straight to his office to make a call to see how he should handle this situation. He was going to do everything in his power to get done what he said he would do. One other thing he did was to call the judge to see if he could let George tell the court what he had heard. He believed that the court just might take some leniency on him.

"Judge Wilson, I don't believe that Mr. Wetzel really wanted to send Phillip Gunn to his death. I mean, I heard his story, and it was really sincere," explained Jennings.

"I'd have to hear him tell the story and, again, let him tell it in the courtroom. Only then could we make it a lesser charge. I know what you're gonna ask, but that's the only way we can do it," the judge answered.

"Well, sir, it took about four to four and a half hours for the story to be told, so when you have the time I'm sure Mr. Wetzel will tell you the same story. I mean, he went through the gates of hell, almost, with that woman, Marge—and even got shot by her," reported Jennings.

"Mr. Jennings, I'll hear the story and will draw my own conclusions, if you please," retorted the judge.

"Yes, sir. I just got carried away, sir," apologized Jennings.

"Let's see—I'll be free for a... Tuesday afternoon. Bring him in at 12:00 p.m. sharp, and we'll go through his story," said the judge.

"We'll be there, sir," answered Jennings.

Jennings went back to the jail cell where George was. "Mr. Wetzel, I've got an appointment with Judge Wilson Tuesday at noon. I want you to tell him exactly what you told me. Okay?"

"Okay," said George. And the wait began again. This was Friday morning—just before lunch. George suddenly lost his appetite. What was this all about? What does the judge want? All I can do is tell him the truth, come what may. He made a vow to himself and to God not to lie anymore, and he won't. Never again.

During the four days George had to wait, he took a real good look at himself. As he looked at the person in the mirror looking back at him, he nearly didn't recognize himself. His eyes were red from crying so much. The stress and pain that he had felt for so long had caught up to him. He had black circles underneath his eyes, and what hair he had left on his head was gray and unkempt. This person looking back at him seemed old and tired-looking. George was sure that man had to be someone else.

Then he knew—no, it was him, and the last several months had taken their toll on him. He then slumped to his bed and just sat there, staring off into space.

As he sat there, his mind drifted back to when he was twelve years old. He was sitting on a pew of an old church with his family. He remembered that the church was just one room—not too big but yet not too small. It held the thirty parishioners that attended. The pews were wood and, as he recalled, very uncomfortable.

Then he remembered the wood floors. He still recalled the creaking of the wood as his mother would walk in and take her seat; then the heavy footfalls of his father, who, at three hundred ten pounds, made the wood groan with his passing. He could still smell the sweet fragrance of the lilacs that were in bloom just outside the windows of the church. The windows were open to vanquish the early August heat. There was still the persistent hum of the bees as they went from bush to bush, looking for the sweet nectar the lilacs gave forth. He remembered Pastor Whittington. He could still see him—beads of sweat rolling down his brow and down the healthy cheeks of his sun-worn face. The pastor started out by taking off his coat. We all knew we were in for a wild sermon when the coat came off. He laid his coat on the chair, loosened his tie, and rolled up his shirt sleeves. Then the hellfire and brimstone started flying. As he started preaching, his face got redder and redder. George remembered two of the scriptures blasted out that hot summer day: Romans 6:23, "For the wages of sin is death; but the gift of God is eternal life through Jesus Christ our Lord." The other one was 1 Timothy 6:10, "For the love of money is the root of all evil: which while some coveted after, they have erred from the faith and pierced themselves through with many sorrows." He could see the pastor's blood vessels bulge in his forehead when he yelled out, "This root of all evil has engulfed many lives! What those people do about it determines their destiny. To some it will be an awakening, while to others it will cause death!" The memories brought tears once again.

How often over the last days—even months—he had wished that he could go back... back before it all happened. George began to relive the ordeal that put him where he now was.

The next three days went by very slowly. George didn't eat much, and sleep was scarce, too. He kept wondering what the judge was going to do.

Tuesday morning, he couldn't eat at all. He did have a couple of cups of coffee and a couple of bites of a sandwich at 11:00 a.m. Then, at 11:30, Jennings walked in and had the jailer open his cell.

"You ready, Mr. Wetzel?" Jennings asked. "Oh—before I forget, I found out that Jody Weinberger— I mean Marge Wetzel was killed in an automobile crash near Mexico City. For some reason, there is a big investigation by the feds on Senator Robinson and his family. Sounds like they were involved in some way."

George felt his gut go tense. Even for Marge, he didn't want to see that happen, but he wasn't concerned with her anymore.

"I guess we might as well get it over with," George said slowly.

They were escorted from the jail cell to the elevator and went to the second floor. From there they went into the judge's chamber down the hall.

And after four and a half hours, George had told the story again, and once again he broke down when he mentioned Phil.

"Mr. Wetzel," Judge Wilson asked as George were about to leave, "what were your thoughts about the rag on fire in the gas tank?"

"Sir, I wasn't even told that it was going to happen. I thought Phil might be in the hospital for a few days from the wreck, but never thought he would be killed. When I saw the fire, I couldn't believe it. It went by me so fast I couldn't even grab it out of the tank." At this George broke down again. "I never meant for him to die. I just wanted to get back at him for making a pass at my wife. The worst part about the whole thing is when she told me later that it was a lie—and that she was going to get the money no matter what it took." George said all this with tears rolling down his face. "Phil was my friend. I never wanted to kill him!" George sobbed.

The judge turned to Jennings and the prosecutor. "I see what you mean. This whole session has been recorded as part of the court proceedings. Counsel, if there is any change in your positions after reviewing it, you may bring that to the court's attention."

"Thank you, Your Honor," said Jennings.

"Very well. Deputy, you may return Mr. Wetzel to his cell," the judge said.

"Sure," replied Jennings, and the deputy took George back. The judge shut the door and returned to his chambers, leaving the attorneys to themselves.

Outside the courtroom, the prosecutor turned to Jennings. "I'd like the family to hear this recording," he said quietly. "If they're open to it, it may affect how we proceed. Can you help me set it up?"

"I can try, sir," replied Jennings.

It took Jennings about four days to get it all set up. When the day came, the prosecutor led Laura, Jeannie, and Jonathon Gunn into a small conference room at the courthouse. A speaker and a simple recorder sat on the table. The prosecutor was already there, waiting for them to enter.

"I called you all here to listen to the recorded statement of George Wetzel," the prosecutor said. "Now, the judge has to stay neutral in this, but I don't think Mr. Wetzel necessarily has to go up for second-degree murder. Please listen to this and let me know your feelings after it's done. It's quite long. It's 9:00 a.m. now, so we can break for lunch and finish afterward if you like, or go straight through and have lunch later. It's up to you."

"Is the family ready for this?" he asked.

They all nodded, and they began to listen to the recording. At first all was pretty sober, but then, when George broke down, their countenances all changed. There was compassion on each face. There was no anger in their faces at all. They felt his pain, his anguish, and they understood the reason he did what he did. They didn't excuse it, but they understood.

By the end of the tape there were tears of sorrow—and much forgiveness.

They didn't go to lunch but chose to listen to the whole thing at once.

"Wow," is all Jonathon could say at first. "I can't let this guy go up for murder. I don't know how you two feel," he added, looking at his mother and sister, "but I can't."

Laura and Jeannie both nodded in agreement. "We can't either," said Laura. "I believe he has suffered enough." And Jeannie nodded.

"Well then," said the prosecutor, "I'll speak with his attorney and let the judge know we're asking for a lesser charge. Shall we say manslaughter with a sentence of seven to fifteen years?"

"That beats life," said Jonathon.

"Okay," said the prosecutor.

No one said a word to George about what was going to take place.

At that point, George was summoned back to the courtroom.

"The court will come to order. The Honorable Judge Wilson presiding in the State of Idaho v. George Wetzel," announced the bailiff.

"We are here this morning on the State v. George Wetzel. Is your client ready to enter a plea, Mr. Jennings?" asked the judge.

"Yes, sir," said Jennings. "He pleads guilty."

"Okay, Mr. Jennings, have you let your client know what second-degree murder consists of in this state—twenty-five to life?" the judge asked.

"Yes, sir," Jennings replied.

"Well then, I guess it's time to get down to business," stated the judge.

"Your Honor," interrupted the prosecutor, "under certain information that has come to our attention, we'd like to change the charge."

"Very well," said the judge, playing along. "What would you like to change it to?"

"Manslaughter, sir," said the prosecutor, "with the term being seven to fifteen years."

"Are all in agreement?" asked the judge. They all nodded in agreement.

"Your Honor, may I speak?" asked Laura Gunn.

"Yes, Mrs. Gunn. Go ahead," said the judge.

"One thing: I don't believe total forgiveness is given until Mr. Wetzel agrees to my proposition."

"What might your proposition be, Mrs. Gunn?" asked the judge.

"May I speak freely to Mr. Wetzel, Your Honor?"

"You may," said the judge.

George was shocked at the way the proceedings were going.

"Mr. Wetzel, you inadvertently took the life of my son. I totally forgive you for that, and so do my children. But now we have a hole in our family. The grief we feel will always be there, but the hole can be filled. We want you to fill that hole—to accept our forgiveness and become one of us. We will visit you and help you in any way we can, before and after you get set free. Is that acceptable to you?"

Laura had tears streaming down her face, because all George could do was weep—in sorrow, fear, and joy.

"Yes, ma'am," George muttered between sobs.

As Laura sat back down, the judge stated, "I order you, George Wetzel, to be remanded to the state until your sentence of a minimum seven to no longer than fifteen years is fulfilled, to include time served. Now, if there is no other reason to continue, this court is adjourned."

For about fifteen minutes, Laura, Jeannie, and Jonathon all talked to George, then hugged him before the deputy took him back to his cell.

As he heard the cell door slam behind him, George stood in confusion—but he felt a burden lift from his shoulders. He turned to look out at the sky through his window, and sitting on the sill was a dove. When George realized what he was looking at, the dove looked back at him—then it flew away. And at that moment, George slid to the floor on his knees next to his bunk and began to pray, thanking God for His mercy.

The End.

Roy Roberts' Testimony

I was raised in the Assembly of God Church in St. Helens, Oregon. After graduating from high school, I entered the Army at age 17.

After serving, I went the way of the world until I turned 40. I was caught up in alcohol, women, and smoking—two packs a day. On October 28, 1990, I cried out to God for deliverance from smoking because I couldn't quit on my own. That night, I threw the cigarettes down and never picked them up again. Along with the cigarettes, He also took the alcohol.

But I still struggled with a familiar spirit I couldn't shake. I eventually spent twenty years in the penitentiary in Idaho. During that time, God not only took that spirit from me—He used me while I was behind bars.

I praise God for His deliverance and for the gospel that not only saved me but continues to save everyone today who believes in Him.

Today, I am a new man in Christ. I write gospel songs, as well as my novel *Of Judgment and Of Mercy*. I thank God for this heavenly gift that only He can give. My hope is that both the book of songs and *Of Judgment and Of Mercy*, when read or heard, will change the lives of those who encounter them—so they might place their trust in Jesus Christ and discover the new life He offers to all.

Roy Roberts